Only GOD Can Heal the WOUNDED HEART

Ed Bulkley

HARVEST HOUSE PUBLISHERS
Eugene, Oregon 97402

The characters in the fictional sections of this book
are composites of various cases and do not
represent any specific individuals.

ONLY GOD CAN HEAL THE WOUNDED HEART

Copyright ©1995 by Harvest House Publishers
Eugene, Oregon 97402

Library of Congress Cataloging-in-Publication Data

Bulkley, Ed, 1947–
    Only God Can Heal The Wounded Heart / Ed Bulkley.
       p.   cm.
    ISBN 1-56507-323-1
    1. Christian life.   2. Spiritual healing–Biblical teaching.
  I. Title.
  BV4501.2.B838   1995   95-515
                                                    CIP

Printed in the United States of America.

95   96   97   98   99   00   01   /   10   9   8   7   6   5   4   3   2   1

To my wife, Marlowe,
and to our children
Heidi, Holly, Heather, and Dan.

I love you more than words can express.
You are my best friends and
truly God's gifts to me!

Acknowledgments

I want to express my gratitude to my close friends, who have made my life full, enjoyable, and just plain fun! We are able to laugh together as we face the challenges of daily living in a broken and plain-filled world. Their loyalty, trust, and love make me want to live up to their expectations—that I be a man of character and integrity—while their firmness in holding me accountable to biblical standards is a blessed defense and point of safety.

They have shared with me the battle for biblical sufficiency and have encouraged me to continue taking a stand for Scripture even when it means going against prevailing thought. They have graciously accepted the time I must spend away from them at the computer and they have supported me in moments of weariness.

I am especially blessed to have as my best friends my wife, Marlowe, and our children, Heidi, Holly, Heather, and Hans Daniel.

Marlowe is the finest partner and co-laborer a pastor could have. She works in our ministries to the point of exhaustion, yet always with a sweet and humorous spirit. She makes our offices a delight for the staff and volunteer workers. She is loved by our people and as long as she's alive, my job is safe.

Our children have delighted us at every stage of their lives. They have validated our ministry by their consistent testimony and godliness. Their spontaneous humor and infectious laughter fill our house with the sweet aroma of joy. Marlowe and I have often thanked the Lord for giving us four easy-to-raise children and have wondered why we have been so blessed. Aside from the pure grace of God, we can only ascribe it to our having been taught to live according to the precepts of the Bible.

I also want to thank my church family at LIFE Fellowship for their prayerful support and loving encouragement in the new ministries God has opened—writing and broadcasting. These dear people have enthusiastically accepted the additional burdens placed upon them due to the time I must spend away from the church. To our members and friends at LIFE, I thank you with all my heart!

Our elders have also been supportive and have had the vision to see the opportunities beyond our local work—opportunities to strengthen and encourage other people far from our community. I thank each of you men for what you mean to me personally as friends and advisers.

I am deeply grateful for the faith and generosity shown to me by our dear friends at the VCY/America radio network, who have joined us in the battle to expose the empty philosophies that are weakening the church from the inside out. To Vic, Jim, Dave, Andy, Ingrid, Gordon, Lou, Gene, and all the others, may God bless and protect you!

Finally, I thank my dear friends at Harvest House, who continue to encourage me to produce the message of hope found in God's word. To Bob, Eileen, Bob, Sr., Teresa, Janna, Mary, Joel, and all my other blessed friends at Harvest House, you are a continual delight to work with. It is no wonder your authors have a fierce loyalty to you.

A special word to a special friend at Harvest House—Steve Miller. Steve is my editor who gently prods and guides me to produce a far better work than I am capable of. He has taken a personal interest in the message I share, and I count him as a dear friend in Christ.

I am so blessed! Thanks to all of you who have enriched my life in ways I never imagined possible.

Contents

A Message of Hope

As you browse through your local Christian bookstore, there is a dazzling selection of self-help books written to help believers deal with their deepest pains. In spite of the exhaustive studies, enlightening findings, intensive therapies, and sincere motives of the authors, complete healing still seems to be an elusive goal.

One of the most controversial and perplexing counseling issues of our day is the recovery of repressed memories. Perhaps you yourself are a victim of abuse so painful that you find it difficult to interact with other people in a comfortable and meaningful way. Maybe you have been wounded so severely that your trust in people and your faith in God are almost gone.

It is more than likely that you have submitted to some sort of psychotherapy and have read a number of books telling you how your wounded heart can experience healing. Yet, after all the time and money you have invested, you may still feel as though you will never fully recover.

This book is different from most other volumes on "recovery" because it asks you to look at your life story through the clear lens of God's Word rather than the dark and distorted spectacles offered by humanistic theories of behavior.

Much of evangelical Christianity has been thoroughly transformed by a philosophy of life that promises healing for the wounded heart. It is promoted by Christians and is called by several names–Christian psychology, Christian psychotherapy, and even biblical counseling.

Yet at the same time, Christians have been told that the Bible does not have all the answers for their inner problems. Rather, they need the insights and wisdom of psychological findings to produce healing for their wounded hearts and experience the peace they so desperately long for.

The results of a weakened confidence in the Scriptures, however, are feeble faith, damaged relationships, paralyzing fear, crippling depression, loss of hope, and inexpressible suffering.

Many "professional counselors" scoff at *genuine* biblical counseling, saying it is simplistic and naive. They say we need to delve into the subconscious regions of the mind to achieve inner wholeness. The sad truth is, such theories lead to increased confusion and further complicate our lives.

I met a young man who had difficulty dealing with the normal pressures of living. He had been told that he needed professional help, and he went into psychotherapy. Within a short time, he was placed on strong psychoactive medications. When his parents saw him only two weeks later, they could hardly believe the change. "He looked like a zombie," his mother said. "He was so drugged that he could hardly communicate."

Fortunately for this young man, his parents believed in the power of God to heal the heart. They placed their son in bed and began playing tapes of biblical teaching as they prayed for his recovery. After two days of listening to the Word, the young man sat up, his eyes clear, and said, "It's all so simple!"

He hurried to the bathroom and flushed his psychoactive medicines down the toilet. His recovery was rapid and total and he is now a productive husband, father, and businessman.

"It's all so simple!" That's the essence of this book.

Dear reader, you may have been told that your depression, your insecurity, your fear of failure, or your unhappy marriage resulted from mysterious secrets buried deep within your subconscious. You may have been told that you will need years of therapy to be healed of sexual or mental abuse. You may have been told that your problem is genetic and that there is nothing you can do except to dull the pain with medication.

Paul writes, "See to it that no one takes you captive through hollow and deceptive philosophy, which depends on human tradition and the basic principles of this world rather than on Christ" (Colossians 2:8). Yet that is exactly what is happening in the Christian "recovery" movement. The tragic result of these hollow and deceptive philosophies is that hurting believers are being led away from a firm confidence in Jesus and the Word of God. Instead of finding healing for their wounded hearts, they are often led into deeper captivity to sin and consequently experience a life of spiritual poverty and sorrow.

It is my firm conviction that our Lord Jesus has pro-vided everything we need for a full and productive walk with God in the Scriptures. I believe this not merely because I have seen it work, but because the Bible makes that claim: "His divine power has given us *everything* we need for life and god-liness through our knowledge of him" (2 Peter1:3, emphasis added).

This book is about *hope*. Hope for the restoration of broken relationships. Hope for the future. Hope for permanent healing. My goal is to convince you that your life does not need to be confused and complicated, but that you can be filled with the joy and peace of God that exceeds our understanding as you follow the plan He has laid out. It is my prayer that you will soon experience God's healing for the deepest wounds of your heart.

–Ed Bulkley

Returning to the Past

"You've just got to attend this seminar on sexual abuse, Miriam!" Wanda's voice came over the phone with deep urgency. "I've finally begun to understand my depressions and how they relate to my childhood."

"Tell me about it, Wanda," Miriam Chase said as she looked over at her husband, Cliff, and shrugged helplessly.

"Miriam, it's like a whole new understanding has opened up for me! I'm beginning to see how it all fits together. You've just got to attend this seminar!"

"Why would I want to attend a seminar on sexual abuse, Wanda?" Miriam replied, glancing self-consciously at Cliff, who had looked up from his paper, taking a sudden interest in the conversation. Miriam blushed slightly and looked away.

"Hey, kiddo, this is Wanda. Michael has told me all about your teen years and what you went through with Frank Jenkins. Miriam, you were an innocent victim, and that's all there is to it! I'll not have you taking responsibility for something that you had no control over."

Just then, Cliff and Miriam's children walked into the house. "Uh, Wanda?" Miriam interrupted. "Can I call you back?"

"What's wrong?" Wanda replied. "Is Cliff there in the room with you?"

"It's not that. The kids just got home from school and I want to fix them a snack. I'll get back to you."

"Well, I just wish Cliff would get over his fanaticism about biblical counseling. Honestly, Miriam, he's so stubborn sometimes! If only he could understand that unless you go back and pick up the pieces of your broken youth, you'll never fully recover. I can tell you from personal experience."

"I really have to go, Wanda," Miriam said tightly. "I'll give you a call."

"What was that all about?" Cliff asked as Miriam hung up the phone and stood to greet the children.

"Oh, nothing, honey," she replied. "You know Wanda. She thinks that I need to go to a special seminar with her."

"But why a seminar on sexual abuse?" Cliff asked.

"Shh, Cliff!" Miriam hushed him with a frown, nodding her head toward the children, who were in the kitchen. "Let's talk about it later," she whispered as she left the room.

Cliff and Miriam Chase had served the Lord at Evangelical Bible Church for more than eight years. For the most part, it had been a wonderful experience. But life had changed considerably in the last couple of years. Cliff had been influenced by a fellow pastor, Dr. John Kryer[1], and had made a commitment to counsel his people from the Bible rather than from psychological theories.

From that time onward, Cliff's preaching had a renewed energy and conviction that moved people as they were confronted by the truths of Scripture. The church had grown spiritually and in number as Cliff faithfully taught the Word. Yet the many demands of caring for a growing church were also claiming more and more of Cliff's time.

Miriam had begun to notice a cooling in the relationship between herself and her husband. *Cliff is under a lot of pressure,* she thought to herself, *but so am I!* And when her feelings got hurt, the pain from her past seemed to flare up.

In all fairness, Cliff never brought up the affair she was involved in during her late-teen years. She had told Cliff all about it before they were married, and he had said, "I understand. I love you and I'll never mention it to you. You asked God's forgiveness, and He cleansed you and made it as though it never happened."

Why, then, had the painful memories from her past suddenly erupted, preventing her from sleeping and laughing and enjoying her husband and children as she had for so many years?

Late one afternoon Miriam stood at the sink, staring absent-mindedly at the dishes and brooding about her growing discomfort. The children had just finished their snack and she sent them out to the backyard to play. *When did all this start?* she thought silently. She reviewed the events of the last two years and to the best of her memory, it seemed that her resentment toward Cliff had first surfaced around the same time as the family vacation in the mountains the year before.

Her cousin Michael and his wife, Wanda, had been there. One evening after all the children had gone to bed, Wanda asked, "Would you like to go for a walk with me, Miriam? It's a beautiful night."

"Sure, Wanda," Miriam replied. "I'd love to. Let me get my sweater."

They took a bright flashlight and walked along the gravel road that circled around the campground. The cool night air was fragrant with the scent of pine and the campfires scattered about cast faint glimmers of light through the deep shadows of the forest. The sweet smell of smoke and the distant pop and crackle of burning logs lent a warm comfort to the nighttime chill.

"I love nights like this!" Miriam said with a deep and satisfied sigh.

Wanda didn't reply and they kept walking. A little further along, Miriam heard Wanda sniff softly. In the dim light of the rising moon, she thought she could see a tear trickle down Wanda's cheek.

"What's wrong, Wanda?" she asked.

"Oh, nothing, I suppose," Wanda said in a suddenly tired voice.

"Of course there is!" Miriam said tenderly. "Come on, Wanda. Tell me about it."

Wanda sighed sadly and stopped walking. She hesitated for a moment, then said, "I'm just so depressed, Miriam!" she said with a broken voice.

"Do you have any idea why?" Miriam asked as she gently brushed a tear from Wanda's cheek.

"Well, Michael says that it's related to my past. He says that the only way I can find healing for my wounded heart is to return to the events that caused the pain, embrace them with courage and faith in God, and work through them under the guidance of an experienced counselor."

"So when did Michael become such an expert on healing the past?" Miriam asked a bit sarcastically.

"Well, Miriam, you know that ever since he finished college, Michael has wanted to go into full-time Christian counseling. He is now training under one of the best-known Christian counselors in the nation. We're planning to open our own counseling clinic after Michael finishes graduate school."

"But I don't understand why Michael thinks you have to go back to your past to be healed," Miriam said.

"The reason is that unresolved pain festers in the heart just like a physical infection does in the body. Unless a person's psychic wound is lanced and the infection is released, true healing can't begin. Think about it for a minute, Miriam. It really does make sense."

"I don't know," Miriam replied, unconvinced. "You make it sound like the heart–man's inner person–can develop an abscess just like human tissue can develop a boil."

"It's not all that different, Miriam. Unless we do something about the pain inside, it just grows and grows, until something has to give!"

They turned around and began walking back toward the large cabin where music and laughter bubbled out from time to time.

"Let me ask you one more question, Wanda," Miriam said. "If lancing your inner boil is so effective, why are you still experiencing depression?"

Wanda didn't answer for a moment. The crunch of gravel under their feet and the soft whisper of a breeze rushing through pine boughs filled the momentary void in their conversation. Finally Wanda replied, "I'm still working through my anger. Michael warned me that the process wouldn't be quick or easy. But I know that I'll be stronger after I work through all the pain and I'll be able to love my husband better when it's all over."

They were almost at the cabin when Wanda stopped and turned to face Miriam. "Michael tells me you went through a rough time yourself in high school and college. He's hoping you'll find a good therapist who can help you work through your memories."

Miriam was shocked. She was sure Wanda could see her blushing even in the dark. "I . . . I . . . I don't think I have anything to work through, Wanda," she stammered. "I asked God to forgive me years ago and I told Cliff all about my past soon after we started dating. He said it didn't matter, that he would always love me, and that he would never bring the matter up. And he never has!"

"But don't you see, Miriam? That puts the entire burden of guilt on *your* shoulders. From what Michael told me, you weren't the one responsible for what happened. You were an innocent victim and the pain you experience is not your fault. It's the fault of the perpetrator who abused you!"

"It wasn't quite like that," Miriam countered softly. "No one made me get involved with Frank Jenkins. I was old enough to know better. But I did ask God's forgiveness and I don't know why I should go back and relive those painful days all over again."

"That's just like you, Miriam," Wanda said as she patted Miriam on the arm. "You always seem so strong and secure. But deep down inside your soul is a little girl longing to be declared innocent. You've got to let her experience freedom and healing. Don't keep her bound up with your pride and false sense of guilt."

"Oh, come on, Wanda!" Miriam laughed. "You make it sound like there's another person trapped inside my body longing to be liberated."

Wanda looked at Miriam condescendingly. "Laugh if you want to, Miriam, but someday you'll understand what I'm talking about."

"I hope not," Miriam replied as she turned to walk into the cabin. "I sincerely hope not."

Since that conversation, Miriam's confident and joyful personality had gradually changed. She had become more introspective and withdrawn. Something within her responded to Wanda's assertion that Frank Jenkins was the one who bore full responsibility for the affair that had taken place so long ago. But if that were true, why did she feel such a deep sense of guilt whenever brief memories of that affair surfaced?

To complicate matters further, Cliff had been so thoroughly influenced by John Kryer's views about biblical counseling that he would, no doubt, oppose her seeking psychological counseling. Inwardly, she was torn by conflicting loyalties–first to Cliff, and then to her cousin Michael. How could two sincere and godly men have such opposing perspectives on counseling when they agreed on so many biblical issues? *Still, if it comes right down to it,* Miriam thought, *I have to be loyal to Cliff.*

Wanda would call from time to time, encouraging Miriam to seek professional counseling. "There's a counselor right there in Denver, Miriam! You've just got to see him!"

"I don't see that I really need counseling, Wanda," Miriam protested. "I'm doing just fine." But she knew she wasn't.

The pain from her past seemed to grow more intense with each phone call from Wanda. One day she had tried to discuss the issue with Cliff, but just as they began to talk, one of the families from their church called with a crisis and Cliff had to hurry to their aid. By the time he returned, Miriam and the children were already in bed.

As the months passed, Cliff began to sense an emotional distance developing between Miriam and himself. They seldom shared spontaneous laughter as they once had, and the romance in their marriage seemed cold and artificial. Arguments, which had once been rare in their relationship, became increasingly common, and there were days when they barely spoke to one another.

Around friends and members of the church, both Cliff and Miriam were able to camouflage their anger, but at home, the rift between them grew deeper and wider.

One day, Cliff came home from the office earlier than usual. The kids were still at school and Cliff knew that he and Miriam needed time alone, away from the responsibilities of the church and the needs of the congregation.

He thought he would surprise Miriam and take her to their favorite restaurant for dessert. When he came into the house, he heard Miriam talking on the phone in the kitchen. Her tone of voice told him that she was tense.

"It's not that he's abusive, Wanda," he heard her say. "It's just that he doesn't understand how deeply hurt I am." For a moment Cliff was tempted to pick up the extension phone and listen in, but he decided against it and remained in the hallway.

"No. I know he wouldn't let me go to the abuse seminar. You know how he feels about psychology." There was a pause as the voice on the other end of the line spoke.

"Because, Wanda, I don't believe I have the right to disobey Cliff in this matter." Cliff sighed, a bit relieved, but angry at Wanda for intruding into their marriage.

"A book?" Miriam asked. "Well, yes, I guess I could read it, but I doubt that Cliff will."

Cliff decided he should make some noise so Miriam would know he was home. He tiptoed back to the door, turned the knob, and opened it. Then he shut it and walked down the hallway to the closet as though he had just come home. "Miriam," he called out, "I'm home." He hung his jacket in the closet and set his briefcase next to the stairway.

"I've got to go now," Miriam said brusquely. "I'll call you later."

She hung up the phone and turned with a somewhat guilty look on her face as Cliff walked into the kitchen.

"You're home early, Cliff," she said, forcing a smile.

"Well, I thought we needed some time together. We've both been so busy lately, we've hardly had time to talk." He walked toward her with open arms to give her a hug and kiss, but Miriam turned away and picked up some dishes from the table.

Cliff swallowed hard and paused to control his emotions. "Who was on the phone?" he asked tightly.

"No one special," Miriam lied, "just one of the women."

"Really?" Cliff said as he pulled a chair out and sat down at the table. "I could have sworn that you were talking to Wanda again."

Miriam turned toward Cliff, her face bright red with anger. "So what if it was Wanda? Don't I have a right to talk to her if I want? What's wrong with that?"

"There's nothing wrong with that . . . unless you're hiding something from me. Why didn't you just tell me it was Wanda?"

"Why should I?" Miriam shot back. "I don't ask who you talk with during the day, and you're never around for me to talk with you. I've got to talk to somebody, Cliff!"

"That's why I'm home, Miriam," Cliff said through clinched teeth. "So let's talk."

Miriam sat down across from Cliff and waited.

Cliff paused for a moment, then broke the silence. "What do you want to talk about, Miriam?"

"Why does it always have to be *me* that starts a conversation?" she responded defensively. "You used to be able to talk with me for hours!"

"I *want* to talk with you! But there's this barrier between us all the time!" Cliff stood to his feet and walked to the sink. He turned and looked Miriam in the eyes. "I feel like Wanda has moved in with us. Every day when I come home you're on the phone with her."

"I am not!" Miriam shouted. "And even if I were, so what? I have a right to talk to anyone I choose."

"Unless that person is coming between you and me! What is it with you and Wanda? What does she want you to do?"

"What do you mean?"

"I heard you tell her that it wouldn't be right to disobey me about something."

Miriam's eyes widened with surprise and anger as she realized Cliff had overheard her phone conversation. "Well, maybe I was wrong!" she said hotly. "Maybe I should just go to that seminar she's been asking me to."

"What seminar? Where?" Cliff stammered.

"A seminar on sexual abuse, if you must know!"

"Sexual abuse?" Cliff repeated, not believing his ears. "Does Wanda think I've been abusing you sexually? Do *you* think so?" He asked, trembling with emotion.

Miriam began to cry and she hid her face in her arms.

Cliff walked over and grabbed Miriam's arm to get her to answer. She jerked her arm away, enraged.

"Don't touch me!" she said through white lips. "Don't you *ever* grab me like that again!"

Cliff exploded in hurt and anger. "What is happening to us?" he asked with tears in his eyes. "I don't understand–"

"That's right!" Miriam interrupted. "You don't understand! You don't understand me; you don't understand the pain I've carried all these years; you don't understand anything!" She began to cry again and ran from the room.

Cliff sighed deeply, shook his head in frustration, and followed her to the bedroom. He stood outside for a moment, listening to Miriam's sobs through the door. He then tried to turn the doorknob, but it was locked.

"Honey?" Cliff said as gently as he could manage. "Please open the door."

"Go away, Cliff!" Miriam cried, face down in her pillow.

"No, Miriam, I'm not going away. We've got to talk about this problem, whatever it is. The Lord can help us solve it. Please, honey, open the door."

He waited as he heard Miriam get up from the bed. After a few moments, the door opened. Miriam turned and walked back to the bed. She sat down, wiping her eyes with a tissue.

"Can I come in?" Cliff asked softly, his eyebrows raised hopefully.

"I can't stop you," Miriam replied coldly.

Cliff walked in, shut the door, and went over to sit on the bed beside Miriam. "Can we talk about this 'sexual abuse' thing?" he asked. "Why does Wanda insist you need to attend a seminar on sexual abuse, Miriam? You know I have never abused you in any way at any time."

Miriam looked over at Cliff with pain in her eyes. "It wasn't you, Cliff."

Cliff was genuinely baffled. "Then who? Surely, you don't mean your dad!"

"No, Cliff! I told you all about it before we became engaged."

"What do you mean?" Are you talking about that college boy you were involved with?"

Miriam nodded, ashamed.

"But, Miriam, I thought you told me that the relationship was mutual. That you were as much to blame as he was."

Miriam looked at him defiantly. "Well, maybe I was wrong about that, too, Cliff! Maybe I took on some guilt that wasn't mine! That's what this seminar, that Wanda wants me to go to, is all about. She's sending me a book called *The Wounded Heart,* which explains how sexual abuse can confuse and victimize a woman for life. I'm going to read it, and I want you to read it, too. Then maybe we'll both understand what's going on in our marriage."

Cliff was stunned. "I thought you resolved all of that before we were married. Now here we are, some fifteen years later, being victimized by an incident already forgiven and long forgotten. It's not fair, Miriam!"

She didn't respond for a moment as she stared down at the floor. Finally, she looked up. "Can I go to the seminar, Cliff?" Miriam asked, her hands shaking.

"You know how I feel about psychological theories of inner healing, Miriam. I thought you believed the same way."

"I thought I did, too, Cliff, but I'm starting to feel that I haven't been honest with you or myself all these years. All I know is that I'm confused and hurting and I want to go to that seminar. If you tell me I can't, then I won't go. It's up to you."

Cliff looked at Miriam sadly. "You know what I believe about it. That's all I can tell you."

Later that night, while Cliff was asleep, Miriam quietly got up and went down to the family room and called Wanda and Michael. She told them about Cliff's response to the seminar.

"It's what I had suspected all along, Miriam," her cousin said. "In many cases of sexual abuse, the husbands of the victims stand in the way of inner healing. They become, so to speak, surrogate abusers. You may have to become more firm with Cliff before he will understand and support the healing process. You can't afford to let him stand in the way of getting your wounded heart healed."

Adult Victims of Childhood Abuse

Across America and around the world, gatherings are taking place for the purpose of helping people to recover from the psychological traumas they have suffered. The concept is fostered by a multitude of twelve-step programs, secular psychologists and, surprisingly, a host of Christian counselors as well.

Therapeutic "experts" have built a lucrative industry around the recently invented term *codependency*. Others specialize in the treatment of eating disorders, depression, phobias, or substance abuse. Perhaps the most rapidly growing counseling specialty is dealing with "adult victims of childhood abuse." This label is troubling and confusing because problems that used to be seen as the normal frictions of daily family living are now often defined as *abuse*. Or, behavior that was once understood as sin is now excused as an addiction that has its origins in childhood abuse. Let me illustrate with actual case histories.

No one would have suspected that a Southern Baptist pastor and his wife near Dallas, Texas, had for years secretly abused their daughter as part of their satanic ritual worship. They seemed so normal. Lee and Jean Grady had maintained the outward appearance of respectable religious leaders for nearly forty years. They had photo albums and scrapbooks that appeared to show their daughter Gloria as a happy and normal child.

Suddenly, however, the story of their horrible deeds was exposed when their daughter entered the Minirth-Meier Clinic in Richardson, Texas, for psychotherapy. Under the guidance of her therapist, Gloria accused her father of having beaten and raped her from the age of ten until she went away to college. Eventually she revealed that her mother, brother, grandfather, and other family members had also abused her and had murdered her three-year-old daughter as a sacrifice to Satan.

> Gloria Grady said [these events] had been hidden from her for years in the clouds of her memory. But during therapy with a "Christian psychologist" who diagnosed her as having post-traumatic stress disorder, flashbacks of the horrors had come to her, and she had remembered. What she remembered made her never want to see her family again.[2]

Accusations of satanic ritual abuse (SRA) have exploded in the United States during the past few years, and a surprising factor is that many of the allegations are coming from within the Christian community.

Lee and Jean Grady claim that they are innocent. They are supported by family members, present and former parishioners, medical records, photographs, and forensic evidence.

Jim, Gloria's brother, describes their childhood home as having "the strongest of commitments to family values, family time, and family unity."[3] He describes Lee and Jean as genuine Christians who "never displayed double standards, much less dual lifestyles."[4]

Yet Gloria was believed by her therapist, a Collin County assistant district attorney, an official with the county department of mental health, a psychiatrist, and a case-worker.

I'll never forget a prominent pastor, author, and conference speaker who visited my office and confessed that he had committed adultery over a period of several years. After he was exposed by his lover, he lost his wife, his church, and the respect he had so carefully earned through years of ministry.

"I'm not trying to excuse what I did, Ed," he said with deep emotion. "It was wrong and I'll be paying for it the rest of my life. But now, at least I understand why I did it."

I sat back in my chair and waited.

"The church I served is paying for my therapy and the counselors have shown me that I was seeking the love and affection that I never received from my father as a child," he said sadly. "You know, Ed," he continued, "I didn't even remember a lot of the pain of my childhood until I entered counseling. Now I realize how emotionally deprived I was. I know that doesn't excuse what I did, but it does help to explain it." Since my meeting with this man, he has married the wife of one of his former associate pastors.

A dedicated couple, serving the Lord with a world-renowned Bible translating missionary organization, was ordered into counseling by their superiors. They agreed to submit to counseling, but asked that it be biblical rather than psychological. Surprisingly, the organization refused to allow the couple to enter biblical counseling and told them that they would be dismissed if they refused psychological counseling. They have since left the mission.

I recently watched a thriving ministry die. It was killed slowly by a form of Christian counseling that leads people into their past in an attempt to heal their "wounded hearts." A marriage was destroyed, a family was broken, and a church was devastated as a direct result of an errant psychology. Instead of leading the counselors to the healing truths of the Scriptures, well-meaning and sincere Christians led them into a hollow psychological philosophy typical of our age, and destruction swept over them with the force of a hurricane.

The scenarios I just described were not the handiwork of secular clinics. They happened in *Christian* organizations and counseling centers, many of which now function within the walls of an overly trusting evangelical church.

The proponents of most Christian psychological theories have good intentions and they genuinely believe that they are providing needed solutions for alleged victims of childhood and sexual abuse. But when they attempt to heal the inner person with psychological tools rather than the Word of God, they often continue the victimization of the very people they try to help.

Let me strongly emphasize this point: I do not dispute the *fact* of all kinds of horrible abuse. I believe that there *are* millions of victims of childhood and sexual abuse in our world. According to *Newsweek* magazine, "80 percent of the girls who arrive at Boys' Town have been sexually abused."[5]

We live in one of the most depraved ages known to man. Jesus predicted it in Matthew 24 when He said, "Because of the increase of wickedness, the love of most will grow cold" (verse 12). I believe He was describing the conditions found in our day.

I frequently counsel with genuine victims and my heart goes out to them. Nowhere in this book will I deny the *fact* of abuse and victimization. But there is a *better* way to deal with the pain of such abuse than revisiting and analyzing the past. Psychological therapies designed to uncover repressed memories can never produce the healing God offers to everyone who will allow Him to work in their hearts.

At this point it would be easy for readers of this book to conclude that I am trying to add to the suffering of those

who have truly experienced the unspeakable pain of childhood sexual abuse and other soul-wrenching experiences.
Some people may feel that I am trying to rip away the only
source of comfort they have found.

Please believe me when I say that I do not want to add
to your pain. On the contrary, my goal is to help you find
a genuine and lasting peace in your heart. I plead with you
to give my words a fair hearing–not for my sake, but for
yours. The stakes are too high to casually toss this book
aside. You can experience genuine healing from God
Himself if you will follow His time-proven solutions.

In the following chapters, we will examine some case
histories of abuse and see how these victims found healing
and victory through faith in God. Come along with me and
I promise you . . . it will be worth your time.

❖ ❖ ❖

Pastor John Kryer bowed his head in prayer as he sat
with a new counselee. "Lord, I ask You to give us wisdom
as we talk about this dear man's problems. Show us what
we need to know and guide us as we seek wisdom from
Your Word. I pray this in Jesus' name. Amen."

"Amen," David Carver agreed. Carver, a professional-
looking man in his late forties, sat across from John. He was
neatly dressed in a dark gray business suit, a crisp white
shirt, and a fashionable tie. Cordovan wing-tip loafers with
tassels completed his ensemble.

"I've looked through the papers you filled out, David,"
John said with a smile. "I noticed that you recently spent
several weeks at Greenway Psychiatric Hospital. How did
you happen to go there?"

"My employer required it. Otherwise, they said I'd be
fired."

"What led to their decision?"

"My sales went way down. Until this year, I had been

the top sales producer in our company. But things started going sour at home, and my sales dropped. I found it hard to concentrate on the job, and I got more and more tense. My vice president came down on me fairly hard one day, and I nearly took a swing at him. I think they would have fired me on the spot if I hadn't been with the company for so long–over twenty years. Anyway, they said I had to visit a counselor. My pastor recommended that I see Dr. West, a psychologist here in Arvada."

"Mm-hmm," John said as he wrote in his notes. "Before you go on, let me ask you exactly what you meant by things going 'sour' at home."

"Well, I'm embarrassed to tell you, but I had a long-term affair with a woman from work, and my wife found out about it."

"Were you a Christian at that time?" John asked.

Carver looked down in shame. "Yes," he said quietly. "I've been a Christian for most of my adult life. I was an elder and a Sunday school teacher in my church. When my wife found out, she went to our pastor, who confronted me. I confessed and was sort of relieved that I'd been caught. I was tired of the perpetual deception and the thrill of having an affair had died out a long time ago."

"What did your church do?"

"The elder board now has me under close supervision. They also required that I get professional counsel. That's where Dr. West comes in."

"I see," John said. "Before we discuss his counsel, could I ask what led you into the affair?"

"It began with cable television, I got in the habit of sitting in front of the television late at night to unwind. I remember scanning the channels one night when an adult movie came in uncoded and showed some erotic scenes. I don't even know how that channel got into our house; I had never ordered it. Anyway, I soon found that I was looking forward to the late hours when I could sit and view adult movies. Then I started buying pornography whenever I was on a trip away from home. After that, I started renting X-rated movies. By that time, I began to lose interest in my wife. Physically, she couldn't match up to the women on TV and in the magazines.

"Then a new secretary was hired at work. Joan was divorced and still hurting badly. I invited her to lunch and we got to talking. I found out that we had a lot in common and we could open up to each other. She seemed to understand me, you know? I mean, she cared about what was important to me. She's in her thirties, she's pretty, and she made me feel young again. I was so attracted to her that I thought about divorcing my wife, Susan. But I just couldn't hurt my kids like that, and then there was my image at church to consider. So our affair just went on and on."

"How was it discovered?"

"My wife found some of the love letters Joan had written to me. Like an absolute fool, I had kept them hidden in the basement. When Susan was doing her spring cleaning, she found them and reported me to the church."

"Then what happened?" John asked.

"The pastor confronted me, like I told you before, and the board suspended me from all leadership. Susan agreed to stay with me on the condition that I receive intensive counseling." David shifted in his chair and crossed his legs. He tapped his shoe nervously.

"And what has been the result of the counseling you have received?"

"Well, Dr. West has cleared up several issues for me. For instance, I now understand that I have a sexual addiction. Just as some people become addicted to cocaine, I became addicted to pornography and illicit sex. It became a compulsion that I had no power over."

"Mm-hmm. What else?" John asked as he looked at David over his reading glasses.

"He helped me to see that the roots of my addiction go

back to my childhood," David said in all seriousness.

"How so?"

"Well, this is the strange part. I had always thought I had a wonderful upbringing. I always enjoyed going back home to visit my folks because all of my memories are so pleasant. In contrast, Susan *hated* going back to see her parents because of the turmoil she experienced as a child. But I loved going back home and Susan always enjoyed the visits, too. You see, Dr. Kryer, I grew up in a loving Christian home. My dad and mom are still together after nearly fifty years of marriage."

"I fail to see the strange part."

"I'm getting to that. Dr. West took me back to my childhood and showed me that I had actually been abandoned as a child–emotionally, that is. My dad was such a hard worker that he didn't have a lot of time to spend with me, except two or three evenings a week and the weekends."

"That sounds like a fairly significant amount of time to me," John said as he took his glasses off and laid them on the desk.

"True, but they weren't quality times. I didn't have his full attention. But that isn't all. When we probed deeper into my memories, we discovered that I had been abused as a child."

"In what way?" John asked as he made a note on the sheet.

"Well, that's the problem–I can't remember," David said, holding his hands up in frustration.

"Can you remember any actual incident of abuse?" John asked.

"No, I can't, but Dr. West suspects that it may have been sexual in nature."

"Why?"

"Because of my current sexual addiction. The two go hand in hand, he tells me. And deeply traumatic events such as sexual abuse are often submerged in the hidden recesses of the mind. The fact that I can't remember the incidents confirms for Dr. West that I was abused."

John sat silently for a moment, thinking. He then looked up at David and said, "Tell me the memory you have that most closely resembles abuse."

"That's another problem, Dr. Kryer. I don't have any specific incidents. I did tell Dr. West of a dream I had, and that seemed significant to him."

"Tell me about it."

"Well, the dream took place in our garage, which was in back of our house. I used to play there all the time," David said with a faraway smile. "I could see the exact location of every tool on the wall. I could see the lawn rake, the shears, the snow shovel, dad's workbench–everything."

"Yes . . . ?" John said, waiting for David to complete the story.

"Then, in my dream, as I looked around the garage, I saw a soft shaft of light in the darkest corner."

"Uh-huh. And . . . ?"

"That's it."

"That's *all?*" John asked incredulously.

"Dr. West says he believes that my sexual abuse took place right there and that my mind is blocking the memory out."

John set his pen down on the desk and leaned back in his chair. "David, I need to ask you a question: Why did you come to see me?"

"Dr. West won't see me anymore."

"Why not?"

"My insurance ran out," David said, a bit embarrassed, "and they kicked me out of Greenway. Do you know how much it costs to stay at a psychiatric hospital?"

"How much?"

"My one-month stay cost the insurance company over $28,000!"

"And are you better now because of their therapy?"

John asked.

David pulled at his ear for a moment as he thought. Then he said, "To tell you the truth, I think I'm more confused now than ever!"

"Why?"

"Because when I thought my affair was simply the result of sinful choices I was making, I had hope. I know that the Lord forgives sin if we are truly repentant, and I was genuinely sorry for what I had done. I had determined that I would come under the close supervision of my church elders and that I would rebuild my shattered marriage. At Greenway, however, I was told that I have no control over my sexual desires. I can't blame myself for what I did. Somehow I've got to uncover the events in my past that have caused me to become this way. But without money, I can't continue therapy." He lowered his head and covered his face with his hands as he began to shake with silent sobs. After a few moments, he regained his composure and looked at John through his tears. "Can you help me, Dr. Kryer?"

With a tender smile John replied, "God can help you, David, and it won't take months of therapy and thousands of dollars. I want to review what you've told me. You shared with me a series of sinful choices you made: to watch X-rated films, to purchase pornography, to focus your mind and your heart on lustful thoughts, right?"

"Yes, that's true," David agreed.

"Then you chose to meet with Joan because she appealed to you sexually. No one forced you to begin the affair with her. Now–follow me closely here–you have been told that you have a sexual addiction. What is the proof for that? That you've had an affair and have been drawn to pornographic literature and movies. And why have you been drawn to the pornography and illicit affair? Because of the sexual addiction. That is circular reasoning, David."

David nodded and said, "I guess you're right."

"The same is true for the assumption that you were sexually abused as a child. You have absolutely no memory of any such event. But according to standard psychological theory, such events are routinely blocked out, and that very lack of memory becomes evidence in favor of the theory. Dream interpretation is so unreliable, David! How can we have any confidence that sexual abuse took place because in your dream you saw a shaft of light in a dark corner?"

"So you think that it's possible that I wasn't abused as a child?" David asked sincerely.

"I think it is not only possible, David, but that it is probable. Instead of the healing of memories taking place in your mind, I think there may have been a *creation* of memories of events that never took place."

"Are you saying that I don't have a sexual addiction?"

"What I'm saying is that the term *addiction* has been twisted and stretched so far by some psychologists that it is now routinely applied to every kind of wrong behavior. In your case, David, the simple fact is that you *chose* to sin. There is always a painful consequence to sin, but the answer is not to give it a new label or to deny it. The answer is to acknowledge it, confess it, and repent of it."

John opened his Bible to 1 John and slid it over to David. "When we come to the Lord Jesus in genuine repentance, He promises to forgive and to cleanse us of all unrighteousness. Look there in chapter 1, verse nine. We are given a fresh start. We don't have to go back and 'work through' our pain."

David sat in his chair as though stunned. His eyes darted back and forth over the verses as he thought through the implications of what John had just said. Suddenly his eyes lit up as the concept penetrated his heart. "Then I don't have to remain this way! I can ask God's forgiveness and begin walking with Him again!"

"That's right, David. You need to genuinely repent of the sinful choices you made. Here, read Acts 3:19 out loud," John said as he took the Bible and turned to Acts. He handed the Bible back.

David took the Bible and read aloud, "Repent, then, and turn to God, so that your sins may be wiped out, that times of refreshing may come from the Lord." David put the Bible down and looked at John. "That's what I want more than anything else in the world!"

"Then let's pray together. You need to confess what you've done and ask God's forgiveness and cleansing. Then I have a few more things to share with you before you go."

They bowed their heads and David prayed. "O dear Lord, I come to You realizing that I have accepted a lie that convinced me that I couldn't do anything about my sinful choices. I confess to You that I have been unfaithful to my wife . . . that I have filled my heart and mind with pornography and allowed myself to lust after other women. I am so very sorry, Lord," he said as his voice broke. Tears began streaming down his face. He sobbed in deep sorrow and anguish of soul as the truth of his sin finally hit deep in his heart. "O God, I am so very, *very* sorry! Forgive me and cleanse my heart." He choked with emotion and could only whisper, "O God! O God!" over and over.

John's head was bowed in prayer and tears trickled down his cheeks as he shared David's sorrow.

After several minutes, David regained his composure and continued in prayer. "O Lord, I thank You for Your forgiveness! I know I don't deserve it, but thank You. Please, Lord, give me the strength to do what is right from this moment on. I ask this in Jesus' wonderful name. Amen!"

David wiped his eyes with a tissue. Finally, he looked up with a smile of joy shining through his tears. "Now, tell me what I need to do, Dr. Kryer."

John smiled. He knew that David's willingness to take further action was a strong indication of sincere repentance. "You need to confess to your wife that you wronged her and ask her to forgive you for what you did." John opened his file drawer and took out a printed sheet. "I also have a Bible study here that I want you to go through this next week, David. I want to you read and meditate on each verse. Write down what you believe they mean and how you can apply them to your situation. Then I want you and your wife to come together for counseling next week to reinforce your decision. We may need to spend several weeks together in counseling to see your marriage begin to heal. I don't want you to expect an instant or easy solution."

David nodded in agreement.

"There's another issue I want to mention, David," John said. "I want you to contact your pastor and ask him if he would be willing to join you and your wife in our counseling sessions."

David sat back with a quizzical look on his face. "Why do you want my pastor to come?"

"Because it is his job to be the shepherd of his own sheep, David. We rarely allow prolonged counseling unless the person's pastor becomes involved. I am willing to counsel you if he can have a part in it. Do you think your pastor would be willing?"

David paused, thinking. "I honestly don't know, Dr. Kryer. He was the one who referred me here because he knows you do a lot of counseling. But I've heard him say that he doesn't consider himself to be a counselor."

"Well, this may be the opportunity he needs to develop that skill. At any rate, I want you to ask him to become involved. Will you do that?"

"Yes," David replied, "I'll ask him. But I don't know what he'll say."

John set the follow-up appointment and wrote it in his book. "Watch out this week, David. Satan is not going to let go of you easily. Expect a great deal of temptation to hit you. When that happens you will want to remember 1 Corinthians 10:12-13: 'If you think you are standing firm, be careful that you don't fall! No temptation has seized you except what is common to man. And God is faithful; he will not let you be tempted beyond what you can bear. But when you are tempted, he will also provide a way out so that you can stand up under it.' If you haven't done so already, I want you to memorize that passage," John said as he wrote it down on the assignment sheet and handed it to David.

John stood to his feet and shook David's hand. "Don't let Satan confuse you again, David. God is able to heal your heart and your marriage as you stay close to Him and fill your heart and mind with His Word."

2

False Memories

After I spoke at a men's retreat in Nebraska, a weary-looking man came up and asked if we could talk. He related a story that has become all too familiar. His wife had gone into therapy with a Christian psychologist because of a general feeling of depression. During the months of counseling that followed, she gradually became cold and angry toward her husband.

"Now her therapist has convinced her that she has some thirty separate personalities inside. She's getting worse as time goes along, and I owe the therapist more than $2,000. What can I do?"

A student at Dallas Theological Seminary called my office and asked, "Dr. Bulkley, can you recommend a biblical counselor who has an office in Dallas? My friend's wife was referred to a Christian psychologist and she is now convinced that she has multiple personalities. It's ruining their home."

A woman in California told me that a therapist had convinced her that she was suffering from MPD (multiple personality disorder)[6] and SRA (satanic ritual abuse). Under the guidance of her counselor, who was recommended by her church, she "remembered" her father abusing her sexually when she was a child. During the three years of therapy that followed, she severed all relations with her parents, accused her husband of molesting their daughter, lost her house, and finally lost her business. Since she could no longer pay for therapy, her counselor refused to see her anymore.

"I praise God I ran out of money," she said to me. "Otherwise I would still be trapped in that horrible lie!" She told me that after her counseling ended, it had taken almost a full year for her to realize that *none* of the events she had remembered during therapy had ever happened.

A heartbroken mother called me and related a similar story. Her daughter began seeing a psychologist at a Christian clinic near Denver. Her counselors recommended that she admit herself to a psychiatric hospital in Florida, where she was placed on powerful psychoactive drugs.

After a period of time, the young woman began to realize how carelessly drugs were being dispensed there and she told her parents that she planned to expose the hospital for its unethical and medically questionable treatment. A short time later, she was found dead in her room. The hospital reported that she had committed suicide, but certain details made the parents suspicious. They were able to obtain their daughter's medical records only through legal action and the hospital subsequently claimed that the young woman was a victim of sexual abuse by her father, but there is no evidence to back up their accusation. The mother said that their house was so small it would have been impossible for her husband to have concealed such abuse. The hospital now appears to be ready to settle out of court.

A couple in Colorado Springs wrote me a letter detailing how their daughter had accused them of sexually abusing her when she was a child. The book that triggered her "discovery" was written by a Christian psychologist from Denver who travels the country preaching a gospel of victimization.

Multiple Stories, All the Same

Story after story, call after call, though the minute details may vary slightly, the essence of the narratives have become routinely familiar: A person submits to general psychotherapy that leads to a diagnosis of possible sexual abuse. That, in turn, is followed by the recovery of repressed memories coupled with multiple personalities.

A caller phoned me on "Return to the Word" (a national radio broadcast produced by our church) to ask a question about her sister, who has been diagnosed as having MPD. She began to describe how her sister's counselor had arrived at the diagnosis. "Wait," I said. "Let me tell you how it was done, and you tell me if I'm wrong, okay?"

"Sure," she replied.

Our conversation went along these lines: "First, your sister probably went to a counselor complaining of general depression, poor self-esteem, a recent weight gain, or something like that. Correct?"

"Yes, that's right."

"During the therapy, the counselor began to suspect that your sister's symptoms were evidence of a much deeper problem and began asking what sort of childhood relationship she had with her parents—especially her father," I continued. "Am I still on track?"

"Absolutely!"

"My guess is that your sister had no specific memories of abuse, but during therapy sessions she began to experience hazy flashbacks of dark sexual and satanic ritual abuse, and eventually accused your father of having mo-lested her when she was a child."

"That's exactly what she did."

"Since then, your sister has 'discovered' that she has multiple personalities."

"Yes," the woman replied sadly.

"As therapy progresses, the number of personalities

keeps rising," I said. "Sometimes therapists have brought out as many as thirty, forty, or even eighty personalities. How many has your sister's therapist found?"

"One hundred and twenty-eight!"

I didn't have time to tell the caller that unless she accepted her sister's new belief in her multiple personalities, the sister would cut herself off from all further contact with the family. That's part of the therapy.

The recovery of repressed memories and the diagnosis of multiple personalities seem to go hand in hand. Stories like the ones I have just shared have been repeated thousands of times in America. Only the names and details vary.

It is worthy of note that multiple personality disorder seems to be a uniquely American ailment.[7] Until recently, it was rarely diagnosed elsewhere. But as the literature on MPD has spread across the globe, so has the "disease." It is now being reported in England, Canada, Mexico, Australia, and New Zealand.[8]

Hopeful signs, however, are now emerging as people who were once firmly convinced of their victimization have begun to recant their claims of having been sexually abused. They are now accusing their psychotherapists of an equally serious form of abuse: the *creation* of false memories.

How False Memories Are Created

A tragic yet common view in Christian counseling today is that to be free from the wounds of the past, a person must *return* to that past under the guidance of a trained counselor. The counselee is told that when he re-experiences the pain and trauma that took place in the past, he will gain the insight and power to "work through" the issues he is struggling with in the present.

A multitude of therapists today are convincing thousands of suffering Christians that they were so horribly abused as children that their memories have been repressed in a self-protective cocoon. Much like a toxic waste dump contaminates underground water supplies, these memories are said to leak "psychic poison" into a person's subconscious so that he cannot function normally. That is why the victim has a weight problem, can't hold onto a job, can't maintain a marriage, can't relate to his children, can't . . . The list can go on forever.

A Downward Spiral

Remember Gloria Grady and her parents Lee and Jean, in the Dallas area? (see pages 23-25). They entered the maze of psychotherapy because of Gloria's weight problem.

> Her mother, Jean, had taken [Gloria] to the well-known Minirth-Meier Clinic, a Richardson counseling service that touts psychological treatment from a Christian perspective. (On religious radio stations, the "Minirth-Meier Hour" features its therapists talking about the treatment of everything from tobacco addiction to serious psychiatric disorders.) . . . Minirth-Meier seemed to Gloria Grady to be just what she was looking for. They were doctors, they were good Christians, they were on [a Christian radio station]: it seemed the perfect place for a 25-year-old Baptist minister's daughter to put her trust.[9]

During her initial five-week stay, Gloria was treated with antidepressants and medication for a thyroid problem. "She was released owing about $11,000 to the hospital and $5,000-$6,000 to Minirth-Meier."[10] She continued indi-vidual and group therapy every week.

Under the care of her psychologist, Dr. Richard Flournoy, Gloria was instructed to write down all of her negative experiences in the past. But she didn't get better.

Her brother, Jim, reports:

> As a family, we began noticing mood changes, small personality changes, and an obsession with the dark side of life—the bad, negative things that happened to others and herself. She slowly became deeply introspective, and was defensive toward anyone who might inquire why or fail to show the same zeal to explore these areas.[11]

Gloria plunged into an ever-deepening depression, so she increased her visits to Dr. Flournoy. As a result, was that she got deeper and deeper into debt.[12]

Flournoy had Gloria purchase a teddy bear and she took it with her to her therapy sessions. "She said her therapist wanted her to go back as close to infancy as she possibly could and write down every bad thing that had happened to her," her brother Jim wrote. "When my wife and I expressed how ridiculous we though that was, we were told that she would have to 'get worse before she could get better.'"[13]

Gloria became increasingly hostile to her family as time went along. Jim said, "I told her I didn't think Flournoy and all those drugs were helping her."[14] She began acting more and more bizarre. Once, she "began flailing at him violently; then, when her parents drove up, she abruptly stopped and began laughing."[15]

Flournoy left Minirth-Meier in 1986, and Gloria followed him to his private practice. Under continued therapy, "Gloria was carrying her teddy bear everywhere. She also had bought a child's punching bag so she could vent her frustrations."[16]

One day Gloria took too much medication, and was admitted to the psychiatric unit at Richardson Medical Center. Nearly two months later, Lee and Jean Grady received a letter from their daughter. In it, she wrote:

> In the course of my stay, I've uncovered
> many horrible memories of my childhood that
> relate to the three of you as well as other family
> members. The pain has been so unbearable at
> times, that I could hardly stand it—that I've liter-
> ally wanted to die at the remembrance of the
> abuse suffered at your hands . . . . Because of
> these horrible memories, I find it necessary to
> remove myself from our family system—a system
> that denies the hurtful and painful memories that
> have haunted me for many years.[17]

Eventually, Gloria sought a restraining order to prevent her family from contacting her. In the three-day court hearing, Jim reports that "we listened to Gloria describe the most heinous, gruesome, macabre, and perverted things imaginable."[18]

> She systematically accused my Father, Mother,
> myself, both grandfathers, her maternal grand-
> mother and uncle and others of being involved in
> satanic, ritualistic abuse, including intercourse,
> sodomy, and object penetration, animal sacrifice,
> sacrifice of numerous babies that she conceived
> through incestuous relationships, including one
> that my grandmother hid until it was three years
> old, dismembering and eating the babies and
> other fetal material, and drinking the blood.[19]

Jim points out that "all of this was patterned almost ver-
batim after a book called *Satan's Underground,* by Lauren
Stratford, which has since been exposed as a fraud."[20]

It didn't seem to matter who disputed Gloria's "recovered" memories. "Anyone we presented as factual witnesses,

such as doctors, law enforcement officers, church officials, and others–all of whom had been intimate friends of our family during the years in question–Gloria would simply lean over the Assistant District Attorney representing her and whisper, 'They were part of it, too.'"[21]

From a weight problem, to depression, to satanic ritual abuse, the revelations of therapy had managed to tear a seemingly loving family apart.

A Destructive New "Disorder"

Other therapists take the concept of repressed memories a step further by introducing the diagnosis of MPD– multiple personality disorder. This theory states that it's possible for inner suffering to become so unbearable that the personality of the patient literally fragments into several separate beings–each having an independent will, personality, and mental process. The therapist then must counsel not just one patient but each separate personality within the patient as well.

I have spoken to people across America who have relatives that were diagnosed as having MPD. Once the patient understands how this "disorder" works, the number of personalities that emerge can multiply at a rapid pace–eighty, one hundred, or even hundreds of distinct entities. Each of these personalities is said to require individual treatment. Some Christian therapists go so far as to teach that each personality must independently receive Christ as his or her Savior!

After reading an article I had written,[22] a missionary in Kenya wrote me a letter detailing the tragedy that this twisted theory has inflicted on her family. Her sister is a patient of a major Christian writer and practitioner of MPD therapy. "Your article captured perfectly the consequences of getting mixed up in this kind of therapeutic milieu," the missionary wrote. "It has been totally destructive to the family unit and has left my sister in a terrible state. Today she is isolated, paranoid, and seemingly far from experiencing a productive life."[23]

She went on to say that "those who do not support this diagnosis or go along with the 'junk' that has been created in the mind of the patient are quickly labeled as 'being in the state of denial.' This appears to be a neat little rationale and defense mechanism which is used as an assurance that [the therapist] and his MPD, SRA, and child abuse theories are correct and that everyone else is totally off base."[24]

The missionary also sent along a copy of the letter she had written to this well-known Christian therapist.

> Dear _____,
>
> I am writing to express my grief over the devastating results of your "therapeutic techniques." To put it quite bluntly, it would appear that you have created a monster inside my sister, [name]. There is no question that she had problems before she met you, but they seem insignificant compared to what she now lives with daily. . . .
>
> If you tell a person she has a certain disease long enough, she will develop the symptoms. (Especially when that person is already vulnerable and most definitely when she is supplied with the manual describing the disease and the symptoms.)...
>
> In the past two-and-a-half years, [my sister] has been brought to the brink of suicide and trapped in an emotional prison of untruth and mental torture. Her precious children have missed out on their mother's love, attention, and relationship. Her husband has lived under the strain of incredible and continual stress ... Family, friends, and church life have long ago been written out of the script. My parents are grief-stricken and wonder daily if they will ever see their daughter again. We three siblings and our families are feeling the

loss of a relationship that once represented the completeness of what used to be a close family unit. . . .

During her time under your care, [my sister] has become so introspective that she has often been unaware of the world around her. She has taken ownership of the seeds of doubt and suspicion which have been sown in her mind. Perhaps worst of all, Satan, rather than Christ, seems to have her undivided attention. This is not progress. This is not healing. This is a tragedy in the making! . . .

There has not been one positive sign along the way; not one sustained glimmer of hope or improvement. In fact, quite the opposite has occurred. [My sister's] behavior and level of functioning has progressively deteriorated to the point of self-destruction, paranoia, and isolation.[25]

Not surprisingly, the doctor doesn't document this sort of tragedy in his book,[26] which has convinced many unwitting Christians of the reality of multiple personality disorder and satanic ritual abuse.

Oddly, it doesn't seem to matter to many "social scientists" that there is not the slightest shred of scientific proof that multiple personalities exist. Beyond that, the only concept in the Bible that even comes close to MPD is demonic possession. If that's what MPD is, then psychotherapy will be no more effective than were the seven sons of Sceva in Acts 19:13-16.

A Growing Skepticism

As this book demonstrates, there is a growing body of evidence suggesting that the theory of repressed memories is absolutely false. A Denver newspaper reported that "at least 80 Colorado therapists have been accused of brainwashing clients into falsely believing they were sexually abused as children."[27]

A few years ago in Philadelphia, the False Memory Syndrome Foundation (FMSF) was started.[28] Its membership has since grown to include thousands of families who claim they are the victims of therapeutic abuse.[29] Critics of FMSF allege that the founders themselves have questionable histories and that the organization is a front for genuine abusers to hide behind. While it is possible that some actual abusers have joined FMSF, the fact remains that thousands of parents have been wrongly accused of abusing their children–all because of incompetent psychotherapy.

Jane Brennan said she went through three years of agony under the guidance of a therapist. She had begun to experience depression after the birth of twins and was suffering from premenstrual syndrome. She decided to see a therapist, who told her that at least one-third of all women experienced sexual abuse as children.

"From the minute I walked in her door, her agenda was sexual abuse by my father. That's all we talked about. I remember saying to her, 'I was never sexually abused by my father.' But she just kept at it."[30] Unwilling to accept Jane's denials of sexual abuse, the therapist eventually convinced Jane, who was subsequently treated with hypnotism and antidepressant drugs.

"At her therapist's insistence, she wrote a letter to her parents laying out the charges and saying they couldn't see her or the grandkids again. Her father had a stroke after reading the letter."[31]

Rather than backing off, the therapist said, "That's a ploy. That's what they all do." Eventually Jane's husband became concerned about her health, which was worsening as therapy continued. He secretly substituted fiber pills for her antidepressant drugs, and to everyone's surprise, Jane's condition began to improve! "Only when she stopped seeing the therapist altogether did she begin to feel better."[32]

Fad Therapies

The theories of repressed memories and MPD are powerful and tragic examples of fad therapies and pop psychology are driven by media attention and incompetent counseling.

An incredible example of the insane behavior fostered by twisted psychological theories involves a woman, Lisa Roth, who visited the Jefferson County Mental Health Center because of depression and alcoholism. Lynda Robinson, the female social worker assigned to her case, diagnosed Roth as having multiple personality disorder and "estimated that it would take from three to 10 years for Roth to recover."[33]

Part of the treatment included having the patient sleep with the therapist and her husband. "Robinson said she first had Roth sleep between her and her husband when she 'regressed' and became unable to talk. 'I considered her at that point to be a child and a member of our family,' Robinson said in a deposition."[34] She said "she became a mother figure to Roth."[35]

To her surprise, Robinson's husband and her patient became sexually involved. Since then, the Robinsons have divorced and the patient, Lisa Roth, has married Robinson's husband. But there's even more: Not content to have her therapist's husband, Roth has now sued Robinson and the mental health center for mismanaging her care.

The therapist–knowing how confused the courts can be when faced with issues of the mind–has pled innocent, saying that "she cannot remember basic concepts of psychotherapy–even the definition of the word–much less the reasons for treating Roth the way she did."[36] And why can't she remember? "Robinson blames her poor memory on toxicity from leaking breast implants that she contends has damaged her brain."[37]

Roth's lawyer, however, says that Robinson's memory

seems to be quite selective; and in court records, psychiatrist Marita Keeling says "that Roth was misdiagnosed and mistreated and that her mental problems worsened as Robinson *became obsessed with her treatment and fostered the creation of multiple personalities*"[38] (emphasis added). "Lynda [Robinson] appears to have been quite enthralled with her role as discoverer and rescuer of Lisa, the (multiple-personality) patient."[39]

Yet when psychological grievance boards examine complaints about malpractice of this sort, they have great difficulty in deciding whether the therapist was at fault. Amos Martinez, administrator for the mental health regulatory section of Colorado state government, admits that malpractice is hard to prove. "The bottom line is the board [doesn't always know] if the therapist acted appropriately."[40]

This is Martinez' conclusion about why some counselors incorrectly diagnose sexual abuse:

> The majority of therapists who diagnose widespread incest "have had problems like this of their own in the past. They have been victimized by their own parents. They have patterns of abuse themselves, and they see everyone's problems through those same lenses."[41]

That shocking opinion comes from no less than a person who is at the heart of the psychiatric industry. Consider the implications of his statement that therapists "see everyone's problems through those same lenses" of the abuse they suffered. In essence, he says that therapists project their own problems on their clients and then make questionable diagnoses. The therapies, therefore, cannot be any better than the unreliable diagnoses of the psychotherapists.

Recently, a "conference was co-sponsored by Johns Hopkins Medical Institutions and the False Memory Syndrome Foundation."[42] According to *The Baltimore Sun*,

Dr. Paul McHugh, chief of psychiatry at Johns Hopkins, said society has been swept by an epidemic of false accusations based on a "fad" theory–recovered memory of sexual abuse. He said the memories often occur while the patients are under hypnosis, a technique that makes them vulnerable to suggestion. "If these practices become standard, then no family that has a member who goes in for psychotherapy is safe from persecution," he said.[43]

What Psychotherapists Are Saying

It is interesting–and at the same time discouraging–that criticism of current psychotherapies is not coming primarily from the Christian camp. Ironically, it is coming from *secular* therapists themselves:

"If [other weird therapies] made us look dumb, this [repressed childhood memories] will make us look totally gullible," says psychiatrist Paul McHugh, chairman of the psychiatry department at Johns Hopkins University. "This [repressed childhood memories] is the biggest story in psychiatry in a decade. It is a disaster for orthodox psychotherapists who are doing good work" (inserts added).[44]

Leon Jaroff asks a necessary question: "Can memories of repeated incest and other bizarre incidents be so repressed that the victim is totally unaware of them until they emerge during therapy or as the result of a triggering sight, smell or sound?"[45]

These memories are debatable, according to Jaroff:

Unlike the countless adults who have lived for years with painful memories of actual childhood sexual abuse, most individuals with "recovered memory" initially have no specific recollection of incest or molestation. At worst, they have only a vague feeling that something may have happened. Others, simply seeking help to alleviate depression, eating disorders, marital difficulties or other common problems, are informed by unsophisticated therapists or pop-psychology books that their symptoms suggest childhood sexual abuse, all memories of which have been repressed.[46]

How are these victims able to recall their repressed memories after a number of years or even decades have passed?

In the course of the therapy, many of these troubled souls conjure up exquisitely detailed recollections of sexual abuse by family members. Encouraged by their therapists to reach deeper into the recesses of their memories–often using techniques such as visualization and hypnosis–some go on to describe events that sorely strain credulity, particularly tales of their forced childhood participation in satanic rituals involving animal and infant sacrifices, as well as sexual acts.[47]

The Problem of Universal Victimization

Some psychotherapists truly believe that nearly every human being was or is a victim of sexual abuse. As one Christian "authority" on sexual abuse writes, "At times, I wonder if every person in the world, male and female, young and old, has been sexually abused."[48] The result of this belief is that sexual abuse can become the ready explanation for every human failure. And the outcome of such false diagnoses is the trivialization of genuine victims.

To give victim status to those who were never abused is a disservice to those who *were* genuine victims. When we reclassify nearly everyone as a victim of abuse, we debase authentic casualties of childhood violation.

In our culture, nearly *everyone* is considered a victim of someone or something. Charles Krauthammer observes that "in a culture of grotesque self-absorption, the criminal's psychic restoration is at least as important as the victim's."[49] The reason this has been accepted, he argues, is that in America, "one no longer sins against God, natural law, the moral order, society or even one's fellow man...but against oneself."[50] Krauthammer hits upon the real problem when he says, "When everyone is a victim—in need of 'healing'—no one is a victim."[51]

Therapist-Induced Memories

Therapist-induced memories are a tragedy of incredible proportions. According to a report in *USA Today,* 31 percent of therapists believe they can help their patients recover memories not only of their past but also from alleged *past lives!* An even larger number—40 percent—believe the claim that patients can recover memories from infancy. According to the report, one out of three therapists surveyed believe that "the mind stores everything; it's just a matter of retrieving the 'facts.'"[52] On the contrary, says Michael Yapko, a San Diego psychologist and hypnotist, "many therapists don't know that memory is responsive to suggestion."[53]

Why the sudden explosion of abuse memories in America today? Could it be the therapists themselves? The summary of an article that appeared in *Insight* magazine states:

> Families are being torn apart as adult children suddenly appear to recall childhood sexual abuse.

Yet there is an eerie similarity among cases. Nearly all the accusers are white, college-educated women in their 30s and 40s, and in virtually every case the memory of alleged sexual abuse occurs only after psychotherapy.[54]

The report asks, "Are the shrinks to blame?" Mark Pendergrast thinks so. He's the author of a new book, *Victims of Memory.* "Pendergrast says he–and thousands of parents like him–are the real victims. His book seeks to prove that his daughters and other 'incest survivors' have fallen prey to what skeptics call 'false memory syndrome.'"[55]

How does this happen?

Therapists who believe memories can be lost and retrieved often say that if you think you were abused, you probably were. But Pendergrast, as well as a significant portion of the mental health community, believes traumatic memories are never forgotten.

He charges that these so-called "memories" that patients are digging up are in fact their imagination, encouraged by therapists who believe incest is as common as chicken pox in the American family.[56]

Some people will no doubt suspect that Pendergrast is only trying to protect himself. As journalist Anne Rochell says, "Some people will see the book as a father's ultimate act of love. Others will see it as a guilty man's obsessive attempt to clear his name."[57]

Though Pendergrast's book is described by some people as "one of the best-researched, most thorough studies of the theory that memories of a traumatic childhood can be fabricated,"[58] others are not so sure. "'He does have a bias,' said Laura Brown, a clinical psychologist in Seattle, who opposes Pendergrast's belief that recovered memories are made up. 'We're assuming he's telling the truth when he says he never did this, but how do we know?'"[59]

Indeed, how *does* a person know the truth about events that supposedly took place years or decades before when the only "evidence" is "recovered" memories? As a female juror in Michigan stated, "I think if you're going to accuse someone, you have to have more evidence than memories."[60]

Though Pendergrast's experience is tragic, it seems to be representative. Joseph P. Kahn comments in *The Boston Globe*:

> Pendergrast's story, while idiosyncratic, is hardly unique. It differs in substance, not form, from thousands who claim to be victims of what is known as false memory, pseudomemory or constructed memory syndrome (even the nomenclature is charged with controversy). And it surfaces at a time when documented cases of incest and child abuse are soaring. In virtually all cases where recovered memory plays a role, the gray areas are stippled in shadow. Only the trajectory of grief is similar.[61]

It used to be that the main critics of the recovery of memories were thought to be insensitive and unsympathetic men. Now, however, women are coming out and declaring that they were victims of psychotherapy itself rather than of sexual abuse.

According to a report in *The Baltimore Sun* by Jonathan Bor,

> Donna Smith once tried to put her father in jail for alleged acts of sexual abuse, some of them supposedly performed during satanic rituals. But

yesterday, she told a gathering of 800 people at a Baltimore conference that the crimes never happened–they appeared in "false memories" coaxed by therapists . . . Two things have put her on the road to mental health: her parents' unconditional love and her resolve to stay out of therapy.[62]

Lynn Gondolf professed that she was victimized by psychotherapy as well:

As Gondolf tells it, she is a victim–not of abuse, but of therapy, which sent her into a two-year tailspin of multiple hospitalizations, familial confrontations, suicide attempts and daily doses of mood altering drugs.

Gondolf believes that she is a victim of an overzealous therapist who used techniques including trance writing and dream guidance to manipulate her into believing that she had repressed the memories of sexual abuse at the hands of her mother, father and grandfather.[63]

The alleged abuse by family members simply had not happened. However, Gondolf had no trouble remembering an event of sexual abuse that had *truly* happened.

"I had actually been sexually abused by someone else," says Gondolf. "But I remembered that. I remember exactly what happened and when it happened. But the rest of this stuff I didn't remember at all."[64]

A young wife who was enrolled in our counseling training program told me a similar story.[65] "I was raised in French Canada," she said, "and I grew up in a home that was involved in witchcraft. I was not abused as a part of the cult itself, but my own father, who was a pedophile, did rape me and I remembered the event. In my counseling at the New Life Treatment Center, however, my therapists were not satisfied with my real story. They insisted that I come up with other even more bizarre stories of abuse. They wouldn't accept the simple truth, as bad as it was. They needed something even worse."

Though she was being treated at a nominally Christian center, *her psychiatrist was an unbeliever* and it was *against ward policy for a patient to study the Bible or to pray!* When she insisted on doing so, she was diagnosed as being "passive-aggressive." An intense interest in spiritual things was viewed as part of her "illness." In their view, her problem was not spiritual; it was sexual.

A Theory Based on Speculation

The current theory among memory-recovery therapists is that if a person has some form of dysfunction (and with virtually every human problem being labeled as a dysfunction, nearly everyone qualifies), sexual abuse is probably a root cause—*especially* if the victim can't recall the abuse.

A research journalist presented this stinging indictment of Christian psychotherapy: "It is no accident that the 'Christian counselors' tend to be the worst kind of suggestive therapists, encouraging memories of satanic ritual abuse."[66]

Perhaps you think I've exaggerated the problem. Actually, I have carefully understated it. As one article points out,

> After all, according to the bible of adult self-recovery from child sexual abuse, *The Courage to Heal*, by Ellen Bass and Laura Davis, it doesn't matter if you actually recall being sexually abused. "If you think you were abused, and your life shows

the symptoms," the book states flatly, "then you were."[67]

When Mark Pendergrast, the author of *Victims of Memory,* visited as a guest on the "Return to the Word" radio broadcast, he made a revealing comparison: "The book *The Wounded Heart* is a very dangerous book. It is the Christian equivalent of *The Courage to Heal.*"

It is tragic that so many people believe these unproved and unprovable claims. An electronic bulletin board on a nationwide computer network is dedicated to the recovery of repressed memories. The messages that flashed back and forth from a self-proclaimed victim named Kathy and her electronic therapists reveal how foolish this thinking can become:

> Dennis: The thing that worked best for me was to tell myself a few times each day that my memories would come back to me in my dreams. Then I would have pencil and paper on my night stand and got in the habit of writing down what I could remember from my dreams the instant I woke up. Within a week I had ten pages of memories from my past that I had forgotten for up to almost 30 years. Within two weeks I had twenty pages.[68]

Kathy related her experience of a flashback of memory:

> The flashback...didn't make any sense to me. I had a flashback of lying in bed in a basement room, and all of a sudden there was such a bright flash at the window that I can't even describe the brightness of it. Then I heard steps coming down the stairs, and I knew someone was coming to get me.
> The weird thing is–I lived in Louisiana when

I was growing up, and there aren't any basements in Louisiana. I didn't live in a basement bedroom until I was twenty. And as for the flash of light, I have no idea what that could have been. I'm puzzled. I thought flashbacks were of things that really happened . . . not symbols to represent things that happened. If flashbacks come in symbol form I'm in BIG trouble, because I can't even interpret my dreams![69]

Others were quick, however, to supply the needed interpretation:

The person coming for you in the basement is you. Houses frequently represent our psyche, as a whole, with various rooms, layers, and structures. Something happening in the basement is at a very primitive level, very deep down in the psyche, perhaps deeper than memory itself. For contrast, something happening at the highest level would indicate the 'thinking' layer, usually too much thinking, or rationality.

The flash that you saw is very much related to the topic you're currently investigating–'Flashbacks.' Symbols often take literal meanings like this. The person going down into the basement is you, going down into yourself, as you investigate deep-rooted memories and flashbacks. You may also literally be going down to rescue a part that wants to be rescued now, perhaps from something that happened as a child.[70]

It is sad that the online therapeutic interpretations the woman received are not that far off from some forms of professional psychotherapy.

Eventually, one cautious person warned Kathy that

one problem with focusing on potentially bad memories is that sometimes things can be "remembered" that never really happened. Within a few months of dealing with my own sexual abuse memories, the minister at the church I sometimes attended was accused of rape. I got really emotionally involved in this case...and one day I found I had a fleeting memory of being raped by HIM! I know for a fact I was never in a room with him alone, so I know for a fact that that could not have happened. But, still, I had something that I could have accepted as a memory if I hadn't analyzed it a little.[71]

A workbook based on the bestselling book *Unlocking the Secrets of Your Childhood Memories* mentions Proverbs 14:8, "The wisdom of the prudent is to understand his way," (NASB) and then says, "To discover where you are going, you must first know where you've been."[72] Is that what the verse teaches? Is it really necessary to understand your past to successfully move into the future? The focus of Proverbs 14:8 isn't memories of the past, but a person's entire manner of life.

The authors then make this astounding claim: "In *Unlocking the Secrets of Your Childhood Memories,* we make the reader a promise, *'Tell us about your earliest childhood memories, and we'll tell you about yourself today'* "[73] (emphasis in original).

One description of the process reveals just how shallow such analysis can be:

Several years ago we did a radio series on memories and their power . . . . In that series Randy Carlson, coauthor of *Unlocking the Secrets of Your Childhood Memories,* turned the tables on Minirth-Meier New Life Clinic psychotherapist Brian Newman and me. We were always analyzing other people; now we were to subject our earliest memories to analysis.

Brian: "My earliest? I used to be an early riser. My parents had to put a lock on the outside of my door or little old Brian would be up and roaming the neighborhood. I would ride with the milkman to a cul-de-sac. There was one gentleman I used to go and wake up, and he'd sit on his porch with his coffee and give me a glass of milk, and we'd talk."

Randy: "What was the emotion?"

Brian: "Excitement. Pleasure and excitement."

Randy's analysis: Brian likes new and exciting things, different things. He's not afraid to step forth. He values relationships highly and is action-oriented.[74]

Another analyst might be tempted to make a big deal of the lock on Brian's door and how he was trying to escape his family because they couldn't successfully communicate with him. Perhaps he was seeking love and friendship that had been denied him in his unhappy childhood.

The point is, there is *nothing* scientific or biblical about this kind of "analysis." It is more akin to sideshow palm reading and circus-tent astrology than to serious counseling! It is so foolish, it's *embarrassing* to realize that it is happening under the guise of Christianity.

Repressed Memories and the Law

It is frightening to see how easily people have bought into this questionable therapy of memory recovery. It has even affected the judicial system in America.

Legislatures in nearly half the states have responded to the widespread public acceptance of recovered memories by applying a strange twist to venerable statute-of-limitations laws. In general, the new legislation allows alleged victims of child abuse to sue the accused perpetrators within three to six years after the repressed memories emerge. This means that with little more than the recollection of the accuser, a parent or other relative can be hauled into court decades after the supposed crime.[75]

Another article shows how American law is being transformed by individuals who accuse their families of past abuse and base there allegations on "recovered memories":

In response to pressure from the incest survivors movement, legislatures in more than a dozen states have responded by changing statutes of limitations to allow adult victims to bring suits based on retrieved memories of incidents that allegedly occurred decades before. For instance, the state of Washington passed legislation that sets the clock ticking only from the date such abuse is remembered.[76]

As a result, parents, grandparents, pastors, and priests are being accused of abusing family members and parishioners decades ago. Think for a moment how *you* would defend yourself if someone accused you of having molested him or her twenty years ago. There would be no physical evidence, no actual proof. But how would you *prove* your innocence?

You see, it's very difficult to prove you *didn't* do something. That's why American courts have traditionally placed the burden of proof upon the accuser. Thanks to psychology, however, that may be changing.

Taking advantage of the newly enacted legislation, some of the supposed victims have successfully brought civil and even criminal actions against members of their own families . . . .

To many critics of the recovered-memory movement, the accusations and convictions are reminiscent of the 17th-century Salem witchcraft trials, in which elderly women and an occasional man were condemned to death, often on the basis of a single unsubstantiated charge that they had demonstrated witch-like behavior.[77]

False Memories Unmasked

A published study by Eric Nelson and Dr. Paul Simpson lists some of the ways that "memories" of abuse are created: suggestions of memories by therapists and members of recovery groups, intense pressure by therapists and group members to produce memories, the reading of recovery and abuse books, watching videos and movies that relate to abuse and recovery, attending seminars which instruct "victims" in the recovery of memories, and intentional "confabulation."[78]

In their study, Nelson and Simpson provide testimonies from people who give a frightening glimpse into the development of false memory syndrome. One subject stated, "[My therapist] became angry because I couldn't get memories; he said I didn't want to. He gave me ten minutes to get a memory. I became scared, and made up a memory to make him happy."[79]

Another reported, "I didn't have SRA [satanic ritual abuse] memories. The therapists put me in the hospital for eight weeks until I remembered SRA. (Finally) I mimicked SRA flashbacks because I had seen them a hundred times in group. I did this to get out."[80]

According to this same report, recovery group members exert pressure on individuals to produce memories. "The group progressed from eating disorders to childhood sexual abuse, to incest, to SRA. Eight out of ten members developed SRA memories, the two who didn't were told they were in denial."[81]

False memories were also induced by the books, videos, television shows, and movies recommended by the therapists. The books included *The Courage to Heal, Suffer the Children, People of the Lie, Michelle Remembers, Sybil, The Rabbit Howls, Satan Seller, Toxic Parents,* and *Secret Survivors*.[82] The movies, videos, and television shows were *Sybil, Three Faces of Eve, The Rabbit Howls,* and "The Oprah Winfrey Show."[83]

Both Dr. Simpson and Mr. Nelson offer seminars about false memories in the hope of alerting the public about this growing menace.[84]

Jumping on the Bandwagon

In spite of the swelling indication that "repressed" memories of childhood abuse are fabricated by therapy, many people in *Christian* counseling have jumped onto this psychological bandwagon enthusiastically.

In a recent study, Nelson and Simpson wrote that sixteen of their twenty subjects "reported that their therapists characterized themselves as Christians. . . . Most subjects reported significant Christian overtones present during therapy," such as "prayer, Bible reading, speaking in tongues, spiritual warfare, and exorcisms."[85]

The victims of therapy-induced memories may find their faith seriously damaged as a result. One subject in the study admitted, "Now I am an agnostic." Another said, "I no longer trust pastors or attend church." Still another reported, "My therapist told me to leave my church because it was satanic, [and] to transfer to his church. I now . . . no longer go to church." Other statements included: "[Therapy] really [debased] my faith. It contaminated it." "My belief system was devalued through my therapy." "I don't know if I will ever go to a formal church again because of it."[86]

Nelson and Simpson summarize:

> The results of this study are disturbing. Though Christian therapy can have many positive and beneficial aspects, it appears that some therapists who are identified as Christians appear to be involved in questionable therapeutic interventions, practices which appear to be detrimental to the mental and spiritual well-being of their clients. Many of the subjects report that though they have remained Christians, they have little trust of pastors or Christian therapists after their therapy experience. . . .
>
> By utilizing trance induction techniques in order to elicit visualizations, Christian therapists have aligned themselves with Freudian theory, new age practitioners, and radical feminist thinking.[87]

In spite of such dangers, one Christian expert on sexual abuse tours America hosting seminars on recovery. Crowds of women have paid hundreds of dollars each to listen to his theories of how a person's wounded heart can be healed through confronting and harassing the supposed abusers. He evidently has more invitations than he can fill, for he has franchised his seminar and other therapists are now spreading his recovery doctrines in meetings across the country.

Recently a man called me from Ohio to ask about his wife's problems, which stemmed from a diagnosis of MPD. Her story followed the pattern of many similar accounts I've heard.

"I'm guessing here," I said, "but your wife's therapist has

probably given her some books to read: *The Wounded Heart* and *Uncovering the Mystery of MPD.*"

"Yes! Those are the exact books she's been reading!" he exclaimed. He went on to tell me about his wife's progressing bitterness and alienation from her family and from God.

A bestselling author and Christian psychiatrist has written a book called *The Power of Memories*, which claims to be the "complete guide to understanding the surprising ways your memories affect your all-around health and well-being."[88] The author believes that "by understanding how memory works, realizing what it will and will not do, and then acting on that understanding" a person can reshape his future. "The techniques . . . can improve anyone's life."[89]

Leaning heavily on the Freudian theory of the unconscious, the book appears to teach that a person can experience wholeness through psychotherapy, and reworking one's memories. Though he acknowledges the fact that "memory does not work like a video camera," the author writes that "there are blank spots in memories that you and others can fill in later. Can you alter actual memories? Yes."[90] It is that very fact that should cause us great concern. Memories *are* being altered and families are being destroyed by people who try to fill in the memory blanks for others.

This author acknowledges that memories are not always accurate:

> Can memories be invented or distorted? Yes. If conditions are right; if the description is vivid enough, and especially if it addresses more than one sense (taste plus vision, perhaps, or smell plus sound); if the desire to remember a described thing is strong enough, the mind can adopt as its own a memory that has been created elsewhere. But that is exceedingly rare.[91]

Not anymore. Now it has become discouragingly common. In reading this text on memories, however, it seems as though the author himself is uncertain about the validity of memory therapy. "Memories can lie. They can play tricks. They can change. . . . You must be careful, therefore about giving extreme credence to any detail of memories . . . It sounds then like memory is not accurate and you shouldn't trust the pictures and stories from your past."[92]

Yes, that's *exactly* how it sounds. But the amazing conclusion of the author? "On the contrary. You would be amazed at how accurate those records are!"[93]

Rather than encouraging Christians to find healing through the Holy Spirit as He applies the Word of God, this world-famous Christian psychiatrist emphasizes the unproven theories of subconscious denial[94] and psychological determinism. "His bad memories . . . were preventing him from living a full life. In ways his conscious mind did not grasp, his memories shaped the way he behaved and even how well he got along in life."[95]

There is little suggestion that a person might be suffering as a result of conscious, sinful choices. In addition, I noted that no biblical references appeared in the book until page 90. Yet thousands of his readers will be convinced that they can find peace of mind by reworking their memories.

What a disaster! Instead of finding the peace that God offers through His divine power, Christians are being offered counterfeit solutions that lead them back into pain, sin, bitterness, and defeat.

Miriam got the book on recovery from sexual abuse that Wanda had recommended and read it desperately. She marked the pages and underlined passages for Cliff to read.

"I'm beginning to understand myself and my pain," she told Cliff one day. "I'm learning to listen to my own heart even when others don't agree, approve, or understand."

"I assume that includes me?" Cliff asked. Miriam didn't answer, and walked quickly out of the room.

As the months passed, Cliff and Miriam found it increasingly difficult to reconcile their diverging views of inner healing. Their relationship grew more and more distant. Whenever Cliff began to express affection, Miriam tensed and made it clear that she was not interested. Finally, she said to him coldly, "I can't stand to think of a man even touching me. It makes my skin crawl!"

One day Miriam informed Cliff that she was going to attend the seminar that her cousin was recommending. "Michael and Wanda have asked me to attend the seminar on sexual abuse this weekend in Detroit. I plan on getting some of my personal issues resolved while I'm out there."

Cliff slumped in emotional weariness. "They just won't give up, will they? How are we supposed to pay for it, Miriam?"

"Is that all you care about? The expense?" she fumed. "Michael and Wanda are paying for it, so you don't have to worry!"

"It's not just the money, Miriam. The more I see of this whole recovery business, the less I trust it. I'm not sure what they might teach in this seminar."

"Well, I trust Michael and Wanda. They love me and want nothing but the best for me."

"And I suppose you think I don't love you?"

"I didn't say that, Cliff! Look, this isn't getting us anywhere. I'm going to that seminar, and that's that!"

The next day, Miriam flew to Detroit. When she arrived, Michael and Wanda were waiting at the gate.

"Miriam!" Michael yelled gleefully as he ran over to her and swept her up in his arms. "Hey, cousin!" He gave her a big hug and set her back down on her feet. Wanda laughed as she watched her husband greet his favorite relative. She walked over and hugged Miriam tightly.

"Oh, it is so good to see you!" Miriam exclaimed. "You have no idea how painful these last few months have been!"

"I'm sure they have, Miriam," Michael said soothingly. "Let's sit down at a restaurant, drink something cold, and talk until we get hoarse!" They drove a few miles and stopped at a quaint little café.

After sharing family pictures and catching up on general news, Michael asked, "How's it going with Cliff?"

"Not good," she said as she looked down at the table. "My pain seems to be getting worse and Cliff just doesn't understand."

"I'm not surprised!" Wanda said. "Preachers can be so dense!"

"Careful, honey," Michael warned gently with a look.

"Well, I mean it, Michael!" she retorted. "We get more resistance from pastors than anyone else and all we're trying to do is help people."

"But we also get our best referrals from pastors, Wanda. Don't forget that. Actually, I can only think of two or three pastors in this whole area who think we're heretics," Michael laughed. Then, trying to return the conversation to Miriam, he turned to her and said, "Now, tell us what's been happening."

"Well, Cliff and I have been drawing farther and farther apart in the past several months. He's preoccupied with the church and he spends so much time ministering to others that he hardly has time for me and the kids. He doesn't understand that he needs to enter into *my* pain," she said as she broke down and cried.

Wanda hurried around the table and put her hands on Miriam's shoulders. "There, there, honey! You're with folks who *do* understand and love you!"

When she had dried her eyes, Miriam turned to Michael and said, "You've told me you think that some unresolved issues from my childhood might be involved in all of this. What did you mean?"

Michael paused for a moment before answering. Then he said, "Well, I don't think you ever resolved all that took place between you and Frank Jenkins. I didn't realize it at the time, Miriam, because I wasn't trained then. But as I told you over the phone, you were a victim of sexual abuse."

Miriam looked confused. "Tell me exactly how you mean that."

"Just what I said. You were a victim, plain and simple. You were not responsible for what took place between you and Frank."

"But I thought I had taken care of that years ago, Michael. I confessed my sin to the Lord and I thought I was forgiven. I thought I was living in peace, knowing that I was fully cleansed. I told Cliff about it before we became married. And he said that it made no difference to him and that he loved me just for who I am."

"But, obviously, it wasn't fully resolved, Miriam," Wanda said softly. "To really be healed of such a traumatic event, you need to go back and work through your grief. There is a young teenage girl inside of you yearning to be released from undeserved guilt. Weep for that young girl, Miriam. Weep for her and release her."

"I still don't understand," Miriam objected. "I was sure I had a wonderful marriage, for the most part, except these last few months. I hadn't even thought about those events until you brought them up to me during that vacation, Wanda. I think that's what brought it all back."

Wanda sat down again, took Miriam's hand in hers, and smiled condescendingly. "Miriam, to be healed fully, you *have* to go back. This seminar can be the tool God uses to heal your wounded heart. One of the country's foremost authorities on sexual abuse is in town this weekend to do the seminar. I know that it will change your life!"

❖ ❖ ❖

Cliff called his friend, Pastor John Kryer, and asked if they could get together. "I've got to talk to you, John, about some problems in my marriage. Are you free for lunch?"

"As a matter of fact, I am, Cliff. Do you want to meet somewhere, or do you want to swing by my office and pick me up?"

"I'll pick you up. What's a good time?"

"How about 11:30? We can beat the rush."

"I'll be there. Thanks, John!"

Right on time, Cliff pulled up to John's church office and waited in the car. John came out a few minutes later and got in.

"Where to?" Cliff asked.

"You name it," John replied as he patted Cliff on the shoulder.

"How about The Ranch House? They have booths, and I'd like some privacy for our discussion."

"That sounds fine, Cliff."

Cliff drove a few miles and turned the car into the restaurant parking lot. He and John made small talk as they walked inside and sat down. After they had ordered, John said, "Now, tell me, Cliff, what's going on in your marriage?"

"I don't even know how to tell you, John, but Miriam is convinced that she is the victim of childhood sexual abuse. She is now in Detroit attending a seminar on that very subject. She knows I don't approve and she resents it deeply."

John shook his head sadly. "I'm sorry to hear it, Cliff. And I'm concerned, because I know how destructive the path she's following can become."

"What do you mean?

"Well, before I answer that, I need to ask a few questions. Was Miriam sexually abused as a child?"

"I honestly don't think so, John. She did have a teenage affair in high school and college, but she told me that she had been a willing participant and had asked God's forgiveness. Other than that, I don't know of any incest or abuse."

"Has she been reading any books that deal with childhood sexual abuse?"

"Why, yes, John. She's been reading several."

"Let me guess. Has she read *The Courage to Heal?*"

"Yes, I believe that is one of the books."

"And *The Wounded Heart?*"

"Yes," Cliff shook his head and smiled wryly.

"Any others?"

"Yes. She has been reading *Sybil* and *Secret Survivors,* too."

John nodded sadly. "I'm not surprised. It's common therapeutic practice to condition the 'victims of childhood sexual abuse' with books and videos that trigger visualizations."

"But, why?" Cliff asked. "Why would therapists intentionally create false memories?"

"I'm not accusing them of intentionally creating memories that they know to be false. These therapists are actually convinced that nearly every personal problem in the lives of their clients is rooted in childhood sexual abuse, incest, or satanic ritual abuse."

"How is it that something as abstract as recovered memories has become tolerated by a profession supposedly dedicated to scientific accuracy?" Cliff asked.

"Well, some psychologists are beginning to question the validity of memories recovered in therapy. But the sad thing is, Cliff, just when secular authorities are dismissing the reliability of recovered memories, Christian therapists are buying into it like it's a revelation from God!"

"What can I do, John? How can I convince Miriam this sort of counseling is unreliable?"

"You might show her some of the studies that have been done. But I have to tell you, once a person becomes convinced she is a victim, it's hard to turn her around. Has she gone so far as to join a support group for survivors of sexual abuse?"

"No, I don't think so, John. But our communication is so shattered right now, that I'm not sure she would tell me if she were."

"Do whatever you can to keep her out of such a group, Cliff. Recovery groups tend to exert a lot of pressure on individuals to conform to the theory. If a person doesn't come up with a memory, the group badgers her until she finally 'remembers,' or else they accuse her of being in denial. If she does produce a memory, the group praises her for her courage and they tell her that the memory is accurate and that she couldn't have made it up."

"So, all I can do is show her some studies?" Cliff asked with a heavy sigh.

"No, that's not all by any means. You need to get her back into the Word. She isn't faithfully reading the Scriptures and meditating on them right now, is she?"

Cliff shook his head. "No. I've told her that she needs to get back into a regular pattern of Bible study, but she says I'm using the Bible as a hammer to beat her into submission."

"Well, you need to keep trying. We also need to get as many people as possible to start praying for her. This is a spiritual battle you're in, Cliff, and the enemy is deceiving Miriam with gentle-sounding messages from sincere people. But they're sincerely wrong."

Cliff sat silently, head bowed for a moment, then looked up at John. "I'm afraid I'm going to have to resign as pastor if something doesn't change soon, John. I don't see how I can be effective if my own marriage is on the rocks."

John sighed deeply. "Don't do anything too quickly, Cliff. Leave room for the Lord to work. He still does miracles today, you know."

"And that's just what it will take, John—a miracle!"

❖ ❖ ❖

All day Friday and Saturday, Miriam attended the sexual abuse recovery seminar in Detroit with Michael and Wanda. She took extensive notes and found herself identifying with the lecturer's description of women who have been abused.

"I am so disappointed with pastors who treat wounded hearts with band-aid solutions!" the lecturer said. "They pull out a Bible verse, quote it out of context, and make people feel guilty when their inner person still hurts." His gentle demeanor and obvious concern for the women made his message almost irresistible.

"I am so grieved over that kind of counseling!" he continued. "Be honest with me, folks. Haven't you ever wanted to just throw your Bible against the wall in anger?" he asked rhetorically. "I have! But God understands my anger. And He understands yours, too."

Miriam found herself enjoying the lecture. At one point she looked around the audience and noticed that of the hundred or so attendees, less than ten were men. *I wish Cliff could be here with me to hear this wonderful man! Maybe then he would begin to understand my heart,* she thought. Her mind drifted for a while as the speaker continued to talk to the enraptured audience.

"I'm going to tell you something now that can liberate each one of you today," he said confidently. "It is my firm belief that more than ninety percent of all women have been abused in some way. And the problem is, these same women are somehow convinced that the abuse they endured was deserved!" Women all around Miriam nodded their agreement.

"Abuse is not something that happens only to children and teenagers," he continued. "The issue is power and control. Let me give you an illustration. Say there is a woman, age thirty-five, who is the executive secretary of a lawyer, who is twenty-five. The lawyer comes on to the attractive secretary and soon they are involved in an affair. Was the woman responsible? Is she guilty? Many would say yes. But I tell you absolutely not! Whenever the man has significant power or influence over a woman, she is not to blame; she is a victim!" Wanda nudged Miriam and smiled.

"Instead of helping the poor woman work through her inner sorrow, too many well-meaning Christians would condemn her and say that she bore at least partial responsibility for the affair. How cruel! How heartless! No, dear ones, don't allow someone to keep you in your prison of guilt. Go back and embrace that inner child that grieves in your heart even as I speak." Several women near Miriam had closed their eyes and tears were streaming down their faces.

During the lunch break, Michael and Wanda asked for Miriam's reaction. "What do you think so far?"

"He's wonderful!" she said. "I just wish Cliff could be here. Then maybe he would understand why I have felt so insecure these past few months." There. She had said it, and she was relieved that her insecurity was finally out in the open.

In the afternoon session, Miriam learned that many husbands become surrogate abusers by not allowing their wives to find healing for their wounded hearts. "Many husbands resist this type of therapy, ladies–oh, and you gentlemen, too," he added with an appealing chuckle. "They feel threatened by any change in the status quo. As an act of love, you women may have to defy your husband occasionally in order to minister to him on a deeper level and to help him understand your inner hurts." *I wonder what Cliff would say about that?* Miriam thought.

"Realize that in the long run, you are actually serving him by forcing him to face your pain with you. If he refuses to join you on this inner journey of healing, he is then taking the place of the original abuser and is perpetrating new abuse. Don't allow that to happen–for his sake, as much as yours."

On Saturday, Miriam learned that to experience full inner healing from sexual abuse she had to confront the person who had hurt her. "Some people will tell you that you have no right to seek vengeance for the wrongs that were poured out on you. They are twisting the Scriptures when they use the verse about vengeance belonging to the Lord. That is true, in the ultimate sense, at the final judgment. But here on earth, we must sometimes seek justice for ourselves so that we can resolve these issues once and for all."

Miriam looked up from her notes, confused. *Surely he can't mean that,* she thought. But she soon discovered that he did.

"Here's how you do it," he said. "First you contact the person who abused you. Confront him with the sin that he committed against you. If he refuses to meet with you personally, call him again and again. Harass him, if necessary, to force him to admit full responsibility for the abuse. Otherwise, you will never achieve full closure." *Maybe he's right,* Miriam thought. *How else can you break the chain or cycle of abuse unless it's confronted?*

When the seminar was over and they went out to eat, Wanda asked Miriam, "Do you feel the seminar was worthwhile?"

Miriam hesitated for a moment, then said, "Well, yes, I think it was." She paused for a moment to collect her thoughts. She sighed deeply, then continued, "I'm going to follow the speaker's suggestions and confront Frank Jenkins. I'm also going to insist that Cliff join me in my search for inner healing. Until I attended this seminar, I had no idea how dead I was inside. I'm beginning to see that for many years I've just been playing the role of the perfect pastor's wife. I didn't realize how miserable I was in my heart."

"Isn't it wonderful?" Wanda said excitedly. "You're finally on your way to recovery!"

Late that afternoon, though she dreaded the resistance

she expected from Cliff, Miriam phoned home. Wanda and Michael sat with her in the room and listened on the speaker phone.

"How was the seminar?" Cliff asked, trying to sound enthusiastic.

"It was good, Cliff," she answered hesitantly. "Really good."

"Do you think you've found some answers that will help?"

"Yes, I think so. But I'm going to need your full support, Cliff."

"You can count on me, honey," Cliff replied warmly. "I want to help you find that old joy you're so famous for."

"But don't know what it is that I'm asking, Cliff."

There was a short pause. Then Cliff asked, "What do you mean, Miriam?"

"At the seminar today, the speaker said that we abuse victims need to confront the perpetrators with what they've done so that we can find closure and true inner healing. I want you to help me do that with Frank Jenkins."

Miriam heard Cliff sigh heavily. "Miriam, don't you remember that Frank asked your forgiveness and your family's forgiveness back when all of this came out? Why should we drop this on him and his family now?"

Miriam's heart sank with despair. Then she felt rage boiling within her as she clenched her jaw tightly. "So you won't help me?"

"I want to help you, Miriam," Cliff said softly, "but I don't believe that dragging Frank back into the past is going to heal your heart. It's just going to make you more bitter. The Lord would want you to forgive–"

"I don't want to hear that!" Miriam interrupted angrily and started crying. "I need your support, Cliff, not Bible verses!"

"I didn't quote any verses, Miriam. All I'm saying is–"

Michael motioned for Miriam to hand him the phone.

"Cliff? This is Michael. Look, this isn't getting us anywhere. I can't allow you to hurt Miriam any further. When you want to talk seriously with her and give her the support she needs, give us a call."

Cliff was astounded. He had no idea Michael had been listening, but he recovered quickly enough to say, "Wait a second, Michael! Miriam is my wife. I'd like to talk to her again—privately!"

"I'm sorry, Cliff," Michael said, hanging up the phone.

Wanda stood to her feet indignantly. "I can't believe that man! How can he continue to be so insensitive?"

Miriam, who had somewhat expected Cliff to resist, turned to Michael and asked, "So now what do I do?"

Michael shook his head angrily. "You'll just have to continue on this journey without Cliff's support, Miriam. The longer you wait, the harder it will be."

That night, after a series of calls, Miriam finally tracked down Frank Jenkins, who now lived in New Jersey. With trembling fingers, she punched in his telephone number and listened to the ring at the other end of the line.

"Hello?"

"Frank Jenkins?" she asked nervously.

"Yes, this is Frank. Who is speaking?

"This is Miriam Chase. You knew me as Miriam Brown," she said, then swallowed hard as her heart pounded furiously. Her hands were wet with perspiration.

"Well, hello, Miriam. I'm surprised to hear from you," Frank said in a friendly but somewhat tense voice.

"I'll bet you are," she said with tight lips, and then continued awkwardly. "Listen, Frank, I don't quite know how to begin this conversation. It's very difficult for me. . . ." She paused, trying to build her courage.

Frank cleared his throat. "Just tell me what's on your mind, Miriam."

Miriam was shaking with emotion as she tried to regain control of the situation. "I . . . I've been attending a seminar. . . ."

"Yes?"

"Well, I've been trying to deal with some of the events in my past and so I came to this seminar."

"What kind of seminar is it, Miriam?" Frank asked warily.

"It's on recovery from sexual abuse."

There was a long pause as Miriam waited for Frank to respond, but he said nothing.

Miriam finally continued, "The lecturer told us that to be totally free from the pain and guilt of our past, we have to confront those who perpetrated the abuse on us."

"What are you *saying,* Miriam?" Frank asked in amazement. In the background, Miriam could hear a woman's voice whispering, "Who is it?"

"I'm saying that I finally realize that I bear no guilt for what took place between us. You *used* me! I reject any responsibility whatsoever for what you did to me!"

"Now wait a minute, Miriam! I'm not proud of what happened between us, but that was many years ago, and I repented of it. Don't you remember the times I asked your forgiveness?"

"Not clearly, I don't," Miriam admitted.

"Well, I do! And I also remember you telling me that it was just as much your fault as it was mine! I never forced you into bed. In fact, if you recall, there were a couple of occasions when you actually initiated the entire thing!"

Miriam felt the old wounds rip open in her heart and a surge of guilt swept over her like a wave of acid. "I did not!" she protested. "It was *your* fault!" She began crying hysterically.

"Miriam," Frank said softly. "I will always carry a certain amount of shame with me for what we did. But we were both young and foolish. I do ask your forgiveness again, right now."

"Not until you meet with me, face to face, mister!" she

said firmly, though she was still shaking with emotion.

"Oh, that's out of the question," he said just as firmly. "I'm not going to drag my wife and children through a cesspool of old sins to somehow satisfy you, Miriam. We're both Christians, you and I. We confessed our sin years ago and received God's full forgiveness. It has been washed away. It was covered by the blood of Christ. Why would you want to dredge it all back up now?"

"Because it is the only way my wounded heart can be healed, Frank! Don't you understand?"

"No, Miriam, I'm sorry. I don't. Again, I ask for your forgiveness. I am truly sorry for any pain I ever caused you. You deserved far better. But right now I think it's best that I close this conversation. I'll pray that God restores your peace. Good-bye, Miriam."

"Wait just a minute–" she yelled, but Frank had hung up the phone.

Miriam sat across from Michael and Wanda, shaking as she still held the phone in her hand. Tears streamed down her face and a hard and desperate look swept over her face. Suddenly, her emotions overwhelmed her and she began weeping with deep, wracking sobs. She felt as though she was going to suffocate as her throat constricted in dry pain.

Wanda hurried to Miriam's side and put her arms around Miriam. "There, there, dear. Let it all out." Miriam continued crying for several minutes before she was able to regain her composure. Wanda handed her several tissues, and Miriam dabbed at her red and swollen eyes.

"Why don't you two go on to bed," Miriam finally said to Michael and Wanda. "I think I'll watch a little television to put me to sleep."

"Are you sure, Miriam?" Michael asked tenderly. "We want to be here for you."

"I know," she replied. "I'm fine. Really. You two need to get some rest. I'll come along to bed soon."

"Okay," Wanda said reluctantly, "but if you need us,

don't hesitate. Wake us up."

"I will," Miriam promised.

Michael and Wanda headed down the hall to their bedroom as Miriam turned on the television. She watched for several minutes, trying to squeeze the pain of the day's events out of her mind, but she simply couldn't. She looked over at her Bible on the coffee table and then back at the TV. After several moments of indecision, she reached out, picked up the Bible, and began flipping through its pages, searching for comfort.

"Oh, God," she moaned. "Please help me!" But her pain only throbbed more intensely. God seemed so distant and uncaring. In her mind she heard the voice of the psychologist saying, *Be honest with me, folks. Haven't you ever wanted to just throw your Bible against the wall in anger? I have! But God understands my anger. And He understands yours, too.* For a moment Miriam was tempted to throw her Bible, and she actually lifted it above her head before she regained enough control to stop herself.

Shaking with emotion, she set the Bible down on the coffee table and walked slowly to her room. There she changed out of her clothes and slipped into bed. She tossed and turned fitfully through the night.

Miriam called Cliff again the following morning. "I'm sorry we hung up on you yesterday," she apologized in a weary voice. "It's just that all of us get so frustrated when you don't try to understand what I'm going through."

"Well, I'm sorry, honey," Cliff said. "I don't mean to be insensitive. I know I need to work on that, and I will." He paused and then asked gently, "When are you going to come home?"

"Later on this week, I think. Listen, Cliff, Michael and Wanda have recommended a counselor for me in Denver.

He's a specialist in recovery from sexual abuse. I plan on setting up counseling with him when I get back."

Cliff hung his head and rubbed the back of his neck as he sighed. "Do you think that's really necessary, Miriam? Don't you believe the Lord can deal with this?"

"That's exactly the kind of insensitivity I'm talking about, Cliff!" Miriam said hotly. "You act like this is a *spiritual* problem I've got. It isn't! It's psychological! And I need someone experienced in sexual abuse therapy to help me recover."

Cliff didn't respond.

"All I'm asking is your support," Miriam pled.

"I'll support you in every way I can, sweetheart," Cliff said. "But I'm not sure I can agree that this counseling is in your best interest. It seems to me that you're more upset now than before you went this route."

Miriam started crying. "It's only because I finally realize how hurt I've been all these years! You just don't understand."

"I'm *trying* to understand, Miriam. When you come home let's work on it together, okay?"

"Okay, Cliff," she said meekly. "I miss you, honey."

"I miss you, too," Cliff replied sadly. "Please hurry home."

The Tragedy of Bitterness

Sexual abuse is traumatic because it violates the victim in a variety of soul-wrenching ways. It is not merely the physical trespass of one's body that makes sexual abuse so hideous. It is even more than pain and the fear of disease. It goes beyond the sense of helplessness and loss of security. Sexual assault victimizes the entire person–physically, mentally, emotionally, socially, and spiritually.

Trauma is not caused merely by the physical act. It is the forced intrusion, the brutal invasion, and the savage violence that makes rape so terrifying. It is the bestial disregard for the victim's emotional and physical well-being. It is the utter contempt and selfishness that devalues another human being.

Paul writes, "The body is not meant for sexual immorality, but for the Lord, and the Lord for the body" (1 Corinthians 6:13). A few verses later he adds, "Do you not know that your body is a temple of the Holy Spirit, who is in you, whom you have received from God? You are not your own" (1 Corinthians 6:19).

Because we understand our material world through the

physical senses God has given us, our view of the world may be distorted by bodily abuse. Physical blows, torture, excruciating pain, and terror are made even more horrendous when the perpetrator experiences pleasure at the event. Job expressed the effect suffering can cause this way: "When I think about this, I am terrified; trembling seizes my body" (Job 21:6 NIV). The verse comes across even stronger in the New American Standard: "Even when I remember, I am disturbed, and horror takes hold of my flesh."

Another tragic consequence of sexual abuse, is the effect it can have on the way a person thinks. Physical suffering does seem to imprint one's emotions and thinking in a major way. I believe that is why God permitted corporal punishment as a means of instilling discipline in children. "Do not withhold discipline from a child; if you punish him with the rod, he will not die. Punish him with the rod and save his soul from death" (Proverbs 23:13,14). This sort of punishment, however, was not to be so harsh as to cause physical damage. Even in civil cases, punishment was limited: "[Do] not give him more than forty lashes. If he is flogged more than that, your brother will be degraded in your eyes" (Deuteronomy 25:3).

The point is, physical trauma usually has an impact on the mental process. It affects how we perceive the world around us–how we view people, their intentions, their tone of voice, their body language, and whether they are to be trusted or feared. It influences the way we accept and develop relationships or the way we resist and reject them. It colors the way we view opportunities, risks, and responsibilities.

In addition to the physical and mental trauma sexual abuse causes, it can produce incalculable emotional damage. Those who have never been abused cannot fully comprehend the sheer terror and sense of total personal violation a victim experiences from the cruel brutality of another human. It can produce a sense of defilement of one's very self.

The Insensitivity of Others

The Bible does not gloss over the emotional distress of an abuse victim. In fact, a classic case of family sexual abuse is found in 2 Samuel 13:

> In the course of time, Amnon son of David fell in love with Tamar, the beautiful sister of Absalom son of David.
>
> Amnon became frustrated to the point of illness on account of his sister Tamar, for she was a virgin, and it seemed impossible for him to do anything to her.
>
> Now Amnon had a friend named Jonadab son of Shimeah, David's brother. Jonadab was a very shrewd man. He asked Amnon, "Why do you, the king's son, look so haggard morning after morning? Won't you tell me?"
>
> Amnon said to him, "I'm in love with Tamar, my brother Absalom's sister."
>
> Go to bed and pretend to be ill," Jonadab said. "When your father comes to see you, say to him, 'I would like my sister Tamar to come and give me something to eat. Let her prepare the food in my sight so I may watch her and then eat it from her hand.'"
>
> So Amnon lay down and pretended to be ill. When the king came to see him, Amnon said to him, "I would like my sister Tamar to come and make some special bread in my sight, so I may eat from her hand."
>
> David sent word to Tamar at the palace: "Go to the house of your brother Amnon and prepare some food for him." So Tamar went to the house of her brother Amnon, who was lying down. She took some dough, kneaded it, made the bread in his sight and baked it. Then she took the pan and served him the bread, but he refused to eat.

"Send everyone out of here," Amnon said. So everyone left him. Then Amnon said to Tamar, "Bring the food here into my bedroom so I may eat from your hand." And Tamar took the bread she had prepared and brought it to her brother Amnon in his bedroom. But when she took it to him to eat, he grabbed her and said, "Come to bed with me, my sister."

Don't, my brother!" she said to him. "Don't force me. Such a thing should not be done in Israel! Don't do this wicked thing. What about me? Where could I get rid of my disgrace? And what about you? You would be like one of the wicked fools in Israel. Please speak to the king; he will not keep me from being married to you." But he refused to listen to her, and since he was stronger than she, he raped her.

Then Amnon hated her with intense hatred. In fact, he hated her more than he had loved her. Amnon said to her, "Get up and get out!"

"No!" she said to him. "Sending me away would be a greater wrong than what you have already done to me."

But he refused to listen to her. He called his personal servant and said, "Get this woman out of here and bolt the door after her." So his servant put her out and bolted the door after her. She was wearing a richly ornamented robe, for this was the kind of garment the virgin daughters of the king wore. Tamar put ashes on her head and tore the ornamented robe she was wearing. She put her hand on her head and went away, weeping aloud as she went.

Her brother Absalom said to her, "Has that Amnon, your brother, been with you? Be quiet now, my sister; he is your brother. Don't take this thing to heart." And Tamar lived in her brother Absalom's house, a desolate woman.

When King David heard all this, he was furious. Absalom never said a word to Amnon, either good or bad; he hated Amnon because he had disgraced his sister Tamar (verses 1-22).

The depth of the emotional pain Tamar experienced was profound. In her anguish and humiliation, she tore her royal robe and made her way home, crying bitterly. Once there, she received the same sort of treatment many victims of rape have experienced. "Be quiet," her brother Absalom said. "Don't take this thing to heart."

Don't take it to *heart?* One reason that sexual abuse is so difficult to deal with is that other people do not fully understand the depth of the pain experienced by the victim. The emotions are intense, deeply heartfelt, and long-lasting. To make matters even worse, *genuine* victims of sexual abuse have found their experience demeaned by therapeutically manufactured memories of abuse that never happened.

As we can see from 2 Samuel 13, one devastating effect of sexual abuse is the social stigma attached to it. The irony is this: Amnon was the one who should have been disgraced for his lust and cruelty. Instead, the family viewed Tamar as the one disgraced. Society's views haven't changed much since then.

Even in our day of sexual liberty and promiscuity, many people still regard a rape victim with a mixture of pity and contempt. Like Tamar, who "lived in her brother Absalom's house, a desolate woman," many victims end up retreating from other people because of a misplaced sense of personal shame and unworthiness. Other victims, in the effort to deal with that shame, become sexually promiscuous. That is why some men begin the homosexual lifestyle after being assaulted by another male.

Doubting God's Love

Perhaps the most critical consequence of sexual abuse is spiritual damage. Feeling personally contaminated by the actions of another, some victims feel as though they no longer deserve anyone's love–not even God's. They fail to understand that God loves us not because we are worthy, but because it is His very nature to love. As John writes, "How great is the love the Father has lavished on us, that we should be called children of God! And that is what we are!" (1 John 3:1).

Knowing how difficult it is for us to believe that God actually loves us, John says, "This is how God showed his love among us: He sent his one and only Son into the world that we might live through him" (1 John 4:9). If we need further proof, John says that we can intellectually know and emotionally count on God's love because of His own character: "And so we know and rely on the love God has for us. God is love. Whoever lives in love lives in God, and God in him" (1 John 4:16).

That truth alone has set millions free from the pain of their past abuse. They no longer identify themselves as victims, but as children of God–pure, clean, and holy.

If you have experienced a deep and damaging personal tragedy, I pray that you will go to the one who really understands your heart. Jesus experienced anger and ridicule from family members. He knew what it was to be hated for no reason. He was violently assaulted by a group of men and beaten so severely that He was hardly recognizable. He was stripped naked in public, hung exposed on a tree, and was laughed at by the religious leaders of His day.

All of His suffering was for *us*. "He was pierced for our transgressions, he was crushed for our iniquities; the punishment that brought us peace was upon him, and by his wounds we are healed" (Isaiah 53:5). Come to the One who loves you. No one understands your pain like Jesus.

Perhaps your heart is aching at this very moment because of the pain you have experienced. I want to share with you one of the most devastating causes of deep inner pain and how you can find real and lasting healing. Read carefully and with an open heart. Allow the Holy Spirit to use His Word to begin the healing process.

The Poison of Bitterness

I have counseled hundreds of people, and I've seen that some of the most wounded persons are those who have allowed bitterness to saturate the innermost parts of their being.

Bitterness is a spiritual cancer that damages the soul as surely as physical cancer consumes the body. It is able to make beautiful women ugly and kind men cruel. Bitterness is dangerously communicable, for it can infect others who come in contact with its soul-rotting toxin. Bitterness is a poison that can literally destroy a person.

What many people do not recognize, however, is the way bitterness can work. When a person is hurt, he or she will likely respond by becoming bitter. This bitterness usually ends up feeding fuel to the fire of pain, and thus causes the person's inner suffering to become even worse.

Defining Bitterness

What *is* bitterness, anyway? The dictionary defines *bitterness* in a variety of ways:

1. Having or being a taste that is sharp, acrid, and unpleasant.
2. Causing sharp pain to the body or discomfort to the mind; harsh: (a bitter wind; bitter memories.)
3. Difficult or distasteful to accept, admit, or bear: (the bitter truth.)
4. Exhibiting or proceeding from strong animosity: (bitter foes.)
5. Resulting from or expressive of severe grief, anguish, or disappointment: (cried bitter tears.)
6. Marked by anguished resentfulness or rancor.[96]

Note some of the key descriptions of bitterness: unpleasant taste, sharp pain, discomfort to the mind, distasteful to accept, strong animosity, anguish, resentfulness. Bitterness is a dark and angry feeling that seems to extend into the very core of a person's being, blinding him to God's blessings and robbing the soul of peace and joy.

When a person is filled with bitterness, it affects all his relationships because bitterness colors the person's thoughts and actions. It even affects the way a person talks. The reason is that what is on the inside eventually erupts into the open. Jesus put it this way: "The good man brings good things out of the good stored up in his heart, and the evil man brings evil things out of the evil stored up in his heart. For out of the overflow of his heart his mouth speaks" (Luke 6:45).

The Causes of Bitterness

Disobedience and Blaming God

Bitterness comes in many forms and disguises. It is usually connected, however, with the notion that someone has failed us. While a bitter person might deny he is angry with God, it is my opinion that anger which grows into bitterness of heart often stems from the belief that *God* is the one at fault. Have you noticed that people who habitually ignore God are tempted to blame Him when tragedy strikes? They reason that since God is all-powerful, He could have prevented the suffering, but didn't. They seldom admit that their problems may have resulted from foolish choices that they made.

God's response to this line of reasoning is clear and to the point: "Your own conduct and actions have brought this upon you. This is your punishment. How bitter it is! How it pierces to the heart!" (Jeremiah 4:18). I know that passage may sound cruel and unkind, but really, it isn't. On the contrary, God's love for us compels Him to be painfully honest with us and warn us that disobedience always results in bitterness and pain. *Disobedience, then, is what truly wounds the heart.*

Spiritual Blindness

I am not suggesting, however, that everything a person suffers is his own fault. Jesus was clear on that point. When his disciples saw a man who had been blind from birth, they asked, "Rabbi, who sinned, this man or his parents, that he was born blind?" (John 9:2).

Jesus replied, "Neither this man nor his parents sinned . . . but this happened so that the work of God might be displayed in his life" (John 9:3). Up until that moment, the poor man had spent his entire life in darkness to eventually glorify the Lord. I'm sure he experienced many days of discouragement and frustration at the "unfairness" of it all. But God made him wait until his appointed day of healing.

Now watch what Jesus did. He treated the man with an unorthodox, unprofessional, even humiliating therapy and then told him to do something seemingly unreasonable–that is, from our finite, human point of view: "[Jesus] spit on the ground, made some mud with the saliva, and put it on the man's eyes. 'Go,' he told him, 'wash in the Pool of Siloam' (this word means Sent). So the man went and washed, and came home seeing" (John 9:6,7).

The suffering was not the man's fault, but obedience to the Lord *was* his responsibility–and his opportunity. Jesus did not spend time analyzing the man's past. Nor did He try to teach him how to cope with his "dysfunction." No, the Lord told him what He still tells us today: Go, wash your eyes, and you will come home seeing.

Imagine what would have happened if the man had bitterly refused Jesus' command. "No!" he could have shouted. "I'm blind. I *can't* go. You don't understand what I've gone through. I'm an innocent victim. God made me this way!"

Returning to the past would not have accomplished healing in the blind man's life. Blaming his parents would not have helped. A course in self-esteem would not have restored his eyes. Years of therapy would not have produced vision. There was only one way to make healing possible in his life: obedience to Christ.

The same is true today for inner suffering. Spiritual blindness robs us of the blessings He offers. Willingly sightless, we refuse to deal with our problems God's way. And when things go sour, as they inevitably will, we blame God.

This is how James explains it: "When tempted, no one should say, 'God is tempting me.' For God cannot be tempted by evil, nor does he tempt anyone; but each one is tempted when, by his own evil desire, he is dragged away and enticed. Then, after desire has conceived, it gives birth to sin; and sin, when it is full-grown, gives birth to death" (James 1:13-15).

Not wanting to accept responsibility for our own choices, we have often allowed the world to convince us that psychotherapy is more powerful and provides better solutions than the Word of God. Peter says that a person who has turned away from the principles of God "is nearsighted and blind, and has forgotten that he has been cleansed from his past sins" (2 Peter 1:9).

Jesus warns us about the effects of spiritual blindness: "If your eyes are bad, your whole body will be full of darkness. If then the light within you is darkness, how great is that darkness!" (Matthew 6:23). Jesus claimed to provide light for that inner darkness: "I am the light of the world. Whoever follows me will never walk in darkness, but will have the light of life" (John 8:12).

Self-Focus

Another cause of soul-damaging bitterness is a focus on oneself. Strange as it may sound, bitterness can be an un-intended by-product of the self-esteem movement. An emphasis on our own needs and desires will inevitably lead to disappointment because few others share our focus.

Though not many of us have suffered like Job, most of us have at one time or another felt like he did when he said, "I loathe my very life; therefore I will give free rein to my complaint and speak out in the bitterness of my soul" (Job 10:1).

Whether we admit it or not, most mental, behavioral, emotional, and spiritual problems are rooted in an unhealthy preoccupation with self. Focus on oneself can become so consuming that a person can even wish himself dead. Think about this for a moment: Suicide can be the ultimate expression of selfishness.

Preoccupying ourselves with self-esteem is like taking spiritual steroids. Steroids can be dangerous substances. Though they are naturally occurring organic compounds, when used inappropriately, they can cause a variety of serious physical ailments. Bodybuilders are famous for using steroids to artificially speed up their muscle development. In a similar way, pumping ourselves up emotionally by declaring how wonderful, beautiful, bright, and awesome we are is as destructive as it is nauseating.

God says, "It is not the one who commends himself who is approved, but the one whom the Lord commends" (2 Corinthians 10:18). Whatever happened to the pursuit of humility? Proverbs 25:6, 7 tells us, "Do not exalt yourself in the king's presence, and do not claim a place among great men; it is better for him to say to you, 'Come up here,' than for him to humiliate you before a nobleman." Or how about this verse? "It is not good to eat too much honey, nor is it honorable to seek one's own honor" (Proverbs 25:27).

I know that humility flies in the face of current therapeutic correctness, but consider this word from the Lord: "Whoever exalts himself will be humbled, and whoever humbles himself will be exalted" (Matthew 23:12). Paul puts self-esteem into perspective when he writes, "Do nothing out of selfish ambition or vain conceit, but in humility consider others better than yourselves" (Philippians 2:3). Even though some people believe that self-esteem is a constitutional right and a road to spiritual health, the Scripture says, "If anyone thinks he is something when he is nothing, he deceives himself" (Galatians 6:3).

One man who came to me for counsel complained of depression and feelings of low self-esteem. He had recently lost his job and felt that he had been treated unfairly by his former company. As time went along, it became apparent that he was angry with God. He felt that God should de-liver him a job quickly—and one that provided even more money than the one he had lost. As he sat at home brooding over his situation, he became more and more depressed, and threatened to leave his family or perhaps even to commit suicide.

Hoping to alleviate his anxiety, he went to a psychiatrist who prescribed a strong antidepressant drug, but things just got worse. "I'm not sure anymore that there is a God," he said to me bitterly. He then added that his wife had urged him to seek biblical counseling; that's why he had come to see me.

I told him that unless he was willing to become obedient to the Word, there was little hope of change. Self-pity had become the crippling characteristic of his entire life, and the resulting bitterness was affecting his job outlook, his marriage, and his children.

Self-pity is an invitation to bitterness. That is why the Scriptures constantly advise us to get our eyes off ourselves and onto Christ.

Injustice

Bitterness can be caused by the belief that we have been denied justice. One of the deepest angers known to man erupts when a person feels he has been treated unfairly. Job expressed it this way: "As surely as God lives, who has denied me justice, the Almighty, who has made me taste bitterness of soul" (Job 27:2).

Such bitterness is not always aimed at God. Children often experience a deep and lasting anger at parents over unfair treatment. It may be related to harsh discipline, unreasonable demands, humiliation before peers, violence, sexual abuse, or a host of other similar actions or attitudes.

Whatever the scenario, the personal desire for justice is often perverted into an individual quest for vengeance. We all can identify with the mother who stalks and kills the man who raped her daughter. We understand her rage and perhaps even applaud the fact that the criminal got what was coming to him. But God has provided two agencies to execute justice: human government and His own judgment throne. Remember, even the "eye-for-an-eye" type of justice was to be administered under the control of civil authorities.

How can we deal with the bitterness that comes from injustice? By imitating Christ. No one was ever treated more unfairly. No injustice was or ever will be greater than the execution of the sinless Son of God. Do you remember Jesus' response as He hung on the cross? He said, "Father, forgive them, for they do not know what they are doing" (Luke 23:34). (We will take a closer look at the healing power of forgiveness later on in chapter 5.)

Unpleasant Circumstances

Yet another cause of bitterness is our reaction to unpleasant circumstances. Chronic pain, an unhappy marriage, a miscarriage, a tedious job, financial problems, disease, natural disasters, loss of loved ones–all of these can generate bitterness of heart. Even the mere lack of material goods has made people bitter. In America we often confuse inconvenience with misfortune because we have been spoiled by

God's continual blessings. We consider a family impover-
ished if they have only a black-and-white television and one
car. Not until we look at what is happening elsewhere in the
world do we realize that our circumstances aren't so bad
after all.

Job describes a man who "dies in bitterness of soul, never
having enjoyed anything good" (Job 21:25). That is true for
millions of desperately poor people around the world who
suffer their entire lives from malnutrition, exposure, disease,
and war. Even now, as I write this, millions of refugees from
wars around the world are dying from wounds, starvation,
thirst, and disease.

News reports showing death and genuine misery should
help us put our psychic woes in perspective, but we have
become hardened by repeated exposure to the horrific
images of actual victims. Our own problems still seem so
great that we quickly forget what real suffering is all about.
Even this hardening toward the suffering of others stems
from our preoccupation with ourselves.

In our self-centered and psychologized age, we complain
about our worries, self-image, weight problems, people who
don't understand us, unhappy marriages, unfulfilled poten-
tial, depression, anxiety, attention deficits, emotional aban-
donment, damaged inner children, the inability to relate,
dysfunctions, or poor self-esteem. We become angry when
we can't have our way, are unable to get what we want, or
don't get the breaks we feel we deserve.

Most of us have more possessions than we need or will
ever use. Our main problem is finding a place to store it all!
Yet we cry and whine and plead for more so we can indulge
our*selves*. Today, more than ever, Jesus would say to us, "If
anyone would come after me, he must deny himself and
take up his cross and follow me" (Matthew 16:24).

A great paradox in Christianity is this truth: To really
experience life, we must first die to self. Some people see preoccupation with self as a relatively benign fault, while others

actually teach that we must increase the attention we pay to ourselves. As one popular self-esteem preacher writes, "the need for dignity, self-worth, self-respect, and self-esteem is the deepest of all human needs."[97]

Paul sees it differently: "Put to death, therefore, whatever belongs to your earthly nature: sexual immorality, impurity, lust, evil desires and greed, which is idolatry" (Colossians 3:5). In this case, idolatry is setting ourselves and our desires in place of God and His will.

Self-centeredness is not a relatively minor infraction. Selfism, moaning, and complaining can have devastating results. Peter warns against "sinful desires, which war against your soul" (1 Peter 2:11). It is not just grumbling about our circumstances that God hates; He also tells us, "Don't grumble against each other, brothers, or you will be judged" (James 5:9).

Difficult Family Relationships

Some of the most intense bitterness we experience comes at the hands of those closest to us–family members. There is no question that the family unit is in serious trouble in this age of selfishness. Jesus predicted it in Luke 12:53 when He said, "They will be divided, father against son and son against father, mother against daughter and daughter against mother, mother-in-law against daughter-in-law and daughter-in-law against mother-in-law."

Most counselors can share about case after case where counselees are so full of bitterness that they can think of little else. Their bitterness has taken on a life of its own and ends up discoloring every perception, every conversation, and every relationship they experience.

One woman called me for counseling and began to relate the story of her divorce and subsequent rejection. The churches she visited let her know that she was not wanted, she said. The women she met was hostile and suspicious of her intentions. The unmarried men who talked with her for even a short time suddenly grew cold and hurried away. She was tired of being alone and raising an adolescent son by herself. She desperately wanted a husband who would share the responsibilities and help to provide.

"I'm so sick of this way of life!" she exclaimed with deep anger. "If God doesn't provide a husband for me within the next two months, I'm going to turn away from Him!"

Her bitterness was centered on the betrayal she had experienced from her ex-husband. On the surface, her attitude seemed justified. The problem was, she was so focused on her loneliness and the unfairness of the hardships she now faced that she could think of nothing else. Her isolation, bitterness, and desperate desire for a husband were so obvious that people were literally scared away from her.

Another woman I counseled decided to handle her heartache differently. She had been abandoned by her husband and was left with two daughters to raise by herself. Instead of becoming bitter, she turned to the Lord for comfort and strength. Though she still experienced deep pain because of her husband's unfaithfulness, she was able to remain a sweet and growing child of God and managed to provide a happy home for her girls.

Her husband eventually came to me for counseling. He told me that he had been a victim of childhood abuse. He described in great detail how his father had humiliated and beaten him so severely that his underclothing had stuck to his skin with blood. As he told me the story, bitterness poured out and he began to weep. "I can *never* forgive him for what he did to me!" he said with deep fury–though his father was now dead. I tried to show him how futile and destructive his bitterness was, but he was unwilling to let go of the hatred in his heart. He left, fully intending to neglect his own daughters and to put them through a similar sorrow.

One friend told me of frightening childhood experiences during which his brothers used to force him to fight bigger children so that he would get over his fear of the bullies at school. Another woman related how her mother would lock her and her sister in a closet while she went out for nights of immorality with her boyfriends. Others have described being locked in trunks, tied to trees, and beaten and humiliated in a variety of ways.

Nearly all of us can relate in one way or another to stories of family bitterness. We have angry memories of a harsh and brutal father who filled us with terror, or a nagging perfectionist mother who was never satisfied, or a brother who teased unmercifully, or a "model" sister to whom we were unfavorably compared.

No matter what the cause of our bitterness, there is no question that its presence in our life can wreak havoc. Indeed, bitterness is such a deep emotion that any therapy short of God's powerful methods will simply fail.

Psychological Approaches to Bitterness

It would be inaccurate to say that all psychologists, psychiatrists and psychotherapists treat bitterness in a standard way. The fact is, there is no standard form of treatment for *any* "dysfunction" since there are as many theories about human behavior and cure as there are therapists.

Some counselors treat the symptoms of bitterness as a physiological condition requiring a regimen of drugs. I recently attended a seminar for Christian counselors cosponsored by a seminary, a counseling clinic, and a drug manufacturer. It seemed that the primary purpose of the presentation was to convince church counselors that drug therapy is spiritually neutral, physically safe, and generally effective. But dulling the ache of bitterness with drugs will not solve the underlying cause.

Another popular way of treating people involves taking

them into their past. I once counseled a woman who abandoned her church, her husband, and her children because of an intense bitterness that began when she contracted cancer. Angry at God, she turned from the Scriptures and began seeking inner peace from psychologists. They led her on a fruitless journey into her past. So far as I am aware, she is still looking for peace. Because she was in a place of influence, her bitterness damaged the spiritual walk of her family and scores of friends. Scripture warns that this can happen: "See to it that no one misses the grace of God and that no bitter root grows up to cause trouble and defile many" (Hebrews 12:15). Bitterness causes unbelievable trouble and contaminates all who come in contact with it.

My point is that returning to the past to shovel through the muck and putrid slime of one's life does not produce healing. Neither does embracing one's pain or comforting one's "inner child." On the contrary, these humanistic techniques produce an even greater bitterness of soul which endangers not only the person who is suffering, but also the people around him.

When we try to "work through" our past with psychological systems, we are *missing the grace of God*. We are neglecting the central truth of the gospel: that God forgives our sins and cleanses us of all unrighteousness through the *finished* work of Jesus Christ. If *we* must work through our past to be healed, then Christ's work on the cross was *not* complete.

The Biblical Solution

Perhaps you have related to this chapter in a special way because you've suffered genuine abuse. Painful events from the past may erupt in your mind at the most inconvenient moments–triggered by certain sounds, smells, or calendar dates. Other traumatic memories may surface when the people around you use certain words, tones of voice, facial expressions, gestures, or in some other way remind you of something or someone who once hurt you.

I have boldly stated that psychotherapy will not produce lasting peace of heart and mind. So *now* what? Please stay with me. In the chapters that follow, we will look at the Bible's counsel for dealing with the bitterness of the past and finding genuine healing and peace that will last. I promise you . . . if you will allow the Lord to apply His Word, you will find a peace you never dreamed possible.

Miriam returned to Denver the following week. Her heart was still full of confusion and anger. Against Cliff's wishes, she began seeing the counselor recommended by Michael and Wanda.

"If you would only come with me, Cliff!" Miriam said after her third session. "He makes so much sense, and he's helping me to deal with the hurts I have been hiding all these years."

Cliff looked at her with deep sadness in his eyes. "You know I don't agree with the psychological viewpoint, Miriam. It seems to me that the further you go on that path, the worse your pain becomes. But because I love you, I'll go with you–at least this once. Don't ask me to agree with everything your counselor says. If I think he's off base scripturally, I'll say so."

"Oh, thank you, honey!" she said. "I think you'll begin to understand where I'm coming from if you will just go with me. But, Cliff, please go with an open mind."

"We'll see," he said.

The following week Cliff and Miriam walked into the lobby of Southeast Counseling Associates. It was a busy place, with people coming and going through the hallway that led to various counseling offices throughout the building. Cliff sat down nervously next to Miriam, picked up a magazine, and began to flip through it.

After a few minutes, the receptionist looked over at

them, smiled, and said, "You may go to Dr. Powell's office now."

Miriam led the way and Cliff followed. They entered an attractive office with comfortable chairs that sat in front of a simple desk. Dr. Jeffrey Powell, a slender man in his early thirties, stood and greeted them. He walked over and shook Cliff's hand. "I'm so glad to meet you, Cliff," he said. "Miriam has told me so much about you."

I'll bet she has! Cliff thought.

"And it's good stuff, too!" Powell added, seeing the look on Cliff's face. "Have a seat and we'll get started right away. My agenda for today, Cliff, is to explain my overall philosophy of counseling and to try to help you understand why sexual abuse is so very difficult for a woman to deal with."

Cliff nodded his head as he sat back and crossed his legs. He noticed that the counselor was not wearing a wedding ring.

Dr. Powell paused and smiled. "I couldn't help but notice your body language, Cliff. You crossed your legs. You're subconsciously shutting me out already. Give me a chance. Hear me out."

Cliff's eyes opened in surprise, but he didn't answer. He set his foot back down and sat up straight.

Dr. Powell looked at him and shook his head with a condescending smile. "Now you're uptight. Relax, Cliff. This isn't going to be so bad!"

Cliff sighed deeply, looked quickly at Miriam, then turned back to face Dr. Powell. "Now, look, Jeff," he said, "may I call you Jeff? I'm not trying to communicate anything to you by my body language. Just tell me what's on your mind."

Dr. Powell cleared his throat and smiled weakly and said, "I think for therapeutic reasons, we probably should keep my title at the professional level."

Cliff scratched his eyebrow as the tension in the office grew. "Okay," he said. "Dr. Powell it is. Go ahead, Dr. Powell."

Miriam looked over at Cliff in irritation. "Cool it, Cliff!" she whispered. "Just listen for a change!" Turning to Dr. Powell, she said, "Preachers aren't very good listeners, doctor."

Powell laughed icily and said, "That's all right. I often find that first sessions with pastors are a bit difficult. I don't know if it's me or them. Well, let's move ahead. I want to point out several of the fallacies in common Christian thinking about sexual abuse. The first is about forgiveness. Traditionally, Christians are taught to forgive and to forget. But unclaimed pain from the past begs for resolution. Hiding from one's past involves denial, and denial of the past leads inevitably to denial of God."

Cliff held up his hand and interjected, "Is it all right if I ask questions as we go?"

"I suppose so," Powell said, displeased with the interruption.

"Can you show me from Scripture that forgiveness is the same as denial of the past, which in turn leads to denial of God?"

Dr. Powell sat back and tugged at his collar. "Well..." he paused. "I...uh...I can't give you a proof text, if that's what you mean."

"Yes, that's what I mean," Cliff agreed. "I was just wondering. Go on."

Dr. Powell wrote a note to himself and continued. "Another major problem confronting victims of sexual abuse is the demand placed upon them by other Christians that they must love and pretend that their relationships are in good order. With that type of Christianity they feel secure, but they also feel dead. Their souls are numb. People need to understand the justified rage of the abused person."

Cliff raised his hand again.

"What?" Dr. Powell asked.

"Pardon me, Dr. Powell, but where do you find that principle in the Word of God?"

"Which one?"

"That abuse victims are not required to love. That the commands of God don't apply to them."

"Now look, Cliff!" Dr. Powell said, frustrated. "If you're going to ask me to proof-text everything I say, this is going to take forever! At some point you have to trust me!"

"At some point, perhaps I might be willing to," Cliff said evenly. "But not until I find out where you are coming from–the Bible or humanism. All I'm asking is for you to back up your statements. I don't know you, Dr. Powell. You may well be a fine Christian man. But I cannot place my trust in you until I know what your ultimate source of authority is."

Dr. Powell looked offended. "Why, my authority is the Bible, of course!"

"Then where is it? I don't even see one in this room."

Powell began to rummage through his desk. "I have one; it's here somewhere. . . ." He stood and looked around his office. "It's on my bookshelf, no doubt." He scanned the shelf quickly and couldn't locate it.

"Never mind, doctor," Cliff said. "My point is not whether you have the Bible at hand, but rather that when you make major propositional statements as a Christian counselor, I would expect that you would be able to support them biblically. I can't accept your scholastic credentials as sufficient authority any more than I would expect my congregation to believe what I say unless I can back it up with the Word of God."

Dr. Powell stood to his feet. "I don't have time for this kind of foolishness," he said haughtily. "If you decide you want help, feel free to call for another appointment." He walked to the door and opened it.

Cliff remained seated and looked at Powell. "I believe we still have another thirty minutes on the meter."

"What do you mean?" Powell said.

"Well, if I'm paying seventy dollars per session, I intend to get the full time."

Dr. Powell frowned. "There won't be any charge, Pastor Chase."

Cliff stood to his feet. "Oh. Well, in that case, I guess I'll leave."

Looking at Miriam, Dr. Powell said, "I can see part of the problem clearly now. Cliff really wants to be in control."

Miriam's face was beet red as she stormed out to their van. "I have never felt so humiliated in my life, Clifford Chase!" she said angrily when they got in and shut the doors.

"Well, I should think you would be," he replied. "I'd be embarrassed, too, if I had brought *you* to someone like that!"

Neither of them spoke on the way home.

A few weeks later, while Cliff was out of town at a minister's conference, Eric woke up in the night, crying, "Mommy! Mommy!" Miriam jumped out of bed and put on her bathrobe. She hurried to her son's room.

"What is it, honey?" she asked as she sat on his bed and pulled him up on her lap. "Were you dreaming?"

"Yes, Mommy!" he cried. "I dreamed you and Daddy got a divorce!"

"Oh, darling," she said as she rocked him gently. "Mommy and Daddy won't ever get a divorce!"

"Then why did he leave us again?" he whimpered as he clung tightly to Miriam.

"Why, honey, he explained to you that he had to go to a conference. He'll be back on Friday."

"I hope so," he said as he sniffed loudly. "I don't like it when you and Daddy fight!"

A pang of guilt pierced Miriam's heart. For a moment, she knew she had been thinking only about herself these past weeks–so preoccupied with her own recovery from abuse that she failed to see she was causing suffering in her own children. Then her jaw stiffened. *No! I'm not the one abusing these dear children! It's Cliff and his stubbornness! If he could only see how deeply I hurt inside! Why does he resist my every effort to find healing for my soul?*

"Well, Eric," she finally said, "I don't like to fight with Daddy. He's making some choices that are hurting me and I can't let him keep doing that."

"Daddy's hurting you, Mommy?" he asked with big eyes.

"Yes, dear, in a way, he is."

"Then I'll tell Daddy to stop it!"

She hugged Eric tightly and set him back down in his bed. "Yes, dear, you tell Daddy that when he gets home." She turned out the light and returned to her room. She hung her robe on a hook, slid into bed, and pulled up the covers.

As she tried to fall asleep, an uneasy feeling began to grow in her stomach. She knew she was violating a primary rule of parenting: Never use your children to get at your mate. But what could she do? Cliff wouldn't listen to reason. Maybe God would teach Cliff through the voice of her children. She turned over in bed, trying to quiet the small voice in the back of her soul.

She tossed fitfully as sleep refused to come. A few blocks away she heard sirens rushing to an emergency. She sighed wearily, got out of bed, slipped into her robe again, and walked downstairs to the family room. She turned on the light and sat down, depressed and angry.

On the table next to her was a book on recovery from sexual abuse. She picked it up and began flipping through its pages. She read that the damage of past abuse subconsciously directs virtually every area of the abused person's life: relationships, the mate chosen, the careers selected, one's religious beliefs, "the fabric of our entire lives."[98] She looked up with tears in her eyes. *The book says I hate myself so much that I'm actually killing my own soul!*[99] As she read on,

Miriam discovered that she would have to open herself again to pain. Otherwise, she would experience "soul deadness–a heart dulled to its own pain."[100] She learned that many abuse victims so effectively bury their trauma that they experience a "dissociation" or "splitting" of their personalities.[101]

Further on, she read that "abuse strips a person of the freedom to choose"[102] and that once abuse has begun, it is impossible to stop.[103] The victim experiences such hopelessness that the only immediate recourse is "the soul-numbing choice to abandon a sense of being alive."[104] She may even "choose to kill the part of her soul that feels pain."[105] Since the book stated that "when we abandon pain, we lose a sense of being intact and alive,"[106] Miriam realized that it was important to hold on to her suffering and experience it fully.

Further in the book, Miriam found that she may have chosen Cliff as a mate as a result of the abuse she had suffered.[107] For just a moment, Miriam began to doubt the teaching. "That's ridiculous!" she said out loud.

She remembered the characteristics that had drawn her to Cliff: his gentleness, his sincerity, and his love for Jesus. It had nothing at all to do with the sexual abuse she had endured. Or did it?

As she continued to read, she found herself wavering between two opinions. Emotionally she responded to much that the book said, for it justified her anger and the desire to avoid personal responsibility for what had taken place between herself and her college-age lover. Intellectually, however, she knew that there was a categorical difference between her case and the actual abuse of a child who had been molested by an adult.

The book said that entering into her past would disrupt her life. She nodded in agreement and underlined the passage with a yellow highlighter. "Marriages will need to be reshaped,"[108] the author wrote. In one sense Miriam dreaded the reshaping. She began to sense a feeling of impending loss. As she reviewed their nearly fifteen years of marriage, Miriam knew that the relationship had been mostly positive. Cliff had never raised a hand to her and he was generally sensitive and kind. He had never given her cause for doubting his faithfulness . . . until now. Suddenly anger flooded into her heart and blocked her growing tenderness toward Cliff.

"Sexual relations may be postponed while the partners devote themselves to prayer and fasting,"[109] the book said.

"Amen!" Miriam said through gritted teeth. She pulled her legs up on the couch and under her nightgown. She failed to note the second half of the sentence–that such postponement was for the purpose of prayer and fasting.

She read on. "The fabric of life will need to be unraveled piece by piece as the Master reweaves the cloth to His design."[110] In the back of her mind, even through her rage, she heard Cliff's voice echo softly. *Where does it say* that *in the Word?*

Miriam shook her head and gritted her teeth with determination. *I will not be victimized again!* she thought. *Never again!*

4

Where Healing
Begins

Recently I talked with a sincere young Christian woman
who had been convinced by a therapist that her parents
had abused her. Later on, however, she realized that the
therapist had misled her and she retracted her accusations.
She told me, "If you talk to many retractors you'll eventually hear the same thing: We are all so embarrassed.
Whenever I talk about what I did, I have to work hard at
not feeling condemned and ashamed."

I had asked her what it would take to awaken other
people who had been lulled into believing therapy-induced
memories. She replied, "I'm not sure what I would say to
someone caught in the false memory trap. I do know they
are hard to talk to and don't easily accept much of anything. Regardless of whether they would accept the Word,
I do know it takes a miracle to get out, and most of them
will eventually tell you they know that."

Whether their memories are real or not, sincere wounded
people are seeking real answers for their problems, yet are
often led into therapies that only make their troubles worse. As
a result, it is not unusual for them to distrust all "authorities,"

including God.

Fortunately, some of the people who have walked that path and seen that it leads nowhere are once again looking to God's Word for help. They sense the answers are to be found in the Scriptures. But oftentimes they are unsure of where to look, and consequently still find it difficult to experience genuine peace and joy.

At the end of the last chapter, I promised we would look at what the Bible says about finding genuine healing and peace. Through the rest of this book, we will look at several key guidelines found in Scripture. I must remind you that these guidelines or steps are not quick and easy answers. Some people will fault them for being simplistic and I understand that. In fact, one dear brother who happens to be a researcher in the study of false memories scolded me for my nonscholastic approach to the issue. He didn't seem to understand that this book is not intended as an intellectual polemic to persuade the academic com-munity. Rather, it is a sincere attempt to direct damaged souls back to the truths of God's Word.

The people who prefer the intellectual approach to mankind's problems often scoff at simple truths. One person specifically questioned whether biblical counsel was too simplistic an approach for dealing with the complexities of false memories. In response, I wrote,

> I'm not sure what you would suggest in helping a person to turn from false memories and woundedness, if not the Word. I am not questioning the fact that you were in the Word during your regression therapy and were genuinely seeking to be obedient, but I still do not see a superior solution. Either God is able or He isn't. At some point [in your therapy], the application of His Word must have been faulty, but not knowing the details, I cannot comment. Please be assured that I am not trying to condemn you or anyone else who has

been caught up in this tragedy. But I cannot believe that the fault was with the Word of God.

As to my "simplistic black and white observations" I genuinely believe that part of the problem with the psychological way is that it complicates and confuses rather than clarifies. The walk with God is far more simple than many would have us to believe. Yet, it is eternally profound. Even so, I do not believe that I have, as you say, offered "easy answers." Simplicity and ease of implementation are not the same.

Choosing Your Authority

It all comes down to this question: Who are you going to believe? Who is worthy of your trust—those who follow the psychological route or the Word of God? I readily admit that there are many pastors, church counselors, elders, and laity who do not handle the Scriptures in an accurate way and they, too, will do incredible harm. This may be because of a general ignorance of the Word, an inconsistent method of interpreting Scripture, a spirit of legalism rather than speaking the truth in love, a lack of confidence in the power of the Holy Spirit to transform the heart, answering too quickly before listening carefully, and so on. The answer, though, is not to turn from God's Word because someone has misinterpreted or misapplied it.

That leads me to our first step toward genuine healing of the wounded heart: *Carefully choose your source of authority and information.* This principle is vital if you are going to move forward toward healing; we find it in the Scriptures repeatedly.

Joshua presented the Israelites with this choice when he said, "If serving the LORD seems undesirable to you, then choose for yourselves this day whom you will serve, whether the gods your forefathers served beyond the River, or the gods of the Amorites, in whose land you are living. But as for me and my household, we will serve the LORD" (Joshua 24:15).

Later on, in the days of Elijah, the people of Israel made their choice. They decided to integrate their faith with the teachings of the unbelieving world: "Even while these people were worshiping the LORD, they were serving their idols" (2 Kings 17:41).

That is precisely what is happening in our day. Many Christians have decided that God just doesn't have the answers for modern troubles and that we need stronger medicine–the wisdom of psychological studies–to heal our wounded hearts.

Confronting Israel was not easy, but Elijah courageously took an unpopular stand. He went before the people and said, "How long will you waver between two opinions? If the LORD is God, follow him; but if Baal is God, follow him" (1 Kings 18:21).

A number of good men and women, well-known as authors and leaders in the Christian world, seem unable to understand this pivotal question: If the Bible really is God's Word and if it is infallible and inerrant as evangelical Christians claim to believe, and if it is our authority for faith and doctrine, how can we deny that it is adequate to deal with the problems of modern life?

We simply can't have it both ways. Either God's Word is absolutely true and dependable or it isn't. Either it is sufficient for our daily lives or it isn't. To try to hold the Bible in one hand and a psychological text in the other is to be what James describes as "double-minded" and "unstable" (James 1:8) because we don't know who or what to believe.

Ultimately, each of us must decide *who* our authority will be. Will we trust the insights of the Holy Spirit as given to us through the prophets of God, or will we place our trust in the ever-changing theories, studies, and therapies of a psychological industry that is based on humanistic foundations?

The first step toward permanently healing of our wounded hearts is to say in response to Elijah, "Since the Lord *is* God, I will follow *Him.*"

Accepting the Truth

The second step toward healing is to commit ourselves to accepting and obeying the truth, no matter how difficult or unpleasant it may seem at the time. Only when we accept the truth will we know freedom; Jesus said that when you "know the truth . . . the truth will set you free" (John 8:32).

Sometimes we humans resist truth because it confronts us with our failures. We may try to shield ourselves by hiding from the truth. As Isaiah laments, "we have made a lie our refuge and falsehood our hiding place" (Isaiah 28:15).

Return with me for a moment to the case of Lee, Jean, Gloria, and Jim Grady. In the court hearing on the restraining order Gloria had requested, Lee, Jean and Jim were "swiftly and completely vindicated."[111] But that didn't change the attitude of Gloria's therapists.

> It was a hollow victory, since my sister left the courtroom in the company of supporters and social workers who had sat through the same three days as the judge and others, but remained as committed to their agenda of keeping Gloria from us and us from Gloria as the day they had walked into that courtroom.[112]

Jim Grady puts his finger upon part of the problem when he writes:

> This entire mindset was unbelievably captured during the hearing when, after learning that Gloria's therapist of the previous four years had suddenly decided the week before the hear-

ing that it was in their mutual best interest for him to no longer see Gloria, the psychiatrist from MHMR (Mental Health Mental Retardation) who was now overseeing Gloria's treatment was called to testify. Under oath, she testified that she had accepted Gloria's previous therapist's diagnosis that all of this had, in fact, happened to her, without questioning its validity or seeking her own verification...and that if she were to find out that very day that in fact NONE of this had EVER happened to Gloria she would NOT CHANGE her treatment of Gloria AT ALL! (emphasis in original)[113]

Whether Gloria's accusations were accurate or not didn't seem to matter to her new therapist. She was intent on protecting Gloria from her family. This kind of thinking and "therapy" is almost beyond belief.[114]

I am not implying, however, that all Christians who look to psychology for answers to their personal problems are intentionally seeking to avoid the truth. Many sincere Christians want to obey the Lord and believe that psychological counseling may provide the key to the healing of their hearts. They are not willfully rebelling against the truth; rather, they are simply confused and unsure of where to turn for help.

And even if we *are* committed to the truth, it is still uncomfortable to undergo examination. I, for example, have never looked forward to a physical exam at the medical clinic. I don't like having a nurse order me onto the scales only to see her slide the balance ever to the right while raising her eyebrows with a smirk and murmuring, "Uh *huh!*"

I don't like having to get undressed and sit in my shorts on a cold stainless steel table waiting for the doctor to arrive just before hypothermia sets in. I don't appreciate the none-too-subtle inference when he asks how much weight I've gained this year. I feel awkward about being told to breathe in deeply, exhale hard, turn my head, and cough. I don't like being thumped and probed like a watermelon or a baked chicken.

But I still go. Why? Because I want to remain healthy as long as possible and I hope to catch any major illness before it becomes serious. While I would dread finding out that I have cancer, I would prefer to know the truth as soon as possible so treatment can begin.

Yet when it comes to our spiritual lives, our character, and our relationships, we tend to hide from the truth. We don't like to have someone point out our flaws. My shame of being exposed in front of the doctor is not due so much because of the extra blubber around my stomach; rather, the embarrassment is from having that blubber exposed. So long as it is covered, I feel fine. Likewise, it is not sin we fear so much; it is the *exposure* of our sin that mortifies us.

As *Newsweek* magazine once reported of police corruption, "Supervisors often fear the impact of a corruption scandal on their careers more than corruption itself. No institution wants its reputation tainted."[115]

We all tend to shrink from the truth as did our original parents. In Genesis 3, we find the first story of man hiding from reality:

> When the woman saw that the fruit of the tree was good for food and pleasing to the eye, and also desirable for gaining wisdom, she took some and ate it. She also gave some to her husband, who was with her, and he ate it. Then the eyes of both of them were opened, and they realized they were naked; so they sewed fig leaves together and made coverings for themselves.
>
> Then the man and his wife heard the sound of the LORD God as he was walking in the garden in

> the cool of the day, and they hid from the LORD
> God among the trees of the garden. But the LORD
> God called to the man, "Where are you?"
>
> He answered, "I heard you in the garden, and
> I was afraid because I was naked; so I hid" (verses
> 6-10).

While it is barely possible that Adam hid out of modesty, I believe the primary reason he hid was that he had disobeyed God. We hide today for the same reason.

The problem is that hiding from the truth does not really protect us. Instead, self-deceit actually damages our ability to mature, to love, and to enjoy fellowship with God and other people. Lies imprison us as surely as the bars of a jail and separate us from the remedy for a hurting heart. As William J. Bennett wrote, "Honesty is of pervasive human importance. . . . Every social activity, every human enterprise requiring people to act in concert, is impeded when people aren't honest with one another."[116]

Truth is vitally important, for it determines one's entire world-view. Josh McDowell makes an excellent observation in his book *Right from Wrong:*

> Without solid convictions about truth...our
> children will buy the counterfeits almost every
> time. It's like a downward spiral. When they
> reject truth as an objective standard, their view of
> life becomes distorted. When their view becomes
> distorted, they easily accept counterfeits. When
> they accept counterfeits, they begin to make
> wrong choices. When they make wrong choices,
> they suffer the consequences. The choice is, quite
> literally, truth or consequences.[117]

It is this downward spiral that concerns me so much. Accepting a lie damages a person's spiritual walk, relationships, and trust of others. Yet, we humans seem so easily led into lies.

Why does deception come so naturally to us? Because it is our fallen nature to protect ourselves from the truth. Jeremiah writes, "The heart is deceitful above all things and beyond cure. Who can understand it?" (Jeremiah 17:9). Isaiah draws a pathetic picture of the person who deceives himself: "He feeds on ashes, a deluded heart misleads him; he cannot save himself, or say, 'Is not this thing in my right hand a lie?'" (Isaiah 44:20).

Because we find it so distasteful to admit that we are truly sinful, we desperately cling to the belief that we are better than we really are. And after years of practicing this charade, we are increasingly unable to identify the sins in our lives. The psalmist put it this way: "In his own eyes he flatters himself too much to detect or hate his sin" (Psalm 36:2).

Humanistic psychology has a way of finding an excuse for every sin: A person who expresses rage is said to be merely venting his anger so that it doesn't build up inside; a man who is given to lust is told he has a sexual addiction and needs our understanding; a woman who is willingly seduced is declared innocent because the man she gave in to had significant power over her life.

With sometimes compassionate motives, psychological counselors often remove the hope of permanent change by supporting the delusion that we are not responsible for our own choices. Knowing that the guilt is real, "friend deceives friend, and no one speaks the truth. They have taught their tongues to lie; they weary themselves with sinning" (Jeremiah 9:5).

Christians are supposed to be people of the truth. Yet in this generation it is accepted practice to redefine sinful behavior as something we have no control over. Instead of feeling guilty about our sin, we are told we need to feel good about ourselves. In doing so we lie to ourselves, to others, and to God. The self-esteem movement that has been enthusiastically embraced by Christian psychology and churches alike is a case in point.

A recent 20/20 broadcast[118] featured the self-esteem movement in public schools, where children are taught to chant self-congratulatory mantras to make them feel good about themselves. When a psychologist was challenged to produce studies to support the theory, she quickly brushed the question aside, suggesting that logic alone tells us that when people feel good about themselves they will treat others kindly.

The biblical doctrine of man's sinful nature is buried under a humanistic philosophy that redefines man as intrinsically good, but dysfunctional, because of what others have done to us. It is one more method Satan uses to keep suffering people in permanent bondage.

An Inaccurate Perception

Sometimes we confuse distortion for depth. Psychological counselors are often repulsed by obvious solutions for inner wounds because they believe that the reasons for our pain are hidden, complex, and obscure, requiring the deep insights of trained professions.

Don't let a counselor make human behavior so complex. Remember that psychological interpretations, theories, and treatments for wounded hearts are generally subjective–and as a result, they are unreliable. Sadly, the longer Christians stay in unbiblical therapy, the more confused they become.

In contrast, the Scriptures say, "We have renounced secret and shameful ways; we do not use deception, nor do we distort the word of God. On the contrary, by setting forth the truth plainly we commend ourselves to every man's conscience in the sight of God" (2 Corinthians 4:2).

The process of inner healing is not as complicated as psychological experts would have us believe. Perhaps the reason that untrained lay counselors are as effective or more effective than trained therapists is because they don't try to see what doesn't exist. There *are* times when truth is simple–but it is always profound.

Real Hope for Healing

Even now as you read, you may have begun to sense a quiet agreement in your spirit that God alone *can* set you free and heal your wounded heart without manmade theories that are doomed to fail.

Healing begins when we commit ourselves to the truth. If we insist that we have done nothing wrong, we are going to continue in our "dysfunctions." Like John wrote, "If we claim to be without sin, we deceive ourselves and the truth is not in us" (1 John 1:8).

Every person must bear his own guilt in proportion to the choices he was free to make. The moment we turn from the truth about our own sin–and God's forgiveness and cleansing–we will be trapped in our guilt again.

Sometimes when friends try to gently confront us with the truth, we angrily turn away from them in a way similar to what the prophet Amos described: "You hate the one who reproves in court and despise him who tells the truth" (Amos 5:10).

Don't get angry at a faithful friend who cares enough to tell you the truth. Remember, "faithful are the wounds of a friend, but deceitful are the kisses of an enemy" (Proverbs 27:6). Respect and love the pastor or elder or friend who has the courage to confront you when you are damaging yourself with sin. Don't make the mistake Jesus spoke of when He said, "Because I tell the truth, you do not believe me!" (John 8:45).

Biblical counselors are often ridiculed for pointing out sin in the lives of those who come for counsel. They are characterized as being harsh and without compassion, but ask yourself this question: Are psychologists being compassionate by keeping a person enslaved to guilt and sorrow when God offers complete forgiveness, cleansing, and healing?

"All those biblical counselors do is spotlight a person's sin and tell him to stop doing it. That is so heartless, simplistic, and naive!" Even if that commonly uttered yet false stereotype were true, is it *really* simplistic and cruel to expose sin? Was Jesus being heartless when He told the woman caught in adultery, "Go now and leave your life of sin" (John 8:11)?

The apostle James was fairly bold about facing up to our sin, too. He said, "Do not merely listen to the word, and so deceive yourselves. Do what it says" (James 1:22). God is not being heartless or impatient when He tells us to quit kidding ourselves, stop sinning, and start living according to His plan. He's telling us the truth because He loves us and wants what's best for us.

The Perfect Counselor

The good news is, God doesn't expect us to change our lives on our own. But neither does He need the help of psychotherapists and hundreds of sessions and thousands of dollars to produce real healing. He has given us our own *personal* Counselor who is on perpetual call–the Holy Spirit.

Jesus promised, "I will ask the Father, and he will give you another Counselor to be with you forever" (John 14:16). Note carefully how this divine Counselor applies His therapy: "When the Counselor comes, whom I will send to you from the Father, the Spirit of truth who goes out from the Father, he will testify about me" (John 15:26). The Holy Spirit deals only with the truth, and the central message of His healing is found in Jesus.

Jesus came to set us *free!* He came to *break* the chains of sin that bind us to guilt, sorrow, bitterness, and pain. He came to transform us from pitiful dying creatures to immortal beings with eternal life. He came to give us *real* life! He said, "I have come that they may have life, and have it to the full" (John 10:10). Paul wrote, "Now that you have been set free from sin and have become slaves to God, the benefit you reap leads to holiness, and the result is eternal life" (Romans 6:22).

Let's not sell our spiritual birthright for a pot full of temporary feel-good therapies. We dare not make the mistake of following our hearts instead of God's Word. Rather, we have been called to seek the truth about God and about ourselves. Otherwise, there may come a day when we have to admit, "All this disaster has come upon us, yet we have not sought the favor of the LORD our God by turning from our sins and giving attention to your truth" (Daniel 9:13).

Finding the Truth

Perhaps you are asking one of the most profound philosophical question of all time: "What *is* truth?" (John 18:38, emphasis added). Jesus anticipated that very question when He said, "I am the way and the truth and the life. No one comes to the Father except through me" (John 14:6). *All* truth–whether it is scientific, historical, archeological, sociological, physical or spiritual–is ultimately related to the Person of Jesus Christ. In that sense, then, I can agree with those who say that "all truth is God's truth." The problem, however, is in *determining* what is true and what is false. Nothing that is true will ever contradict the written Word of God.

We will never find truth by looking inward, contrary to what Eastern religions, New Age cults, and psychology teach. We will not find truth by going to the "experts" of the human mind. If we want to find truth for our souls, we only have to look to Jesus and His Word.

His coming underscores our desperate condition–our need of a Savior. If our hearts could be healed without

Jesus, then His coming, His death on the cross, and His resurrection would be meaningless. In fact, they would be *foolish* if we can somehow achieve peace of soul without Him.

God has chosen to reveal the truth of Christ through His written Word. And the Holy Spirit works through Scripture to transform our lives as we begin to grasp His truth. This process is the fulfillment of Jesus' prayer for us in John 17:17: "Sanctify them by the truth; your word is truth."

A Healthy Pain

Self-examination is not a pleasant process, but the end result is worth it. Surgery is not something we look forward to eagerly, but at times it is necessary so we can remove a life-threatening cancer.

Paul had to reprove the saints at Corinth because of rampant sin. They were wise enough to listen to him and they took action. In his second letter to the Corinthians, Paul wrote,

> If I caused you sorrow by my letter, I do not regret it. Though I did regret it–I see that my letter hurt you, but only for a little while–yet now I am happy, not because you were made sorry, but because your sorrow led you to repentance. For you became sorrowful as God intended and so were not harmed in any way by us. Godly sorrow brings repentance that leads to salvation and leaves no regret, but worldly sorrow brings death (2 Corinthians 7:8-10).

Look especially at this incredible statement: "Godly sorrow brings repentance that leads to salvation and *leaves no regret*" (emphasis added). Facing the truth with a sincere heart leads a child of God to repentance and produces genuine peace in the heart.

How to Begin

A healing relationship with God begins with the truth. John reminds us, "God is spirit, and his worshipers must worship in spirit and in truth" (John 4:24). Subjective interpretations of our dreams, suggestions to draw out our repressed memories, and bizarre explanations for our behavior will never accomplish permanent healing of our hearts.

Do we really *want* to get better? Do we want to be free from the burden of guilt that weighs heavily on our souls? Then we must face the *truth* about ourselves. We must allow the Lord to begin His healing work by asking Him to reveal what we are *really* like. We cannot hide behind psychological labels and excuses. Instead, we must allow the brilliant light of God's Word to illuminate every corner of our being so that God's cleansing can begin.

Miriam continued meeting with Dr. Powell. He was concerned about the radical mood swings he observed in various sessions, yet overall, he was pleased with the progress she was making in understanding herself.

During one session, he began their discussion in an unusual way. "Miriam," he said, "I think you're ready to go deeper in your search for healing. I have observed that sometimes you come in all cheerful and lighthearted, and at other times you seem deeply depressed. Sometimes you're talkative, and at other times you hardly say a word. It's like I'm talking to several entirely different people."

Miriam blushed with embarrassment. "I know, Dr. Powell. Sometimes I feel I'm making progress, and then at other times I feel like I'm going crazy. Sometimes I don't think I even know myself."

He nodded sympathetically. "That may be truer than

you realize, Miriam."

She looked at him quizzically. "What do you mean?"

"I mean that you have some of the symptoms often associated with a condition called MPD–multiple personality disorder."

"I don't understand."

"Well, let's review what your therapy has revealed so far," he said, leafing through his notes. "You are a victim of sexual abuse and your husband has perpetuated the abuse–unintentionally, to be sure–by not nurturing you, right?"

"Well, yes, I guess so," Miriam agreed hesitantly.

"Then we discovered that you have an unusually high level of creativity and a wonderful ability to fantasize."

Miriam nodded in agreement, wondering where Dr. Powell was leading her.

"I have noticed in various sessions that your facial expressions seem to change radically at times and your tone of voice and even your vocabulary become quite different from normal. When Dr. McCall prescribed tranquilizers for your anxiety, you did not seem to improve at all, remember?"

Miriam nodded, still uncertain of where the conversation was going. "The tranquilizers just seemed to make me groggy."

"Exactly. And do you remember telling me how you sometimes experience blank spots in your days, when you feel as though you have lost some time?"

"Well, not exactly, Dr. Powell," Miriam corrected. "I believe you suggested that someday I might have the experience of feeling as if I had lost time, and that if it happened I shouldn't worry about it."

"Oh, yes," Dr. Powell said, writing on his pad. "Let me ask you, though, is it possible that you have had episodes of amnesia?"

"Well, if I have had amnesia, I certainly don't remember it," Miriam laughed.

Dr. Powell didn't see the humor in her reply. "That's my point exactly, Miriam. You wouldn't remember it, so it is impossible to say for sure that you have not experienced it."

"Well, I suppose," Miriam replied meekly, a bit miffed that her joke had been unappreciated. She shifted in her chair uneasily and asked, "Just what are you suggesting, Dr. Powell?"

"I'm saying that we have a great deal more work ahead of us. I have come to believe that we are dealing with more than simple depression and recovery from abuse. I believe we need to explore far deeper into your heart than we have gone so far. I think we will find that a lot of dissociation has taken place."

"Dissociation? What is that?" Miriam asked

"Dissociation is a defense mechanism that victims use to separate themselves from the memory of painful events. The inner personality creates an alternate personality who did not experience the trauma. This 'alter personality' has absolutely no memory of the horrible event the host personality suffered."

Miriam looked confused. "I simply don't understand what you're talking about."

"Of course you don't, Miriam," Dr. Powell said with a sad smile, "but you will. It's my job to help you uncover the painful memories you have buried in your heart."

"Why can't we just leave painful memories buried, Dr. Powell?" Miriam asked sincerely. "If I can't remember them, why stir them up?"

"Because, Miriam, a fragmented person cannot experience the full joy God meant for us to have. Your marriage can be restored, you can become a better mother, you can find peace again through a unified personality. Though it sounds paradoxical, sometimes you have to get worse before you can get better. I believe a better life is worth the pain, don't you?"

"Well, yes, if that's what it takes," Miriam replied with

tears in her eyes. "But how do we begin?"

"It starts with you placing your trust in me as your therapist," Dr. Powell said gently, with deep sincerity. "Can you do that?"

"I...I think so," Miriam replied. She was impressed with his deep concern and his confidence. He knew what he was talking about.

"Then let's begin," Dr. Powell said, leaning back in his chair. "Haven't you sometimes felt as though there is a little girl inside of you longing to get out and play again?"

Miriam thought for a moment, then replied, "Yes, I think all adults have occasional longings to return to their childhood, don't you?"

"Perhaps. But this may be different. Now relax and close your eyes for a few moments, Miriam. Have you had any unusual dreams lately?"

"No," Miriam answered almost sleepily. "Well, not anything terribly strange."

"I didn't say strange. I said unusual."

"I'm not even sure it was unusual."

"Just tell me about it," Dr. Powell said gently.

"Oh, there's nothing special about it," she said as she leaned back into the comfortable overstuffed chair. "It's hard to recall it in detail."

"Just relax and tell me the images that flash on the screen of your mind."

Miriam smiled slightly. *This is kind of fun,* she thought. "I can't remember anything specific."

"Just try."

"Okay. Oh, there *is* one. I was lying on the little hill by my grandparents' house in Indiana, looking up at the clouds. I used to do that all the time as a kid. I loved it. I pretended that I could see animals and other shapes in the clouds."

"Good, good. Go on."

"That's all there is."

"No, Miriam," Dr. Powell said softly. "Try harder."

"That's all I can remember. It isn't much, is it?" she said, looking up at Dr. Powell.

"Keep your eyes closed and relax. Do the clouds grow dark?"

Miriam closed her eyes again and thought for a moment. "No, I don't think so. It's a sunny day and the birds are chirping happily. I loved those times when I could be by myself imagining all kinds of wonderful adventures."

"What kind of adventures?" Dr. Powell asked as he wrote in his notepad.

"Oh, the usual kind of things girls dream about–being a princess, having a handsome knight fall in love with me, and going off to his castle to live happily ever after," she laughed.

"Were there ever any sad or scary dreams?"

"Of course. All children have nightmares from time to time, don't they?"

"Some do. Tell me about a nightmare you remember."

Miriam squeezed her eyes shut even tighter and tried to recall. "I remember one weird dream I had several times as a child, especially when I had a fever."

Dr. Powell leaned forward. "Tell me about it."

"It's kind of dumb," she said apologetically. "I had this big storybook when I was a little girl. The main characters were a pair of elves–a tall skinny elf and a short fat elf. They both had pointed stocking caps and shoes with long, floppy points. Whenever I had a fever, I would see them in a nightmare, dancing around me."

"Did they ever do anything to you?"

She shook her head. "No, they just danced and then I'd wake up crying because they kind of scared me."

"Why?"

"I don't know. They just seemed strange."

"They never tried to touch you or make you lie down?"

"Well, maybe," Miriam admitted. "I can't remember. Yes, they probably tried to touch me."

"Where did they touch you?"

"I can't remember," she said, and then suddenly blushed.

Dr. Powell noticed and gently asked again, "Where did they touch you, Miriam?"

"I...I don't want to say."

"Was it in an intimate spot?"

Miriam swallowed hard and nodded. "But I'm not sure I really dreamed that or if it just came to mind now."

"Trust your heart, Miriam. It will never lie to you," Dr. Powell said soothingly. "Don't be embarrassed. Now tell me, where did they touch you?"

Miriam sat up and blinked her eyes. "I don't think that's appropriate, Dr. Powell," she said with a firmness that surprised her.

Dr. Powell sat back in his chair with a gentle smile. "I understand how you must feel. I think we've gone far enough this session." He turned to his bookshelf and pulled out a paperback book. "I want you to read this before our next session."

"What is it?" Miriam asked.

"It's a book about multiple personality disorder," he replied. "I think it will help you to understand what's going on in your life right now. Believe me, Miriam, we're finally getting somewhere."

5

From Victim to Victor

Recently I was the phone guest on a Christian radio talk show and the topic was the recovery movement. During the program, some callers asked my opinion of Alcoholics Anonymous (AA). I explained my concerns that the "higher power" of AA is not the God of the Scriptures and that the twelve steps are not based on the biblical pattern of total transformation through the power of the Holy Spirit.

One man phoned to say that he strongly supported twelve-step programs and had been in AA for seven years. When I asked him if he was attending a Bible-believing church on a regular basis, he admitted that he was not, but said, "I do read my Bible every day." For him, AA *is* his church, but it is a church without power.

Lisa called in to say that she was sober and that God had used AA to bring her to Christ. "God is much bigger than you make Him out to be," she said reprovingly. Her point was that we should not limit God; if He chooses to use AA to free people from the disease of alcoholism, we should rejoice.

I do indeed rejoice whenever someone is truly freed from bondage to alcohol. But what I see in AA is a new bondage–perpetual victimization–because one of the central doctrines of AA is that once a person becomes an alcoholic, he is forever an alcoholic. Furthermore, alcoholism is viewed as a disease over which a person has no control. It is seldom suggested that God is able to *completely* deliver a person from alcohol when he becomes a new creation in Christ. Instead, AA congregations are taught that they are diseased victims with a genetic disorder. Their hope for permanent healing is removed; instead, they are given an excuse for every problem in their lives.

The Problem of Victimization

Universal victimization–that's where we're headed in a society that devalues the legitimate goal of protecting the truly handicapped by extending the protections of the 1973 Rehabilitation Act and the Americans with Disabilities Act to those who are voluntarily overweight.

In 1993, a federal appeals court ruled that Rhode Island had to pay $100,000 in damages to a 320-pound woman because she was refused a job. It appears that her condition was not glandular, for in its statement to the court, the Equal Employment Opportunity Commission argued, "It is not necessary that a condition be involuntary or immutable to be covered."[119] In other words, just because the woman chose to overeat and could reverse the condition if she were to exercise discipline–or to discipline herself and exercise–does not change the fact that she is a victim.

An essay in *Time* magazine made this observation: "Treating the discrimination against someone who is fat alongside that of someone who is a paraplegic is part of an effort by special-interest groups to make all suffering equal so that all remedies will be."[120]

Other people are noticing the problem of universal victimization as well. Kristin Leutwyler writes in *Scientific American:*

Do you use grammar and punctuation poorly? Is your spelling horrendous, and penmanship bad, too? You may be mentally ill–that is, if your diagnostician believes you are truly impaired and adheres strictly to the guidelines laid out in the latest edition of the "Diagnostic and Statistical Man-ual of Mental Disorders IV (DSM-IV)," published by the American Psychiatric Association. The manual lists these indications under Code 315.2, the "Disorder of Written Expression."

The DSM, or "the psychiatrist's bible," catalogues the behavioral traits associated with some 290 different psychoses and neuroses. The newest version is the third update published in the past 15 years, and critics charge that it shares a problem with its predecessors. "The criteria open a wide bag, and a lot of healthy people fall in," explains Herb Kutchins, a professor of social work at the California State University at Sacramento. Kutchins notes that tomboys could be diagnosed with gender-related personality disorders, or college students as alcoholics.[121]

ADHD, or attention deficit hyperactivity disorder, is an example of diagnostic excuses running amok. A report in *Time* magazine reported this:

Fifteen years ago, no one had ever heard of attention deficit hyperactivity disorder. Today it is the most common behavioral disorder in American children, the subject of thousands of studies and symposiums and no small degree of controversy. Experts on ADHD say it afflicts as many as 3 1/2 million American youngsters, or up to 5% of those under 18. It is two to three times as likely to be diagnosed in boys as in girls.

The disorder has replaced what used to be popularly called "hyperactivity," and it includes a broader collection of symptoms. ADHD has three main hallmarks: extreme distractibility, an almost reckless impulsiveness and, in some but not all cases, a knee-jiggling, toe-tapping hyperactivity that makes sitting still all but impossible. (Without hyperactivity, the disorder is called attention deficit disorder, or ADD.)[122]

It is intriguing that as "information" about psychological diseases becomes widespread, so do the symptoms. This is precisely what has happened with ADHD: "Ten years ago, doctors believed that the symptoms of ADHD faded with maturity. Now it is one of the fastest-growing diagnostic categories for adults."[123]

This new discovery has been a source of great comfort to a growing number of people:

Many adults respond to the diagnosis with relief–a sense that "at last my problem has a name and it's not my fault." As more people are diagnosed, the use of Ritalin (or its generic equivalent, methylphenidate), the drug of choice for ADHD, has surged: prescriptions are up more than 390% in just four years.[124]

There is a price to pay, however, for adding to the victimization of America:

Adults with ADHD are beginning to seek special treatment. Under the 1990 Americans with Disabilities Act, they can insist upon help in the workplace. Usually the interventions are quite modest: an office door or white-noise machine to reduce distractions, or longer deadlines on assignments.

Another legal trend that concerns even ADHD advocates: the disorder is being raised as a defense in criminal cases. Psychologist Barkley says he knows of 55 such instances in the U.S., all in the past 10 years. ADHD was cited as a mitigating factor by the attorney for Michael Fay, the 19-year-old American who was charged with vandalism and caned in Singapore.[125]

Is ADHD really an illness, or have we just renamed bad behavior so that its "victims" have an excuse? Consider the fact that ADHD is primarily an American disease:

Other than the name itself, there is nothing new about this suddenly ubiquitous disorder. The world has always had its share of obstreperous kids, and it has generally treated them as behavior problems rather than patients. Most of the world still does so: European nations like France and England report one-tenth the U.S. rate of ADHD. In Japan the disorder has barely been studied.[126]

How can a person know whether he actually has ADHD? And just how is it diagnosed? The evidence suggests that ADHD is more of a cultural and educational disease than a distinct physiological condition:

In the absence of any biological test, diagnosing ADHD is a rather inexact proposition. In most cases, it is a teacher who initiates the process by informing parents that their child is daydreaming in class, failing to complete assignments or driving everyone crazy with thoughtless behavior. "The problem is that the parent then goes to the family doctor, who writes a prescription for

Ritalin and doesn't stop to think of the other possibilities," says child psychiatrist Larry Silver of Georgetown University Medical Center. To make a careful diagnosis, Silver argues, one must eliminate other explanations for the symptoms.[127]

A Case Study of Victimization

A sweet 64-year-old woman named Grace called in on our radio broadcast seeking information about ADD. "There was recently a lot of publicity in the paper about ADD in adults and it seems like I have the symptoms. Just recently I obtained Ritalin; I have not started to take it, and I'm kind of reluctant to take it, because I think that maybe God can heal me. I'd also like to know your opinion about my situation."

"What was it that led your doctor to say that you have ADD?" I asked.

"Apparently it's because I handle my daily activities in a disorganized way," she replied. "I mean...I'm severely disorganized. That's basically the biggest symptom."

"And what do you mean by 'seriously disorganized'?"

"I mean keeping my apartment neat and doing all the things that have to be done. And I'm not a working lady, so there's no reason to be short on time. But when I received my prescription, it seemed like the Lord was telling me, 'Don't take it. I'm able to help you in this area.' After that I had a couple of wonderful days where I got a lot accomplished. But now I'm slipping back into some of my bad habits . . . and I'm just wondering if you think I should give it [Ritalin] a try. I have not tried it yet."

"Let me encourage you to consider some other things first," I replied. "I'm not trying to countermand any medical orders that a doctor has given you, but I think you have the right to understand what Ritalin can do. You have the right to ask your doctor for information. And you need to keep in mind that God expects us to be good stewards of our bodies."

As we continued our discussion, I said, "Grace, I want to comment about the use of Ritalin for an 'organizational disorder.' That's basically what they're trying to treat. You have not given me any *organic* reasons for taking Ritalin. They've prescribed it simply to try to help you become more organized and be able to focus better. But there are other ways to do that–like learning how to make lists, writing things down, and working through and checking off the items on the list. Rather than trying to treat this with a drug, we need to look at what God's Word says about self-control."

"Like discipline!" Grace interjected with excitement in her voice.

"Like discipline," I agreed. "That's really the issue, isn't it?"

"I think it is!" she said with relief. "Over the years it has been overwhelming for me to assume that there was something wrong with me. I wondered if maybe my problem was self-discipline, sin, anger, or something else."

"It also may be, Grace, that you're just the kind of person who doesn't like to file everything alphabetically. There are some people who enjoy having a little more freedom in their life, and that is not a disorder or sickness. That's just your personality. Don't let anybody tell you that you're sick because you don't put all of your magazines in binders and you don't dust and clean your house the way they think you should."

"Well, that's exactly what I had felt. When I was ready to start the Ritalin, I felt like the Lord was saying, 'Don't. I can help you." And I had the most fantastic day! I got so much accomplished! So I am thinking that God can help me overcome this." Grace was relieved to find that her problem was a lack of discipline rather than a psychological dysfunction.

As *Time* magazine pointed out,

> [M]any if not all adults have trouble at times sticking with boring tasks, setting priorities and keeping their minds on what they are doing. The furious pace of society, the strain on families, the lack of community support can make anyone feel beset by ADD. "I personally think we are living in a society that is so out of control that we say, 'Give me a stimulant so I can cope,'" says Charlotte Tomaino, a clinical neuropsychologist in White Plains, New York. As word of ADHD spreads, swarms of adults are seeking the diagnosis as an explanation for their troubles. "So many really have symptoms that began in adulthood and reflected depression or other problems," says psychiatrist Silver. In their bestselling new book, *Driven to Distraction*, Edward Hallowell and John Ratey suggest that American life is "ADD-ogenic": "American society tends to create ADD-like symptoms in us all. The fast pace. The sound bite. The quick cuts. The TV remote-control clicker. It is important to keep this in mind, or you may start thinking that everybody you know has ADD."[128]

To be fair, not all victims are faking their symptoms; there *are* genuine victims who deserve our pity and support. Our hearts go out to an innocent child who is molested by a perverted adult. We are moved by the images of starving civilians who are caught between two armies in a civil war. We empathize with hemophiliacs who contract AIDS through blood transfusions. But to equate some of the popular, psychologically driven discomforts with the pain and trauma of actual victimization is unwarranted and unfair.

The Disappearance of Personal Fault

A major step toward genuine healing of the wounded heart is accepting responsibility for our choices and actions, and one of the surest ways of preventing complete healing is to provide excuses for our sinful behavior.

Years ago, there was a useful phrase that seemed to put it all in perspective: "It's his own fault." We knew that there were tragic circumstances over which a person had no control and we were right to feel compassion for anyone who suffered from such. But we also knew that many problems people faced were brought on by their own foolishness or rebellion. And that's when we heard, "It's his own fault."

Today, however, common sense like that is considered harsh, insensitive, and perhaps even un-Christian. And may the Lord pity any pastor who dares suggest that some people may be suffering because of their own sin. People get angry when you call sin what it is.

In the book of Malachi, God said, "You flood the LORD's altar with tears. You weep and wail because he no longer pays attention to your offerings or accepts them with pleasure from your hands. You ask, 'Why?'" (Malachi 2:13,14). God answers the question, what He says goes against our natural bent. He says it anyway: "It's because of your sin." That's what the context of Malachi 2 tells us.

I applaud the courage and common sense Dr. Henry Brandt shares in his book *Breaking Free from the Bondage of Sin.* He writes that some people choose to hold onto their bitterness even though it causes them great pain.

> For many people yielding bitterness and hatred in exchange for a tender heart toward someone who doesn't deserve it would not be a blessed relief but rather a great sacrifice. . . . Untold numbers of people would like to be free from their aches and pains. But if you say

that means they must relinquish a long-standing grudge, they say they would rather ache.[129]

I remember sitting in on one of Brandt's lectures more than twenty-five years ago in Chicago and thinking at the time that for an old guy, he made a lot of sense. Now I'm probably older than he was then and I *really* appreciate his wisdom. Listen to what he has to say:

> To see your own sin is disturbing to you only if you fight what you discover. If, instead, you admit it and seek help from God, the result is not guilt but an overwhelming sense of forgiveness, cleansing, renewal, and peace. The Scripture states it this way: "Through Christ Jesus the law of the Spirit of life set me free from the law of sin and death" (Romans 8:2).[130]

Genuine biblical counselors are often accused of over-simplifying the causes of personal problems and inner wounds by looking for sin in the counselee's life. On the contrary, it seems that too few Christian counselors have the courage to confront sin head-on for fear of confirming the stereotype.

Brandt explains why this has happened:

> Psychological explanations for personal un-rest eventually filtered down to the churches of this nation. . . . [D]ealing with sin was totally ruled out in the psychological world and was rapidly disappearing in the church as well.
>
> The emphasis among Christians was slowly changed from dealing with sins to coming to terms with past experiences.[131]

The Issue of Sin

Sin–such a simple word. Yet sin is a foundational concept that truly separates Christianity and the gospel of Christ from humanism and psychological counseling. If the Bible is true, sin is what has separated man from a relationship with God. In the ultimate sense, sin is the original cause of all disease, depression, and death. Sin is why Jesus came to earth. Sin is what He came to save us from.

Pause for a moment and think about this verse: "Fools mock at making amends for sin" (Proverbs 14:9). Hard as it is to believe, some Christian counselors actually make light of the concept of sin and arrogantly dismiss biblical counselors as naive. "All you do is try to identify sin in a person's life and tell him to stop it," they say. "You don't try to understand the subconscious motivations causing him to act in his dysfunctional way. It is ridiculous to approach psychological problems as though they are sin."

Who would have dreamed a decade ago that Christian leaders, evangelical seminaries, Bible colleges, and even many local pastors would abandon biblical solutions for psychological theories? Yet this is exactly what has happened. Psychology has swept through Christendom with such speed and force that those who question its validity are viewed as ignorant, simplistic, and out of touch.

Is it any wonder, then, that modern believers shy away from Biblical counsel and seek psychological solutions instead? We don't want to hear that we have sinned. We are comforted to find that we are victims. We want to be told that our inner problems are caused by disorders, dysfunctions, addictions, wounded hearts, neuroses, psychoses, repressed memories, painful pasts, oppressive theologies, manias, phobias, and a host of other soul-numbing factors. We want psychiatrists, psychologists, and psychotherapists to try to remove our pain without treating the actual "disease." As sincere as they may be, however, they often seem more interested in subjective feelings than biblical truth.

I say this as gently as I can, with genuine sympathy for those who are suffering deep pain and confusion. But I would not be loving if I failed to share this truth: sin is frequently at the center of our problems. Thus counselors who neglect to consider sin as a possible reason for your problems are not necessarily helping you; they very well could be misleading you.

In fact, any Christian counselor who fails to confront a counselee with his sin will be held accountable by God. Ezekiel writes, "When I say to a wicked man, 'You will surely die,' and you do not warn him or speak out to dissuade him from his evil ways in order to save his life, that wicked man will die for his sin, and I will hold you accountable for his blood" (Ezekiel 3:18).

God's View of Sin

Have you ever done a word study about sin? The words *sin* or *sins* occur some 681 times in the New International Version of the Bible. A study of those verses reveals that sin is no laughing matter. God takes sin seriously, and so should we. John writes:

> If we claim to be without sin, we deceive ourselves and the truth is not in us. If we confess our sins, he is faithful and just and will forgive us our sins and purify us from all unrighteousness. If we claim we have not sinned, we make him out to be a liar and his word has no place in our lives (1 John 1:8-10).

Let's examine just a few of the verses dealing with sin and see how they relate to the healing of our hearts. First, however, we need to understand what sin is. The dictionary defines sin as "a transgression of a religious or moral law, especially when deliberate."[132] The Bible says that whether it is deliberate or not, "Everyone who sins breaks the law; in fact, sin is lawlessness" (1 John 3:4).

Did you know we are held accountable even if we break God's law unintentionally? The Bible clearly tells us, "If a person sins and does what is forbidden in any of the LORD's commands, even though he does not know it, he is guilty and will be held responsible" (Leviticus 5:17). Any time we break a law of God, we have sinned. John puts it this way: "All wrongdoing is sin" (1 John 5:17). Whether we agree with God or not, whether we understand His law or not, whether we like His law or not–none of these change the fact that we have sinned.

Understanding God's Laws

The Categories

In any discussion about God's laws, it helps to know that His laws can be divided into three distinct categories: moral, civil, and ceremonial. God's moral laws transcend time, culture, and location–that is, they are universal. They are in force at all times, for all people, in all places. God's moral law preceded the Law of Moses and remains in force through all time. It is the moral law that God has written on the hearts of all humans (Romans 2:15).

Civil law, though entrusted to government, is also under the direct authority of God (Romans 13:1). Its purpose is to protect society and individuals from criminals and to produce fear of punishment that is enforced by the governing authorities (Romans 13:1-5).

God's ceremonial law, however, was in force only from the time of Moses until Jesus fulfilled the law through His death on the cross (Colossians 2:14). The ceremonial law, which dealt with rituals, feasts, dietary regulations, cleansing, and sacrifices, was limited to the nation of Israel

(Malachi 4:4; Romans 9:4).

God has not given His laws to hurt us, aggravate us, or keep us from having fun. He has given them to us for our good. His laws protect us and guide us in our relationships with Him and our fellow human beings.

The Purposes

A primary purpose of God's law is to make us conscious of sin so we will avoid it. Sin damages everything it touches, and God wants to spare us the suffering that sin inevitably brings. He wants to *keep* us from becoming victims.

When my children were little, I warned them to stay away from the kitchen stove. I made it a law: "You must *never* touch the stove!" I was not trying to stifle my children's curiosity. I was not trying to keep them from enjoying our house to the fullest. Rather I was protecting them. My fear was that one of the children might pull a chair next to the stove, climb up, and accidentally turn on the flames. I wanted them to be aware–to be conscious–of the danger.

That's exactly what Paul meant when he wrote, "No one will be declared righteous in [God's] sight by observing the law; rather, through the law we become conscious of sin" (Romans 3:20). He emphasizes this same point a few chapters later: "I would not have known what sin was except through the law" (Romans 7:7).

A second purpose of God's law is to show us our need of a Savior. Sometimes we have to be desperate before we will listen to counsel and change our ways. We have to understand our hopeless condition before we can fully understand the grace of God. "So the law was put in charge *to lead us to Christ* that we might be justified by faith" (Galatians 3:24, emphasis added).

A third purpose of God's law is to provide a framework for relationships in a fallen world. The Ten Commandments list four laws which are to guide our walk with God and six that deal with our interactions with others. In direct proportion to the extent people have taken God's laws seriously, societies around the world have enjoyed relative peace and stability.

We are now seeing the erosion of modern social stability as people have turned their backs on God's law. Secularism has turned to contempt for God, which has led to lawlessness in general. The seeds of humanism are finally bearing their hideous fruit of immorality, illegitimacy, abortion, euthanasia, and cold-blooded violence.

Sin has actually blinded our modern era. What the psalmist said of himself individually describes our nation collectively: "For troubles without number surround me; my sins have overtaken me, and I cannot see. They are more than the hairs of my head, and my heart fails within me" (Psalm 40:12).

What to Do About Sin

God would heal our nation if we would repent of our rebellion and turn back to Him. The Bible promises, "If my people, who are called by my name, will humble themselves and pray and seek my face and turn from their wicked ways, then will I hear from heaven and will forgive their sin and will heal their land" (2 Chronicles 7:14).

Be Troubled

Fortunately, we do not have to wait for the rest of our country to kneel before God to find peace in our own individual lives. But we must recognize the real source of our suffering: sin. The psalmist wrote, "I confess my iniquity; I am troubled by my sin" (Psalm 38:18). Some people have hardened their hearts so deeply that they are no longer troubled by their sin. Until they regain spiritual sensitivity, there is little hope for permanent change.

Confess Our Need

When we admit our sinful condition, God gives us hope that genuine and lasting change is possible. David wrote, "I acknowledged my sin to you and did not cover up my iniquity. I said, 'I will confess my transgressions to the LORD'– and you forgave the guilt of my sin" (Psalm 32:5).

We are always tempted to deny our sin, to claim that we didn't intend to lie or cheat or be unfaithful. For example, some husbands claim that their adulterous behavior is justified because their wives are unresponsive and frigid. Some wives attempt to justify their bitterness by pointing to their husbands' insensitivity and harshness.

We often try to find excuses for our wrong behavior and look for others to blame. We claim to be victims and we find Christian counseling authorities who will agree with us. But until we admit our own rebellion, we will never find the peace we so deeply desire. As happened to Israel, "Many times [God] delivered them, but they were bent on rebellion and they wasted away in their sin" (Psalm 106:43).

Denying our sin does not remove our guilt. Neither will all our efforts at self-improvement. No amount of therapy, self-discipline, or resolution of new behavior will change the basic nature of our sinful heart. "'Although you wash yourself with soda and use an abundance of soap, the stain of your guilt is still before me,' declares the Sovereign LORD" (Jeremiah 2:22). God simply cannot be fooled. "My eyes are on all their ways; they are not hidden from me, nor is their sin concealed from my eyes" (Jeremiah 16:17).

What, then, can we do? We can trust God! He is the one "who forgives all your sins and heals all your diseases" (Psalm 103:3). "He does not treat us as our sins deserve or repay us according to our iniquities" (Psalm 103:10). He *loves* us! He wants our lives to be full of joy and peace. If we will learn to obey Him, trusting His wisdom and love, we will enjoy genuine healing in our souls.

Face the Penalty

As Christians, we know that our sins are so serious that nothing can satisfy a righteous God except a holy sacrifice. Hebrews 9:22 tells us, "The law requires that nearly everything be cleansed with blood and without the shedding of blood there is no forgiveness." We either have to pay for our own sins or someone else must pay for us. We can pay for our sin by eternal separation from God in hell, or we can ask God to forgive us because Jesus has already paid by dying in our place. Paul wrote, "For the wages of sin is death, but the gift of God is eternal life in Christ Jesus our Lord" (Romans 6:23).

Believe God's Provision

Christ's payment for sin is worthless to an individual until he personally believes God's promise and trusts Jesus as his own Savior. A person is not saved from eternal death until the instant he actually *believes* that Christ's sacrifice on the cross is sufficient to bring him to heaven and he places his trust in Christ. Paul wrote, "If you confess with your mouth, 'Jesus is Lord,' and believe in your heart that God raised him from the dead, you will be saved" (Romans 10:9). John 3:18 tells us, "Whoever believes in [Jesus] is not condemned, but whoever does not believe stands condemned already because he has not believed in the name of God's one and only Son" (John 3:18).

Why God Values Faith—God delights in hearts that believe, *especially* when we don't comprehend what God is doing. Jesus told us that "the work of God is this: to believe in the one he has sent" (John 6:29). The kind of faith that brings joy to God is an unshakable trust in His loving character. That means having this attitude: "Though I do not understand what God is doing in this situation, I believe in Him. I know He loves me and has only my best in mind. I will trust Him and watch how He works in my life."

God attaches a blessing to this kind of "blind" faith. Jesus had to appear physically to convince Thomas that He had actually risen from the dead. Jesus then said to him, "Because you have seen me, you have believed; blessed are those who have not seen and yet have believed" (John 20:29).

That is the kind of belief Jesus spoke of when His close friend Lazarus died. Jesus said to Lazarus' sister, "Whoever lives and believes in me will never die. Do you believe this?" (John 11:26).

"Yes, Lord," she told him, "I believe that you are the Christ, the Son of God, who was to come into the world" (verse 27).

Mary and Martha had no idea that Jesus was about to raise Lazarus from the dead, yet they believed that someday Lazarus would indeed live again. God *loves* people with that kind of faith. Jesus said, "The Father himself loves you because you have loved me and have believed that I came from God" (John 16:27).

Faith's Role in Our Lives—Belief is the element that connects our material world to the spiritual realm. It is the only part we play in salvation; and even then, faith that saves is possible only when God enables us to believe. Paul wrote in Ephesians 2:8,9, "It is by grace you have been saved, through faith—and this not from yourselves, it is the gift of God—not by works, so that no one can boast."

Belief is the key to salvation and peace with God. It is that same kind of faith that we must exercise in our daily walk if we are to experience healing for the wounded heart.

Live in Freedom

I once counseled a woman who appeared to have a genuine and sincere belief in Christ. Yet she seemed unable to enjoy the forgiveness and cleansing of God. She suffered from bouts of self-condemnation and depression, and she claimed that no amount of Bible study or prayer provided long-term relief. She eventually entered a Christian psychiatric clinic at a cost of over $100,000 for a few months of therapy. Once out, however, she was no better, for she had not learned the secret of living in the freedom of Christ. She felt as though she just couldn't be good enough to deserve God's love. And she is not alone; there are multiplied thousands of Christians who live in despair and seek comfort for their inner pain.

What is the problem? Apparently they have either forgotten or never fully understood the value of Jesus' blood–His sacrifice for us when He died on the cross in our place. The writer of Hebrews says, "How much more, then, will the blood of Christ, who through the eternal Spirit offered himself unblemished to God, cleanse our consciences from acts that lead to death, so that we may serve the living God!" (Hebrews 9:14).

Did you catch that? It was Jesus' sacrifice that *cleanses our guilty consciences.* This truth alone can free our hearts from the burden of accumulated sin! We don't need therapy to help us "work through" our traumatic pasts. We don't need to claim victim status. And we don't need to continue suffering from our guilt. Ephesians 3:12 says that "in [Christ] and through faith in him we may approach God with freedom and confidence." What a liberating truth that is!

No psychiatrist, no psychologist, no counselor who neglects the central truth of God's forgiveness in Christ can hope to deliver suffering patients from their inner misery. Yet millions of Christians are seeking healing for their souls from an industry that claims it has better solutions than the Bible.

Paul would write today as he did to the Galatians: "I am astonished that you are so quickly deserting the one who called you by the grace of Christ and are turning to a different gospel–which is really no gospel at all. Evidently some people are throwing you into confusion and are trying to pervert the gospel of Christ" (Galatians 1:6,7). We are willingly trading God's forgiveness for man's feeble attempts to heal the soul through psychotherapy.

I am not accusing all Christian psychologists and psychiatrists of deliberately perverting the gospel of Christ. I have generally found them to be sincere people who want to comfort others. The problem is that many have become convinced that the Bible is simply insufficient for our modern age and that we need the "scientific insights" of psychological studies to liberate the suffering saint.

Paul pleads with us: "It is for freedom that Christ has set us free. Stand firm, then, and do not let yourselves be burdened again by a yoke of slavery" (Galatians 5:1). That's what psychotherapy produces–a new form of slavery.

A woman named Catherine called me during a talk show and said, "A minister told me that I was powerless over alcohol and that I should get involved with Alcoholics Anonymous. The problem was, I found that it just replaced one addiction with another."

Another caller, June, told how she had been in therapy three times a week for two years without receiving inner healing. "Now I'm putting that same effort into the Word of God and I'm doing much better." The Bible, then, was her key to freedom.

Walk in Righteousness

Living in the freedom of God's forgiveness is not a license for sin. On the contrary, real freedom is power for righteousness. Paul addressed this issue in Galatians 5:13: "You, my brothers, were called to be free. But do not use your freedom to indulge the sinful nature; rather, serve one another in love."

Since we are naturally sinful creatures, how is it possible for us to live a life pleasing to the Lord? Paul explained it this way: "Just as you received Christ Jesus as Lord, *continue* to live in him" (Colossians 2:6, emphasis added). We are to live in Christ the same way we received Him. And how did we receive Jesus as Lord? By *faith.* Again, the key is belief in God. He is the one who enables the believer to overcome continual sin.

A man came to my office to talk. During our conversation, he revealed that he was constantly struggling with a desire to read pornography. "I got started when I was in junior high," he said, "and I just can't seem to get victory in this area of my life."

We talked for some time, and I shared with him a truth that has given hope to countless believers through the ages. It is found in 1 Corinthians 10:13: "No temptation has seized you except what is common to man. And God is faithful; he will not let you be tempted beyond what you can bear. But when you are tempted, he will also provide a way out so that you can stand up under it."

God *will* provide a way out. What a wonderful promise! So why doesn't it work for so many people? I believe it is because oftentimes we are not looking for a way out of our sin, but for a way to justify our sin so we can continue to enjoy it.

Obey the Word

Whenever people tell me that biblical counseling didn't work for them, I know that it failed for one of two reasons: 1) the counsel was not biblical to begin with, or 2) the counsel was not followed.

Many Christian counselors claim to be biblical, but in reality much of their counsel is rooted in psychological concepts rather than the Word of God. They may sprinkle a verse here or there and may even pray with their clients, yet often their counsel is not truly biblical.

Genuine biblical counseling seeks to determine God's will for every situation by examining circumstances, attitudes, actions, and reactions by the standards of Scripture instead of human theories and opinions. While certain solutions may seem wise from man's point of view, they can lead to disastrous results. "There is a way that seems right to a man, but in the end it leads to death" (Proverbs 14:12).

I should also point out that genuine biblical counseling does not always end successfully. The reason is that uncommitted counselees seldom like the solutions the Bible presents. The only treatment for such counseling failure is what I call "James 1 Therapy"–which we can sum up in the well-known phrase, *Just do it!*

Let's look at the passage:

> Do not merely listen to the word, and so deceive yourselves. Do what it says. Anyone who listens to the word but does not do what it says is like a man who looks at his face in a mirror and, after looking at himself, goes away and immediately forgets what he looks like. But the man who looks intently into the perfect law that gives freedom, and continues to do this, not forgetting what he has heard, but doing it–he will be blessed in what he does (James 1:22-25).

Some people say, "I read the Bible all the time but it hasn't helped me!" My answer to them is, "Have you *done* what it says?" Have you forgiven that brother who sinned against you? Have you prayed for that enemy who lied about you? Have you forgiven that unfaithful husband who walked out of your life? Have you made restitution for the money you stole? Have you asked forgiveness for sinning against your friend? Have you overcome evil with good?

Notice that James tells us, "Anyone who listens to the word but does not do what it says is like a man who looks at his face in a mirror and, after *looking at himself,* goes away and immediately *forgets what he looks like*" (verses 23,24, emphasis added). Psychological counsel focuses on one's *self,* and when we look at ourselves we forget what we are really like—sinners in need of redemption.

James contrasts self-focus with Word-focus: "But the man who looks intently into the perfect law that gives freedom, and continues to do this, not forgetting what he has heard, but doing it—he will be blessed in what he does" (verse 25). Look at the healing sequence James lists for us: 1) we must study the Word of God intently; 2) we must *continue* to look into the Word intently; 3) we must not forget what we have studied; 4) we must put the Word into practice—we must *do* it; 5) the law will give us freedom; 6) we who obey the Word will be blessed in what we do.

The psalmist wrote, "I have hidden your word in my heart that I might not sin against you" (Psalm 119:11). Then he prayed, "Direct my footsteps according to your word; let no sin rule over me" (Psalm 119:133). We need to pray like that today if we want to know healing in our hearts.

Victory Is Possible

A husband called from another city in Colorado and told me that his wife had just discovered that she had been ritually abused as a child. She had recently been in psychiatric care for cutting and burning herself. She was now on a strong medication and seemed to be doing better. Now the husband felt it was time to confront his wife's father, who was in his seventies.

I asked several questions about his wife's background. He described some of the bizarre behavior he had personally witnessed while he was with his wife's parents. It seemed as though it was truly possible that the wife had suffered some form of severe abuse as a child. I question whether we can trust the memories that emerged only with the help of therapy, but I do not doubt the fact that she has suffered incredible torment throughout her life.

Like this woman, you may have been a genuine victim of a horrible crime. Perhaps you were a childhood victim of sexual abuse, or your husband was verbally and physically abusive. Maybe your mate was unfaithful and left you to raise the children by yourself. Perhaps you have suffered the consequences of alcohol or other substance abuse in your own life or in a loved one.

If so, I grieve with you for what you went through. I am not trying to give you simplistic answers for your sorrow and pain. Rather, I want to hold out this hope for you: You do not have to *remain* a victim!

I am not discounting your anguish and suffering. Our world is a dark and cruel place where abuse and violence scar the bodies and souls of men and women, boys and girls. The pain and sorrow that untold millions of people have experienced is incomprehensible. But through the finished work of Jesus, there is hope! "Everyone born of God overcomes the world. This is the victory that has overcome the world, even our faith" (1 John 5:4).

Paul knew the suffering that accompanies abuse, yet he wrote this powerful passage:

> Who shall separate us from the love of Christ? Shall trouble or hardship or persecution or famine or nakedness or danger or sword? As it is written: "For your sake we face death all day long; we are considered as sheep to be slaughtered." No, in all these things we are more than conquerors through him who loved us. For I am convinced that neither death nor life, neither angels nor demons, neither the present nor the future, nor any powers, neither height nor depth, nor anything else in all creation, will be able to separate us from the love of God that is in Christ Jesus our Lord (Romans 8:35-39).

Read that again. Is there *any* type of suffering left out of the list? No, dear friend, God *does* understand what you have gone through, and He *loves* you. He has provided healing for your wounded heart through the work of the indwelling Holy Spirit.

Don't let anyone keep you in your prison of pain. Determine right now that you will no longer be a victim, but a victor in Christ. Continue on in the upcoming chapters, and you'll see how the Lord can make this real in your life.

The coordinator for the pastors' association, Larry Hinderman, called the meeting to order. Pastors from around the metropolitan area were engaged in friendly conversation, sitting at tables while they sipped coffee and caught up on news of what was happening in other ministries. Cliff had not seen John Kryer for a while and had wanted to talk with him, but that would have to wait until after the meeting.

"Let's go around the group and introduce ourselves," Larry said in his gentle way. Larry was an experienced former pastor with a sincere love for the pastors under his care. His eyes clearly showed his genuine spirit as he interacted easily with the other men.

One of the guests was a younger man–tall, thin, with a well-trimmed beard. "I'm Peter Jenkins and I'm new to your area. I've just graduated from seminary with a degree in counseling and I'm looking for a staff position in a church."

"It's great to have you with us, Peter," Larry said warmly. "I hope you'll like our area."

Turning to the pastors, Larry said, "I hope one of you will consider Peter for a staff position. And I want to make a special point that Peter brings to mind. I want to warn you against counseling in the church; it is dangerous and can cause division."

John looked over at Cliff and sighed deeply as their eyes met.

Larry continued, "I have seen so many people leave churches because pastors insisted on counseling. Frankly, men, most counseling is simply out of our league. That's when we get into trouble–trying to deal with problems that are beyond our experience and expertise."

John swallowed hard. He wanted to raise his hand to disagree, but, out of courtesy, he restrained himself.

"If you insist on counseling, however, I advise you to place your counseling room away from the church, or at the very least, as far away from the sanctuary as possible. You don't want people to confuse counseling with worship."

John couldn't believe his ears. He glanced at Cliff again, who was looking down at his coffee cup in deep disappointment. Other pastors, however were nodding their heads in agreement.

John sat through the meeting grieved that pastors had once again been discouraged from fulfilling their role as shepherds. He wanted to talk with Larry to share his deep concern over Larry's philosophy of counseling, but there were too many other pastors who were talking with the coordinator. John decided to talk with him later in private.

John and Cliff went to lunch after the meeting and discussed what Larry Hinderman had said.

"What do you think about today's meeting?" Cliff asked John.

John shook his head sadly. "I don't know, Cliff. I can't believe Larry said that people shouldn't confuse counseling with worship. That's exactly what we want people to do! We want them to connect their personal problems with God's solutions as the answers are presented in the context of worship and Bible study."

Cliff nodded in agreement as the waitress brought their meals.

"What good is preaching if it doesn't connect with our

people's daily lives?" John continued. "That is precisely the problem modern Christians face: failing to couple theology with practical living. No wonder people see church as irrelevant to their day-to-day existence."

The waitress came back to fill their water glasses, and they both sat back and waited until she left.

"Larry just doesn't seem to know how to deal with real-life problems, John," Cliff said. "Especially when they involve pastors. I told him about Miriam and the damage that psychology is causing in our home. His response was that I should go in for psychological testing! He brought a book entitled *Men Who Hate Women* to our elders' meeting and implied that I am an abusive husband who simply doesn't understand my wife's inner needs."

"Have you asked Larry to look into the details of Miriam's accusations?"

"Yes. Our elder board has thoroughly investigated Miriam's criticisms. They feel that the problem is lack of submission on her part rather than a case of my having emotionally abused her."

"Did he listen to your board?"

"Actually, no. He said he wasn't interested in the details, but that it was obvious our problem was relational and that we needed professional counseling."

John sat quietly for a few moments, thinking as he ate. Finally he looked up at Cliff and said, "I am convinced that Larry is a godly man, Cliff. He truly loves the Lord. He just doesn't understand the damage that psychological counseling is doing. We just have to pray that the Lord will open his eyes."

"I know," Cliff said. "But in the meantime, Miriam senses his support and is becoming more determined every day to follow psychological therapy. And she won't be satisfied until I join her on that road."

❖ ❖ ❖

Miriam Chase entered Dr. Powell's office hesitantly yet with anticipation. She had been uncomfortable during the last session when her therapist had probed for sexual memories. Nonetheless, at his direction, she had read the book *Uncovering the Mystery of MPD* and wondered how he would relate her emotional distress to the cases described in the volume.

Dr. Powell began the session eagerly. "Did you read the book?" he asked.

"Yes, I did," Miriam replied, "but it seemed to me that it was mostly about satanic ritual abuse. My situation is different, don't you think?"

"What makes you think your situation is different?"

"Well, for one thing, I wasn't a child. And two, the abuser wasn't a close relative."

"That seems to be true on the surface, Miriam," Dr. Powell agreed, "but in our last session, we began to uncover some dark memories. They were so uncomfortable for you that you declined to discuss them with me. Remember?"

Miriam nodded her head and looked down with embarrassment.

"If you are going to experience full healing in your heart, you are going to have to remember what happened–even if the memories produce a great deal of pain. Do you understand?"

Miriam nodded sadly and said, "I wish there were another way."

"I do, too, Miriam, but there is no other way," Dr. Powell said compassionately. "Are you ready to begin?"

"I guess so," she answered stiffly.

"All right, Miriam. I want you to close your eyes and relax. Lean back in the chair and empty your mind." For several minutes, Dr. Powell talked soothingly to help Miriam relax. "That's it, Miriam, take a deep breath. Now let it out slowly. Again. In and out slowly. Feel your body relaxing like you are on warm sand in the shade of a palm tree by the ocean. You can hear the waves roaring and crashing on the shore. Relax...relax. That's it. Now I want you to see a large blank movie screen on the wall in front of your mind. Is it there?"

"Yes."

"Now I want you to see the two elves that were in your nightmare we discussed last time. Do you see them?"

"Yes," Miriam said as she frowned slightly and changed positions on the chair.

"Stay relaxed, Miriam. They can't hurt you anymore. Now you are on the screen with them. Last time you said they had touched you in an intimate area. Are they doing that to you now?"

Miriam shook her head slightly. "No. They're gone now."

"Who is there with you?"

"My mom and dad."

"What are they doing?"

"Mom is holding me and washing my forehead with a cold washcloth. Dad is sitting on my bed, holding my hand."

Dr. Powell was writing as fast as his hand could move. "How do you feel about him holding your hand?"

"Fine. He held my hand a lot when I was a little girl."

"Is your mother gone yet?" Dr. Powell asked.

"Yes. She was tired and had to go to bed."

"What is your dad doing now?"

"He's leaning over and kissing me on my forehead."

"Is that all?"

"No."

"What else does he do?"

"He takes my hand and–"

"What? What does he do with your hand?"

"He kisses it and says I'll feel better tomorrow. I shut my eyes and fall asleep. A little while later I suddenly awaken. I'm startled to see him kneeling beside my bed."

Dr. Powell leaned forward. "What is he doing?"

"I think he's praying," Miriam answered slowly. "Yes. He's praying for me."

Dr. Powell sat back in his chair and sighed. "Praying?"

"Uh-huh."

"Are you sure?"

"Well, I can't make out the words," Miriam said sleepily.

"How is he dressed?"

"It's too dark. I can't see. I think he has a robe on."

"A robe?" Dr. Powell asked. "What color?"

"I don't know."

"Is it black?"

"It could be," Miriam agreed.

"Can you see his face?"

"No. It's too dark."

"All right, Miriam. Now let the movie play. What's happening?"

"Nothing. I roll over and fall asleep."

"And your dad?"

"He leaves the room."

"Are you sure?"

"Yes. He's gone."

"Try hard, Miriam. Does he come back later?"

Miriam stirred, opened her eyes, and sat up. "That's all there is. I don't remember anything else."

Dr. Powell closed his notebook and sat back in his chair. He rubbed his eyes wearily and looked at Miriam. "I think you remember more than you're telling me."

Miriam sat up, confused. "What makes you think I'm holding back? I told you—that's all I remember."

"I don't mean you are intentionally holding back a memory, Miriam," Dr. Powell said gently. "What I'm about to say may be hard for you to accept at first, but you have to be open to the possibility if you are going to be fully healed."

Miriam looked at Dr. Powell nervously and swallowed

hard. "Just what are you suggesting?"

"I think you may have had a childhood experience so painful that your subconscious has repressed it to protect you. The fact that your mind is working so hard to erase the memory convinces me that it's in there trying to get out."

"What kind of memory could be that painful?" Miriam asked.

"Well, before we get into that, let me ask a few questions, okay?"

"Okay."

"Have you ever felt uncomfortable around men? I mean, for some unexplainable reason have you felt repulsed if a man happened to brush against you in a crowded elevator?" Dr. Powell asked.

"Well, sure, I suppose so," Miriam agreed.

"Mm-hmm. And have you felt that men seem to have only sexual interests around you?"

"Sometimes. Not all men, though."

"What about your husband? Have you ever felt used or cheapened by him?"

Miriam grew increasingly uneasy with Dr. Powell's line of questioning. She cleared her throat and paused. "I think every woman has felt that way from time to time, Dr. Powell. Really, I don't like these kinds of questions. What are you trying to get at?"

Dr. Powell leaned forward with genuine concern. "I think it is possible that the abuse you suffered as a teenager may have had its beginnings in childhood sexual abuse. I also think your marriage has been deeply affected."

"But I don't remember any abuse as a child!" Miriam said almost desperately.

"I know you don't. I wouldn't expect you to. Abuse that serious can cause such deep emotional trauma that the mind has to protect itself by dissociating."

"Who could have abused me?"

"I don't know, Miriam. You tell me. Could it have been

a neighbor? An uncle? Your father?"

Miriam was genuinely shocked. "You can't be serious! My father? Absolutely not! He was the most loving, most protective father any girl ever had!"

"Then why are you so defensive about him?" Dr. Powell asked pointedly. "Is it possible that he was too loving? Think back, Miriam. Did he ever hold you too close, too tight? Did he ever kiss you in a way that made you feel uncomfortable? Think! It's important that you remember."

Miriam stood to her feet. "I will not have you accuse my father of molesting me as a child! That is a lie and I won't stand for it!"

"I'm not accusing him, Miriam," Dr. Powell said softly. "I am just trying to help you remember. Now, please...sit down. If your father never did anything, we'll find that out, too."

Miriam slowly sat down, her eyes burning with anger and fear. "It's not possible!"

"It may not be, Miriam, but you'll never know unless we explore those deep, hidden moments. I want you to allow your mind to roam free this next week. You will experience sudden images flashing across your mind. Some will be almost too horrible to believe, but you must allow them to come out. I want you to write them down so they won't resubmerge. Then we will discuss the flashbacks and try to make sense of them."

"But why is this necessary?" Miriam pleaded.

"We have to know who abused you so that you can confront him. The perpetrator has to be identified and exposed, or inner healing will never come. You don't want to have to suffer this inner turmoil the rest of your life, do you?"

"Oh, no! Of course not!" Miriam exclaimed. "But how could I have forgotten something so traumatic as child abuse? I just don't understand."

"No one fully understands how the mind works, Miriam. Sometimes the mind creates another personality that takes over when abuse happens so that the host personality can remain safe."

"Another personality, like in the book, right? You mentioned that possibility at our last session. It seems as though you believe there's someone else inside me that remembers abuse that I have forgotten."

"That's fairly close, Miriam. The soul or spirit seems to fragment under intense emotional pressure, and several personalities may emerge. If that has happened in your case, we will need to become acquainted with each personality so we can help them resolve their own traumas and memories."

"That sounds so bizarre!" Miriam objected. "How do we meet these...these personalities?"

"If I'm right, they'll begin to introduce themselves in the weeks ahead. You will sense different personalities wanting to come to the surface. Don't fight them. Let each one come out. Let them speak for themselves. I will keep careful notes and help you become familiar with each one."

"How many do you think I might have?"

"It's hard to say, Miriam. Some people have discovered three or four alter personalities. Others have found even more."

Miriam smiled slightly and shook her head. "I don't know if I can believe any of this. It sounds absolutely crazy!"

Dr. Powell smiled and nodded his head. "Miriam, as hard as it is to believe, it really happens. Trust me, okay?"

In the weeks that followed, Dr. Powell's prediction began to come true. Miriam was introduced to one personality after another. One was a little girl who called herself Sally. When she surfaced, Miriam's voice became high and squeaky and her vocabulary was childish. Later in the session, Dr. Powell explained that this was Miriam's "inner child" trying to get out and that she needed to talk to that little girl and comfort her.

At other times, Miriam's eyes would seem to go blank and her posture stiffened as her voice changed. Another personality, Hillary, would come to the front of her conscious and speak loudly and angrily about the general evils of the male sex. And then with hardly a pause another personality would appear. She called herself Mazie and always folded her arms tightly across her chest in a self-protective manner. Dr. Powell explained to Miriam that even though the mind may forget abuse, the body remembers.

In a period of a few weeks, more than thirty personalities were discovered by Miriam and Dr. Powell. Each one had an increasingly bizarre story of horrible abuse and trauma. During one session Dr. Powell asked Miriam, "Have you sensed any male personalities trying to surface?"

"I don't think so," Miriam said hesitantly.

"Don't be surprised if that happens. Most MPDs experience both male and female alter personalities regardless of the host's sex," Dr. Powell explained.

Soon thereafter Miriam did indeed encounter a male alter who called himself Aristotle. He seemed to represent Miriam's intellectual side, and Dr. Powell was impressed with his wisdom and honesty. While talking with Dr. Powell as Aristotle, Miriam came across as confident and secure, treating the psychologist almost as an equal.

"I like you, Aristotle," Dr. Powell said, speaking to Miriam's male alter. "I think we could make a great team."

"Only if you learn more of my ways," Aristotle replied mysteriously.

Another alter, Betty Ann, was extremely vulnerable to the verbal attacks of the other personalities. She seemed to feel it was her responsibility to bear the guilt for the entire group.

As time went along, the variety of personalities that emerged became confusing. Terry was a creative alter who loved art and literature. Alberta was an older woman who helped to direct the activities of the others. Louisa was a writer who authored some short stories and poems that Miriam placed on paper. Basil was a malignant character who delighted in mocking Betty Ann.

Dr. Powell became familiar with each personality, for they had distinct traits, interests, tones of voice, facial expressions, emotions, vocabularies, and desires. Each one seemed to have a job to perform and a personal agenda.

One day Miriam said to Dr. Powell, "Sometimes I hear their voices talking to each other and then to me. I'm having trouble keeping all of these alters straight."

"I can understand that," he replied with a chuckle. "Here's what I want you to do this week: Take a sheet of paper and a pencil and begin mapping your alters in any way that represents their relative importance or dominance. Alongside each name write the primary characteristic of the alter. That will help us to deal with each one as an individual."

That following week Miriam faithfully drew circles and arrows, labeling each alter personality with a name and description. When Dr. Powell saw the chart, he smiled broadly and said, "Good job, Miriam, good job!"

"So, where do we go from here?" Miriam asked.

Dr. Powell explained that his job was to validate the feelings of each alter and to give support. "I try to feel exactly what each alter is feeling so that I can understand where each is coming from. My objective is to help each alter personality to have a positive experience in therapy. It is important for each alter to trust me so that I can teach them about MPD. My job is to help uncover the painful memories that have created these alters so they can work through the pain, achieve resolution, and eventually reunify with you, the host personality. Isn't the hope of a better life worth the pain?"

"I...I guess so," Miriam replied wearily.

Dr. Powell smiled knowingly. "It is, Miriam. You know it is. There is no other way to heal the contaminated alters unless we can help them to regain the abilities they were meant to experience."

"The 'contaminated' alters?"

"Yes, Miriam, those alters that remember the trauma of abuse. As we decontaminate them, their memories erupt and are drained away. Their inner burdens are lifted. It isn't easy, Miriam, but it is worth it!"

Miriam nodded in confused agreement. "Yes," she said numbly. Then she looked into Dr. Powell's eyes and asked the same question she had asked a dozen times before: "All of this happened because of what my father did to me when I was a little girl?"

"Yes, Miriam," Dr. Powell said sadly. "As hard as it is for you to believe, your alters have exposed his hideous abuse. The question now is this: What are you going to do about it?"

"What do you mean?"

"I mean exactly that. What are you going to do? Are you going to allow Sally and Mazie to suffer forever because of what your father did, or will you liberate them by confronting him and demanding a confession?"

"Confronting him? Oh...I could never do that!"

"You *must*, Miriam, if you want to be healed."

"But why can't I just forgive him and move on with my life? Think of what this will do to my mother!"

"You can't just forgive him, Miriam, until he confesses and makes it right. That wouldn't be fair to Sally and Mazie and the others. Don't you see? Without confession, your forgiveness would be meaningless."

Miriam thought for a moment and then tightened her lips as she nodded in agreement. "I guess you're right. I owe it to them."

❖ ❖ ❖

That night, feeling extremely agitated, Miriam swallowed the medicine that Dr. Powell had prescribed with the help of Dr. McCall, a consulting psychiatrist. "You need it, Miriam," Dr. McCall had said. "It will help you deal with the anxiety you've been going through, but it will take a few weeks before you notice much relief. Don't stop taking it without consulting me, okay?"

"Okay," Miriam had said with a sad voice.

Now, as she lay in bed, separated from her husband and children, tears of sorrow streamed down her face onto her pillow. Her bitterness and anger toward Cliff had never been more intense as she cursed him. "Oh, Cliff!" she sobbed. "If only you had tried to understand the depth of my woundedness! Why couldn't you have come with me into this dark valley? I'm so alone! I'm so frightened!"

She began to sweat profusely, as she had for several nights, and she groaned as she felt her muscles stiffening. She breathed rapidly, feeling as though she couldn't get enough oxygen into her lungs, and it seemed as if her heart was racing out of control. Her mouth was so dry she found it difficult to swallow.

She rolled over on her side, and a deep masculine voice rumbled out of her lips. "He doesn't care for you, Miriam! He is home with your children, while we suffer here alone! We can never forgive him for that! Never!"

Miriam sat up in terror and groped for the light next to her bed. With trembling fingers she switched it on as she jumped to her feet and hurried to the mirror in the bathroom. She was shocked beyond words as a strange face with blood-red eyes peered back at her. She screamed, and fell to the floor unconscious.

The Power
of Forgiveness

"I was told that I could not forgive my parents until they confessed that they had abused me," victims often say. "My therapist told me that my parents would deny the facts and that I would have to cut off all contact with them and with anyone else who didn't believe my story of abuse."

This standard psychotherapeutic technique has separated daughters from parents, wives from husbands, mothers from children, and friends from other friends. Some victims of this unbiblical counseling practice have even been encouraged to hold mock funeral services for their parents.[133]

"Protection" That Damages

Today's therapists often intervene in the lives of their patients, becoming their authority in place of parents, husbands, and church leaders. Some therapists encourage their clients to bring all letters to the counseling office–unopened–so the counselor can screen the messages to "protect" the counselee from those who dispute the accusations of abuse.

This leaves no room for godly admonition or encouragement to take place, since anyone who disagrees with the counselor is cut off from all communication. Had the early church subscribed to current theory, Paul would have been declared a toxic church leader because he regularly confronted believers with their sin. He wrote to the Corinthians, a church full of abuse victims, "I am not writing this to shame you, but to warn you, as my dear children" (1 Corinthians 4:14).

My wife and I were acquainted with a woman who got caught in the whirlpool of psychotherapy and began to cut herself off from family, friends, and fellow church members who gently confronted her with the sin of her anger and bitterness. Some people had been close friends with her for many years. Yet because they cared enough to admonish her with biblical truth, she turned away and cut off all communication. Even when her own children talked with her on the phone and confronted her with their concerns, she would hang up on them.

Admonition—a Proof of Love

God reminds us that "better is open rebuke than hidden love. Wounds from a friend can be trusted, but an enemy multiplies kisses" (Proverbs 27:5,6). A person who really cares about you will tell the truth, even when it hurts. And a wise Christian will accept correction. David wrote, "Let a righteous man strike me—it is a kindness; let him rebuke me—it is oil on my head. My head will not refuse it" (Psalm 141:5).

In contrast, Solomon said that "a fool spurns his father's discipline, but whoever heeds correction shows prudence" (Proverbs 15:5). Accepting correction is a mark of a wise person. "A rebuke impresses a man of discernment more than a hundred lashes a fool" (Proverbs 17:10).

Has a trusted friend been trying to tell you something

you don't want to hear? Are you turning your back on loved ones who have a proven record of their care for you? As a Christian, it is vital that you keep your ears and your heart open to the biblical admonitions of those who love you.

The "Expert" Myth

You might be thinking, "But my friends aren't experts in counseling. They are just ordinary Christians." I have met many "experts" and have studied the writings of numerous scientists and professional counselors, yet I have far more confidence in the wisdom of ordinary people who know God's Word than I do in the insights of the experts.

Though we might assume that professional counselors are more effective at helping people to solve problems than untrained laymen, studies have shown that laymen are often *more* effective than professionals! One prominent Christian psychologist reported on an important study done by J.A. Durlack entitled "Comparative Effectiveness of Paraprofessional and Professional Helpers":

> [The research] reviewed forty-two studies that compared professional counselors with un-trained helpers. The findings were "consistent and provocative. Paraprofessionals achieve clinical outcomes equal to or significantly better than those obtained by professionals. . . . The study, on the whole, lent no support to the major hypothesis that . . . the technical skills of professional psychotherapists produce measurably better therapeutic change."[134]

I know a man who never graduated from college and has no impressive degrees. He has never written a book and he is not in great demand as a speaker. He has never made a fortune and the world would not call him a success. Yet he knows the Word of God as few men I have met. And what's more, he lives it. I have gone to him for advice and he has admonished me when I needed it.

Don't be intimidated by the "expert" myth. A humble fellow believer who shares from God's Word may be the only counselor you will ever need. Paul wrote the believers in Rome, "I myself am convinced, my brothers, that you yourselves are full of goodness, complete in knowledge and competent to instruct one another" (Romans 15:14).

Forgiveness Therapy

I know of nothing that is more therapeutically effective than forgiveness. Are you looking for the "silver bullet" of counseling? You need look no further. Forgiveness is the "miracle drug" that can heal the heart of bitterness, anger, pain, hatred, violence, and other deep and abiding wounds.

Forgiveness is a foreign concept to many people. When we are hurt by someone, our natural response is to hurt that person in return. Some people claim that getting even is biblical and point to Exodus 21:24, which speaks of "eye for eye, [and] tooth for tooth." If we look at the context of that passage, however, we see that Moses gave that law to *limit* vengeance, not to encourage it.

According to the dictionary, *forgive* means "to excuse for a fault or offense; to pardon; to renounce anger or resentment against; to forgive is to grant pardon without harboring resentment."[135]

Forgiveness and God

Forgiveness is a vital part of our relationship with God. Indeed, unless God had forgiven us of our sin, we could never have a relationship with the Father. That's why Paul reminds us, "Be kind and compassionate to one another, forgiving each other, just as in Christ God forgave you" (Ephesians 4:32). He repeats the thought in Colossians 3:13: "Bear with each other and forgive whatever grievances you may have against one another. Forgive as the Lord forgave you."

God warns us that He will not accept our worship when we refuse to forgive other people. Jesus said, "When you stand praying, if you hold anything against anyone, forgive him, so that your Father in heaven may forgive you your sins" (Mark 11:25). His promise is this: "If you forgive men when they sin against you, your heavenly Father will also forgive you" (Matthew 6:14). Then He adds a warning: "But if you do not forgive men their sins, your Father will not forgive your sins" (Matthew 6:15).

Do you want God's forgiveness for the wrong things you have done? Then you must be willing to forgive. "But Ed," you might say, "you don't know how terrible my [husband, wife, brother, boss, friend] has been to me! You can't expect me to go on forgiving him forever!" *I* might not expect you to, but God certainly does.

Peter felt the same way we do when someone continues to take unfair advantage of us. We don't know what led him to ask Jesus this question, but there seems to have been some family tension in Peter's house: "Lord, how many times shall I forgive my brother when he sins against me? Up to seven times?" (Matthew 18:21).

Forgiving an erring brother seven times sounds commendable, doesn't it? You have probably heard the old saying, "Fool me once, shame on you; fool me twice, shame on me!" Or how about this one: "Once burned, twice shy." I myself have a low tolerance for being treated unfairly and I can understand someone who says, "I just can't forgive him again!"

Jesus, however, will have none of that. He looked Peter in the eye and said, "I tell you, not seven times, but seventy times seven" (Matthew 18:22). Is He saying that we are to forgive someone 490 times? Yes. And 500 times, and 1,000 times. The point is that forgiveness must never stop if we want to be pleasing to the Father.

Forgiveness and Justice

As we talk about forgiveness, please understand that I am *not* suggesting that we let an abuser get away with his crimes. You should report genuine abuse to the proper authorities so they can mete out appropriate civil and criminal punishment. Forgiveness does not mean that the civil law is to be ignored.

A murderer may well accept Christ as Savior while in prison, but he should still pay the penalty for his crime. We may share many of the convictions and concerns of the anti-abortion crusader who murdered an abortion doctor in Florida; yet, if we are consistent as believers, we should also support the appropriate penalty for murder.

It seems, however, that many abusers are not adequately punished. We feel that justice has not been served, and are reluctant to offer forgiveness. That's when it is comforting to know that God will eventually punish every wrongdoing. That's what Paul says in Romans 12:19: "Do not take revenge, my friends, but leave room for God's wrath, for it is written: 'It is mine to avenge; I will repay,' says the Lord."

Likewise, Proverbs 24:29 tells us, "Do not say, 'I'll do to him as he has done to me; I'll pay that man back for what he did.'" Yet some of us don't like to hear that. After all, isn't it only fair to make the abuser suffer as he made the victim suffer?

Forgiveness and the Victim

As hard as this may be to understand, forgiveness is more for the sake of the innocent victim than for the sake of the wicked abuser. Scripture gives us at least three reasons why this is so. First, a vindictive spirit in a Christian is a miserable testimony. Paul writes, "Do not repay anyone evil for evil. Be careful to do what is right in the eyes of everybody" (Romans 12:17).

A second reason that forgiveness is to our advantage is that God promises to bless those who forgive others. "Do not repay evil with evil or insult with insult, but with blessing, because to this you were called so that you may inherit a blessing" (1 Peter 3:9).

A third reason to forgive is that God tells us He will judge us the same way as we judge others. Jesus said it clearly: "In the same way you judge others, you will be judged, and with the measure you use, it will be measured to you" (Matthew 7:2). James said, "Judgment without mercy will be shown to anyone who has not been merciful. Mercy triumphs over judgment!" (James 2:13).

Forgiveness and Feelings

A final reason to forgive others is that it produces the inner healing we so desperately seek and it just feels good! That's especially interesting because the Bible says so little about our "feelings."

Notice that God does not tell us to *feel* as though we have forgiven someone. He simply *tells* us to forgive. It's a *choice* of obedience. There is a seemingly illogical but real pleasure in doing things God's way and trusting Him to make it turn out right. That's the basic message of Habakkuk 3:17,18, "Though the fig tree does not bud and there are no grapes on the vines, though the olive crop fails and the fields produce no food, though there are no sheep in the pen and no cattle in the stalls, yet I will rejoice in the LORD, I will be joyful in God my Savior."

Imprisoned to Bitterness

There is joy in the presence of God. His ways produce peace and healing. That's what David was saying when he wrote, "You have made known to me the path of life; you will fill me with joy in your presence, with eternal pleasures at your right hand" (Psalm 16:11).

The alternative is bitterness and continual victimization. Peter confronted the sin of bitterness in Acts 8. He told a man, "Your heart is not right before God. Repent of this wickedness and pray to the Lord. Perhaps he will forgive you for having such a thought in your heart. For I see that you are full of bitterness and captive to sin" (verses 21-23). Do you see in that passage the poisonous fruit of bitterness? A person *remains a captive* to sin.

It is sad to see a victim who imprisons himself behind bars of unforgiveness. That's what a lack of forgiveness does. And that's why we need to ask ourselves, "Am I full of bitterness and captive to sin?"

One way we can tell if we're bitter is by examining the way we talk. Though a person may be able to mask his evil character for a time, eventually it will be exposed by his words. Jesus said, "The good man brings good things out of the good stored up in his heart, and the evil man brings evil things out of the evil stored up in his heart. For out of the overflow of his heart his mouth speaks" (Luke 6:45). Bitter people spew out bitter talk.

A woman in a suburb south of Denver called me to tell me that her pastor was ruining her church. Her tone of voice was harsh and bitter as she detailed one accusation after another.

After a few minutes, I asked, "Has your pastor done anything that is unbiblical? Are you aware of anything immoral or unethical? Or are you upset merely because you don't like his style of leadership or the decisions he has made?"

Reluctantly, she admitted that she just didn't like the way her pastor was leading the church, even though there were obvious signs of God's blessing on it—such as the qua-drupling of attendance in a matter of a few years. Anger and bitterness had stolen her joy.

I have seen it again and again. Marriages are damaged, friendships are broken, churches are split, and hearts are deeply wounded. There simply is no peace of mind when one is filled with unforgiveness and bitterness. These emotions can actually prevent a person from experiencing the healing God offers. That's why the Bible says, "See to it that no one misses the grace of God and that no bitter root grows up to cause trouble and defile many" (Hebrews 12:15).

Learning How to Forgive

Forgiveness is not easy, but the healing results are worth the effort. Here are some ways we can make forgiveness a reality in our lives: 1) committing ourselves to Jesus Christ; 2) being filled with the Holy Spirit; 3) submitting our will to the Spirit's; 4) choosing to forgive; 5) putting our feelings in their place; 6) practicing by repetition; and 7) performing specific acts of kindness. Let's look at each one.

Commitment to Christ

Spiritual disciplines always begin at the same place—the foot of the cross. Before we can walk with God, we must kneel before Him. Until we have personally accepted Christ as Savior and become children of God, we simply cannot enjoy the healing salve of forgiveness. Have you accepted Jesus as your Savior and Lord? If not, I urge you to call a mature Christian friend, elder, or pastor and ask him to help you make this most important decision right *now*.

Filling of the Holy Spirit

When we commit our lives to Christ, the Holy Spirit enters our hearts and begins the work of enabling us to live the Christian life. Our part is to yield ourselves to Him completely. That's what it means to be filled with the Spirit. Paul makes this clear in Ephesians 5:18 when he says, "Do not get drunk on wine, which leads to debauchery. Instead, be filled with the Spirit." Paul's comparison of wine and the Holy Spirit is intentional: When a person is filled with alcohol, it affects his thinking, speech, coordination, eyesight, and interaction with others; it literally controls every area of that person's life.

In the same way, when a believer is filled with the Holy Spirit, his thinking, speech, eyesight, and interaction with others are thoroughly changed because he is controlled by the Holy Spirit. This happens the moment we consciously submit our wills to His direction and seek to obey Him in every possible way as He directs us through His Word.

With the filling of the Holy Spirit comes a new inner power. Paul spoke of it in Ephesians 3:16, "I pray that out of his glorious riches he may strengthen you with power through his Spirit in your inner being." It is this incredible new resource that enables the believer to do things he cannot do on his own–such as forgiving someone who has wronged him.

Ongoing Submission to the Holy Spirit

Being filled with the Holy Spirit is a *continual* act of surrender as we renew our commitment day after day. That's what Jesus meant when He said, "If anyone would come after me, he must deny himself and take up his cross *daily* and follow me" (Luke 9:23, emphasis added). I recognize that the concept of self-denial flies in the face of modern therapeutic theory, but it is an essential part of healing nonetheless.

Choosing to Forgive

Even with the filling and power of the Holy Spirit, a person must make the *conscious decision* to forgive those who have sinned against him. You see, even after we become Christians, God never removes our free will. We always have the opportunity and responsibility to choose what we will do. God will not *make* us forgive, but He will *help* us to forgive if we choose to obey Him. David wrote, "May your hand be ready to help me, for I have chosen your precepts" (Psalm 119:173). When we make the conscious decision to forgive others, God will help us.

Putting Feelings in Their Place

There is a big difference between the *decision* to forgive someone and *feeling* as though we have forgiven someone. You may be tempted to doubt that you have really forgiven someone until you no longer *feel* any anger, sorrow, or pain when that person comes to mind. But just as love is a series of decisions and actions and not primarily an emotion, forgiveness also is first and foremost a *choice* that leads to actions. Keep this principle in mind: The *feeling* of forgiveness will never precede the *choice*.

If you have been in standard therapy, you are aware of the emphasis that is placed on feelings. You have, no doubt, heard phrases such as, "You have to learn to follow your feelings," or "How does that make you feel?" or "I want to validate your feelings."

God, however, does not put as much emphasis upon feelings as He does upon obedience, and there is a reason for that. Our feelings are an untrustworthy barometer of reality. Sometimes we feel happy and content, and other times we feel sad and dissatisfied. Those feelings can be triggered by any number of unrelated factors: the weather, the amount of sleep we had the night before, physical cycles, a cross word from our spouse, disapproval from the boss, extra weight, or a bad-hair day.

I once received a call from a concerned lady whose friend was depressed and unable to function successfully in society. She told me that the woman was suffering from MPD and needed professional help. She wondered if I would be willing to meet with them, and I said yes.

When they came to my office, I asked the troubled woman how she knew she had multiple personalities. "My therapist told me so," was her reply.

"Why did you stop seeing your therapist?" I asked.

"I ran out of money. The strange thing is, I don't feel as though I have other personalities inside me. Sometimes I have different emotions and moods and I react to different situations in a variety of ways, but I don't think those are distinct personalities, do you?"

"No," I said. "I think you're suffering from HDS."

Her friend quickly wrote my diagnosis on her notepad and looked up for an explanation.

I smiled and said, "I think you have human deficiency syndrome."

Their expressions showed that they didn't understand my point.

"What I mean is that you have different moods, emotions, and feelings because you're human–just like the rest of us."

This woman's emotions were not an accurate indicator of reality and she illustrates how careful we must be about what kind of emphasis we place upon feelings.

Practicing Forgiveness

Forgiveness becomes easier and more natural each time we make the choice to overlook a wrong. Proverbs 19:11 says, "A man's wisdom gives him patience; it is to his glory to overlook an offense."

That sounds fine in theory, but how many times do we have to choose to forgive? Jesus answered that when He said, "If he sins against you seven times in a day, and seven times comes back to you and says, 'I repent,' forgive him" (Luke 17:4). That is to say, we must forgive continually.

The habit of forgiveness doesn't happen automatically. Paul says that we must practice the spiritual disciplines, which includes forgiveness. And that begins when we learn to focus our minds on things that please the Lord: "Finally, brothers, whatever is true, whatever is noble, whatever is right, whatever is pure, whatever is lovely, whatever is admirable–if anything is excellent or praiseworthy–think about such things" (Philippians 4:8). Forgiveness matures as we practice it. As a result, we will know God's peace: "Whatever you have learned or received or heard from me, or seen in me–put it into practice. And the God of peace will be with you" (Philippians 4:9).

Doing Deeds of Kindness

Romans 12:20 tells us, "If your enemy is hungry, feed him; if he is thirsty, give him something to drink. In doing this, you will heap burning coals on his head."

I have heard different interpretations of that verse. One says that heaping coals on a person's head was an oriental expression describing the kindness a host showed to a departing guest. The host would place some burning embers in a metal container that the guest would carry on his head so he could start a fire when he arrived at his own home. That interpretation makes sense in view of the next verse: "Do not be overcome by evil, but overcome evil with good" (Romans 12:21). I also believe Paul was suggesting that showing kindness to another person can burn deeply into that person's conscience and help to turn him around spiritually.

A Giant Step to Inner Healing

My dear friend, I know that forgiveness is a difficult pill to swallow, and it seems so unfair because it appears to place one more burden upon the victim. The world says that we should seek vengeance, but God says that we must forgive. Is it unrealistic? Foolish? Simplistic? No, it is a giant step on the path toward healing the wounded heart.

It was late at night. The children were in bed and Cliff sat alone in the family room, tears streaming down his face. Just hours before, Miriam had called to tell him she was not coming back.

"Until you're ready to listen to my heart and enter into my grief with me, Cliff, we're through!" she said.

"But what about the children, Miriam?" Cliff pleaded. "Surely you can't walk away from them!"

"I don't want to be away from them!" she snapped. "It's not my choice. It's yours! *You're* the one who's making me do this."

"What do you mean?"

"I don't want to talk about it, Cliff! Dr. Powell says that I need to protect myself from continued abuse and that I need to get into a support group for survivors of abuse."

"Miriam," Cliff said with a sigh, "we're the only support group you need–I and the kids. We love you and want you back!"

"If you really loved me, you wouldn't have put me through this suffering! I'm done talking. Since you refuse to vacate the house, I'm going to take whatever legal action I have to."

"Do you mean you would actually consider divorce?"

"I didn't say divorce. I'm talking about a separation until you understand what you're putting me through."

"What *I'm* putting you through?" Cliff agonized. "Have you ever thought about what *you're* putting *me* through?"

"We've been over this a thousand times, Cliff. I'm done talking!" she said as she hung up.

His hands shaking with grief, Cliff dialed John Kryer to ask for prayer and advice. "John, I'm sorry to call so late, but I don't know how much longer I can go on. Miriam has left us. She walked out on the entire family. She says she needs time to sort everything out. Her therapist also told her that she needs to spend time with a support group of fellow victims."

"Is she talking divorce?"

"If you had asked me a few months ago, I'd have said absolutely not. But now she's a different person, John. I actually think she might divorce me!"

"But doesn't she realize that she is now victimizing her own children? Even with the conditioning she's undergone, I still can't believe Miriam would be that selfish. That's just not like her."

"It's more than mere selfishness, John. It's like she's joined a cult. She's been brainwashed into believing that I am her enemy and that I have abused her by not accepting her claim of absolute innocence."

"Where will she go?" John asked.

"I don't know. I suppose she might stay with one of her friends." An involuntary sob escaped and Cliff fought his emotions for a moment before continuing. "I just can't believe it, John! It doesn't seem possible that a woman as strong and godly as Miriam could be deceived so easily. I would never have believed this could happen to us!"

Miriam did indeed move into the home of a friend–a woman from the church, Susan Byers. Susan was married and a graduate student at the Baptist Seminary, studying to be a therapist. She and her husband, Al, were missionaries with a Bible translating ministry and worked with the organization's staff counseling department. They had been members of Cliff and Miriam's church for a couple of years while they were in training.

"Tell me what happened, Miriam," she said sympathetically as they sat down in the living room.

Miriam began to relate the events of the past few years and how her marriage with Cliff had been growing more and more strained. "You know how controlling Cliff can be," she said as tears welled up in her eyes.

Susan nodded her head slightly in agreement. "Well, Al and I have discussed how opinionated he seems to be at times. Of course, all leaders tend to take strong positions, I suppose."

"And I want Cliff to remain strong in his convictions," Miriam said genuinely. "But there are some areas that he is just stubborn about, and one of them is psychology. He absolutely rejects anything connected with it, even though I have told him that nothing else can take care of the wounds and pain in my heart. He acts like my problem is spiritual instead of psychological."

"I know," Susan murmured. "I've heard Cliff preach about psychology. He just doesn't understand the dynamics of the mind, Miriam. And it does sound so right to say that the Bible has all the answers to life's problems. I mean, how can any Christian argue against the Bible?"

"But what he's doing by spiritualizing everything is *adding* to my suffering. It's not enough that I have to deal with an abusive past; now I have to experience a whole new form of abuse—and from my husband!"

Susan stood to her feet. "Let's go into the kitchen and I'll fix us some tea." Miriam nodded, followed Susan into the kitchen, went to the table, and sat down. Susan heated some water and got two tea bags out of the cupboard. When the tea was ready, Susan brought the cups to the table and sat down across from Miriam. "So what are your plans?" she asked.

"I don't know," Miriam said softly as her lips trembled. "I can't go back home for now. I can't deal with any more pain."

"I understand," Susan said gently. "Are you seeing a counselor?"

"Yes. Dr. Powell, from Southeast Counseling Associates."

"Oh, he's a good man!" Susan said enthusiastically. "I heard him lecture at the seminary. He deals with some difficult cases. Can you tell me about his counseling? You don't have to, of course...."

"Yes," Miriam said eagerly. "I'd like to talk with you about it. That's why I came here. I knew you would understand."

"Well, I don't want you to think that I'm prying. I want to help, Miriam," she said as she reached across the table and patted Miriam's arm.

Miriam took Susan through the counseling procedure Dr. Powell was using, but stopped short of mentioning the multiple personalities. She wasn't sure Susan was ready for that. "Now Dr. Powell has asked me to join a support group for victims of childhood sexual abuse. What do you think, Susan? Is it a good idea?"

"By all means, Miriam!" Susan replied. "You will find that the problems you have experienced are not just yours alone. It helps to talk about problems with people who truly understand and can share their insights and solutions with you. When do you begin?"

"I'm supposed to go twice a week, on Tuesday and Thursday evenings, starting next week. In the meantime, can I stay here?"

"For the time being," Susan agreed. "Ultimately, of course, I'd like to see you and Cliff get back together. I'm afraid that a prolonged separation will damage his career, aren't you?"

Miriam gritted her teeth. "That's not my choice, Susan. That's in his hands and God will hold him responsible, not me. I'd go back home in an instant if he'd just wake up!"

"Still, not everyone will understand your position, Miriam," Susan warned. "You're going to have to be strong to stand up to the criticism of those who don't know the whole story."

"That's a risk I'll have to take," Miriam said firmly. "It will be worth it to gain real peace of mind and relief from the pain I feel in my heart. Eventually, I think Cliff and I will be able to help others who are going through this same sorrow."

"Oh, I hope so!" Susan said.

On Tuesday evening, Miriam went to Old Mill Community Church and found her way to the room where the support group met. About fifteen women were talking in little groups as they drank coffee and snacked on cookies. At the designated time, a facilitator called the meeting to order.

"Come on, ladies," Alice Gooden said with a beautiful smile. "Let's sit down and share together."

Miriam was impressed with the caliber of the women in the group. They weren't the losers she had somehow pictured. Most were in their thirties or forties and were neatly dressed and groomed. Two or three were a bit overweight, but several seemed almost too thin.

"Tonight, I've asked Janet to share her story," Alice said. "I know that many of you will relate to what she has gone through. Janet?"

Janet stood up, cleared her throat nervously, and smiled with embarrassment. "I hardly know how to begin. I'm not used to being believed. But here goes. My name is Janet and I'm a survivor of childhood sexual abuse.

"I wasn't aware of this until about a year ago, when I felt I needed some professional help. I was experiencing depression and I began to suffer an eating disorder. I also found that I dreaded my husband's advances and I began to look for any excuse to avoid intimacy.

"I was watching a talk show one afternoon and I heard women describing feelings just like mine. They explained how traumatic memories can be repressed in the mind and how the body remembers sexual abuse and causes a woman to hate sex. They pointed out that if you can't remember being abused but have the symptoms, then you probably were.

"It made sense to me, and I was almost relieved to find out why I was so miserable all the time.

"I went to see a Christian psychologist and over a period of several weeks, with hypnosis, she helped me to remember events that I had pushed deep into my mind." Janet swallowed hard and her lips trembled momentarily. "Memories and flashbacks began to emerge and I discovered that my father had molested me when I was less than a year old and continued doing so through my early adolescent years. When I confronted him, he denied everything. And my mother backed him up, saying it could not have happened!"

The other women nodded with understanding as they looked at one another with shared sorrow.

"My sisters have also denied that Dad could have molested me and have accused me of being brainwashed! That was almost more than I could handle. My therapist advised me to cut off any further contact with family members until I'm stronger. So that's what I've done. She suggested that I might find a new family here."

Janet sat down and the group applauded.

Alice leaned forward and said warmly, "You have found a new family, Janet, right here. A family of choice."

As others told their stories, Miriam noticed that the details seemed almost identical–even to the alter personalities they introduced. They seemed to have shared the same patterns of lights and shadows and painful body memories. As one woman would share after the other, everyone would nod knowingly and say, "Yes, yes! That's just what happened to me!"

Miriam began to feel a bit left out because she had not had the same experiences the others had related. Yet, she found that the more graphic and emotional the stories became, the more she felt her memories emerging. It seemed like such hard work to recover the memories that had been buried by the trauma of the past!

Miriam listened carefully to every word as various women shared their stories of incest and abuse. She knew she would have to confront her father soon, but she dreaded the very thought. It still seemed impossible that the man she had admired for his deep walk with God could have violated her childhood so viciously. But she knew that denial would only lead to more pain, and she couldn't bear to think of allowing that to continue. She had to find relief, no matter what the cost.

A few months after Miriam moved out of their home, Cliff resigned as pastor of Evangelical Bible Church. "I don't see how I can continue," he explained to the board of elders. "It is fairly obvious that I no longer meet the qualifications of a pastor, because my family is so out of order."

"Isn't there some other way, Cliff?" Wallace Kramer asked. "Can't you compromise and meet Miriam halfway in her decision to follow psychological therapy?"

"If I thought it would heal our home, I'd probably do it, Wallace," Cliff replied sadly. "But so far, nothing has worked. Miriam's bitterness is so deep that she sees *me* as the enemy. I've offered to go to counseling with her, but she insists on a psychologist or no one. I even attended a seminar on sexual abuse, which was led by her 'expert' on the wounded heart, but what I heard was so unbiblical that it made me sick."

The leaders and the church worked hard for several months to find a way to retain Cliff as pastor. But the board finally agreed that it was time for the church to move on, and they accepted Cliff's resignation with deep sorrow.

They graciously offered to continue his salary until he was able to find another means of support.

Cliff began looking for a job, but found that from a secular standpoint, his qualifications were limited. There were few jobs that called for skills in preaching and Bible study. Each day, Cliff became more discouraged, and oftentimes, after the children were in bed, he would sit in the dark in the family room, crying in loneliness, anger, and confusion.

He longed to have Miriam beside him, hear her laughter once again, and feel her warmth as he held her in his arms. He found it hard to believe that she was gone. Surely one day Miriam would come to her senses and realize that she was destroying her own family. But as the months dragged into years, Cliff realized Miriam wasn't going to come back, and for the sake of the children, he had to make a new life for all of them.

7

The Gift
of Forgetting

One tragic result of therapeutically induced false memories is that they crowd out the cries for help from *true* victims of sexual abuse. There are many *actual* victims of sexual abuse whose suffering is discounted because of false claims of victimization and these false claims (based on false memories) have led some people to assume that *all* claims of abuse are false.

While it is important for us to question the accuracy of hazy memories, we must also have deep compassion for genuine victims. They need our love and acceptance. They need to be taught from Scripture that victims can be healed through the power of the Holy Spirit and the Word of God. What they don't need is to be revictimized by lack of compassion or by elevating false claims to the status of true abuse.

Real memories don't have to be resurrected through hyp-nosis, dream interpretation, body-memory analysis, or other pseudotherapies. Memories of actual abuse are painfully vivid and detailed. As one woman told me of a traumatic event in her distant past, she said, "I can remember every second of that day."

Another devastating result of false memories is the heart-wrenching sorrow that innocent parents, relatives, and friends experience when they are accused of abuse that never happened. As we learned earlier, there are thousands of families across America that have been destroyed by the insidious teachings of fad therapies.

A Pervasive Influence

One of the most damaging doctrines of the recovery movement is that we must never allow a memory to die. The theory is that unhealed memories have substance, and until they are resolved by psychotherapy, they fester and grow like spiritual infections that must be lanced by hypnosis, dream interpretation, or other forms of analysis before healing can take place.

That is the underlying foundation of the psychologized recovery movement that has swept into evangelical Christianity. There are thousands of self-help support groups meeting in churches week after week across the country. Many of these groups follow the twelve-step pattern of Alcoholics Anonymous to deal with every sort of emotional pain. Proponents of using AA's methods in the church point out that "ironically, John Bradshaw began his now nationwide recovery program in Episcopal churches in the 1970s in Houston."[136] Hardly a glowing recommendation for Christians concerned with biblical truth.

I was astounded to see the list of support groups offered by one large Baptist church in New Mexico. They have special "affinity groups" for soon-to-be parents, parents of toddlers, parents of kids, parents of adolescents, parents of teens, parents of home schoolers, parents of adopted children, single parents, blended families, families dealing with attention deficiency syndrome, teens with substance abuse, parents with an empty nest, divorce recovery, remarriage, those who have moved beyond divorce, divorce recovery for children, divorce after long marriages, disability, lost children, those suffering from grief, children of aging parents, families of homosexuals, those in pain, recovery from sexual abuse, those who have drinking problems, those who gamble, women who overeat, men who overeat, women who have had abortions, women who have had miscarriages, those who have had cancer, veterans of war, four groups on self-esteem and relationships for adults, and three groups on self-esteem and relationships for students. This church offered more than forty specialty support groups!

People who are sold on self-help groups often state that they are patterned after Alcoholics Anonymous, which they believe was "founded in the 1930s by a group of evangelical Christians [although the plan] contains no reference to Christ."[137]

Dr. William L. Playfair shatters this supposedly Christian connection in his book *The Useful Lie*. He writes:

> Many within the Christian community believe that the founders of AA were Christians and that AA's Twelve Steps are based on the Bible . . . However, nothing in AA's history supports these beliefs. In fact, the myth is actually denied by the founders themselves as well as by the official literature of AA and spinoff organizations.[138]

Playfair makes a strong accusation: "As a matter of fact, AA's Twelve Steps are more akin to the Bahai faith than to Biblical Christianity. That is, they are eclectic–a hodge podge of different, and even conflicting, philosophical and religious systems."[139] Playfair then carefully documents his point.

In spite of such evidence, evangelical churches are welcoming with open arms groups that are built on AA philosophies.

The Focus on Self

One pastor in Texas who is enthusiastic about support groups admits that "individuals who have come primarily to have their hurts ministered to...may need to be self-focused for a while, and we need to understand that."[140]

The problem is, self-focus leads to increased pain and misery rather than healing, and the Bible tells us to focus on the Lord instead of on our suffering. Paul writes,

> Since, then, you have been raised with Christ, set your hearts on things above, where Christ is seated at the right hand of God. Set your minds on things above, not on earthly things. For you died, and your life is now hidden with Christ in God. When Christ, who is your life, appears, then you also will appear with him in glory (Colossians 3:1-4).

Look at the text carefully. Paul is saying that the result of our having been born again is that we have been *raised* with Christ. Because of that, we are to set our hearts and minds on things above, not on the pain and sorrow of our earthly existence.

The writer of Hebrews takes up the same thought when he says, "Let us fix our eyes on Jesus, the author and perfecter of our faith, who for the joy set before him endured the cross, scorning its shame, and sat down at the right hand of the throne of God" (Hebrews 12:2).

Where is there even a hint that we are to look within for healing? Instead we are told, "Consider him who endured such opposition from sinful men, so that you will not grow weary and lose heart" (Hebrews 12:3). And what was it that Jesus did that we are to do so we don't lose heart? He dealt with deep inner pain and suffering by focusing on the joy before Him.

The Ability to Forget

What is rarely considered in psychologized Christianity is the possibility that God has *already* allowed healing of the soul to take place through the gift of forgetting. God has created within us the ability to move on from painful events and circumstances. One old adage expressed it this way: "Time heals all things." For the believer, however, healing is related not only to time, but also to the active work of the Holy Spirit.

Jesus vividly illustrated this point in John chapter 16: "A woman giving birth to a child has pain because her time has come; but when her baby is born she forgets the anguish because of her joy that a child is born into the world" (verse 21). Joy overcomes suffering. And for the child of God, joy is directly related to our walk with Jesus.

Leaving the Past Alone

There is nothing in Scripture that tells us we need to return to the past to accomplish inner healing. Instead, the Bible says that God Himself "heals the brokenhearted and binds up their wounds" (Psalm 147:3). If Christ's death on the cross has no bearing on our psychological well-being, then Isaiah 53:5 is meaningless: "He was pierced for our transgressions, he was crushed for our iniquities; the punishment that brought us peace was upon him, and by his wounds we are healed."

When we come to Christ, we *are* healed! How it must grieve the Lord when His children are told that they aren't healed, but that they are in denial and need to return to their painful past and reopen the wounds He has lovingly closed.

Looking to What Is Ahead

Through Isaiah, God writes a refreshing passage about the suffering the Israelites experienced because of their failures. Instead of telling them to meditate on their inner pain, He says, "Forget the former things; do not dwell on the past. See, I am doing a new thing! Now it springs up; do you not perceive it? I am making a way in the desert and streams in the wasteland" (Isaiah 43:18,19).

Have you been led back into the wilderness by psycho-therapy? Instead of the peace and joy the therapists promised, have you found dryness and spiritual thirst? Then come back and drink from the streams of living water that flow from the throne of God.

Paul, who once called himself the worst of sinners and knew the true meaning of suffering, wrote, "One thing I do: Forgetting what is behind and straining toward what is ahead, I press on toward the goal to win the prize for which God has called me heavenward in Christ Jesus" (Philippians 3:13,14).

Dear friend, our time on this earth is too brief to spend it gazing inward. Those who are being taught to look for healing within are being cheated of the healing that comes from the Lord when we press on toward the real goal.

What It Means to Forget

Originally, the term *forget* meant "to lose one's hold" on something. In English, we sometimes think of forgetting as being unable to remember, but the concept Paul describes in Philippians 3 is far more active. The forgetting he talks about is an active choice of refusing to mention again or determin-ing to banish from one's thoughts–that is, *to cease remembering.*

This doesn't mean that a painful event or a bitter moment never again crosses your mind. It simply means that by for-getting an offense you have chosen not to dwell upon it, but rather, to exercise forgiveness and to focus your mind on Christ, His kingdom, His people, and the needs of others.

Controlling Our Thoughts

Years ago, a couple got into a bitter argument and became so angry with one another that they could barely speak a civil word for several days. As time passed, the details of their disagreement began to fade and neither could remember exactly what their anger was about.

Finally, with a half-smile, the husband said, "What were we arguing about, anyway?"

The wife replied with a full grin, "I don't remember, and I don't want to try!" That's right: The couple was me and my wife.

Had we tried to remember, there is no doubt we could have brought each ugly detail to the surface, but we chose not to. Some people would say that my wife and I went into denial and that our unresolved problems are bound to erupt again. But that does not have to happen. We can exercise a measure of control over our thoughts. In Romans 12, Paul called it renewing the mind. Let's look at how we can control our thoughts so we can find inner peace.

Acknowledging Our Mental Limitations

The first step toward renewing our mind is to acknowledge our mental limitations to ourselves; God is *already* aware how puny our minds are. According to Psalm 94:11, "The LORD knows the thoughts of man; he knows that they are futile." Our minds are so distorted by sin that we continually deceive ourselves.

Psychologists, psychiatrists, psychotherapists, and other "experts" of the mind are equally confused when it comes to understanding another person's mental condition. No human can look into and fully understand another person's heart. That's what Jeremiah was writing about when he said, "The heart is deceitful above all things and beyond cure. Who can understand it?" (Jeremiah 17:9).

According to the first chapter of Romans, sin debilitates the thinking process: "Although they knew God, they neither glorified him as God nor gave thanks to him, but their thinking became futile and their foolish hearts were darkened. Although they claimed to be wise, they became fools" (Romans 1:21,22).

While I was writing this, my wife, Marlowe, called me upstairs to watch a segment on ABC's "20/20" broadcast.[141] Dr. Brian Weiss, a psychiatrist with impressive credentials from Columbia University and Yale Medical School and the former chairman of psychiatry at Miami's Mt. Sinai Medical Center, was interviewed because of his new technique for helping people experience inner healing. He uses "regression therapy" by which he takes patients back into "past lives" under hypnosis.

Whether reincarnation is true is beside the point, because, according to Weiss, "to accept the idea of past lives has great healing power." One patient who had recently lost her husband expressed comfort in the belief. "If we have multiple lives, we'll meet again. You're either a believer or a nonbeliever," she said.

Weiss indicated that he has been getting a lot of support from medical colleagues, though they are reluctant to back him publicly. The American Psychiatric Association has no official position on past-life therapy, but a psychiatric journal did a study of 100 students which showed that the best subjects for regression therapy were already believers in past lives or were influenced by their therapists' suggestions.

Their recollections were clearly inaccurate, said Nicholas Spanos, professor of psychiatry at Carlton University in Ottawa, one of the writers of the study. He said that some patients would, for example, give their past-life dates as "54 B.C." Had they lived back then, they would not have known to refer to the year by using a B.C. label.

Dr. Spanos explained that regression therapy can help people even if it may not be true in the scientific sense. "Therapies can be effective even though the theory behind the therapies isn't true." Did you catch that? If the theory isn't true, how can we place confidence in it?

Dr. Weiss added, "I'm not here to tell anyone that reincarnation is real or is not real, but as regression therapy or that part of it that seems to heal people–that's very real."

Whether Dr. Weiss is practicing science, medicine, or voodoo doesn't seem to concern his patients, because, according to the report, Weiss has a client waiting list of more than 2,000 people and he is now getting calls from Eastern Europe, Japan, and Korea. His book *Many Lives, Many Masters* is a runaway bestseller.

According to this sort of psychological thinking, it doesn't matter whether therapy is true or not so long as it works. And how are we to know whether something "works" or not? All that matters is how a person *feels.*

Such distorted thinking produces a deep alienation between people and God—the exact condition of a person before he accepts Christ. "Once you were alienated from God and were enemies in your minds because of your evil behavior" (Colossians 1:21).

This sinful condition explains why people—without the power of the Holy Spirit—are rarely able to permanently overcome their addictions, fears, and bizarre behaviors. You see, "the sinful mind is hostile to God. It does not submit to God's law, nor can it do so" (Romans 8:7).

Recognizing God's Infinite Wisdom

Once we have admitted our intellectual limitations, the next step in renewing our minds is to recognize the supreme intelligence of God. It isn't even a contest. God says matter-of-factly, "My thoughts are not your thoughts, neither are your ways my ways. . . . As the heavens are higher than the earth, so are my ways higher than your ways and my thoughts than your thoughts" (Isaiah 55:8,9).

Recognizing God's infinite knowledge helps us to accept the inerrancy and infallibility of the Scriptures, which reveal the thoughts of God to man. Indeed, we can come with absolute confidence to the Word of God for guidance and wisdom for our daily lives. As David said, "Your word is a lamp to my feet and a light for my path" (Psalm 119:105).

God's Word is food for our famished souls; acknowledging His absolute supremacy humbles us enough to accept His Word as life-giving truth. Moses explained this principle when he wrote, "He humbled you, causing you to hunger and then feeding you with manna, which neither you nor your fathers had known, to teach you that man does not live on bread alone but on every word that comes from the mouth of the LORD" (Deuteronomy 8:3).

The danger in seeking "truth" outside of God's Word is that we are risking our lives on it. That's why I am so concerned when Christians seek solutions for their problems in the manmade systems of psychology.

Allowing God to Search Us

No one other than God can really know what is going on in your heart. No one else can truly make sense of all the conflicting desires and emotions. David knew this and wrote, "Search me, O God, and know my heart; test me and know my anxious thoughts" (Psalm 139:23). Only God is able to accurately analyze our anxieties. Paul wrote in 1 Corinthians 2, "Who among men knows the thoughts of a man except the man's spirit within him?" (verse 11). Not even the self-proclaimed experts of the mind are able to look inside their patients, but God can. Let Him look freely into every corner of your being to see what is keeping you from the peace you so desperately desire.

Forsaking Unbiblical Thoughts

Once we have accepted theories and principles as true, we find it hard to turn from them. Maybe it is a matter of pride—our reluctance to admit that we were wrong. But to transform our thought process, we must abandon that which disagrees with the Word of God.

The doctrine of self-esteem, for example, is accepted as

unquestioned truth in our psychologized culture. Churches across America now proclaim self-esteem as a primary need, yet you will not find that view supported in the Word of God. Another example is the teaching that we must follow our hearts wherever they lead us. Yet the Bible says that the heart is deceitful and absolutely unworthy of our trust.

It doesn't matter how sincere your instructor may be. If he is teaching concepts that are foreign to the Bible, run from him. Whether a concept has come from your childhood upbringing, a trusted relative, your traditional faith, your racial heritage, or national culture, unless it agrees with the Scriptures, it must be abandoned. When a counselor says you must work through your past before you can know healing in the present, ask him where the Bible teaches that. If he can't support this claim, then turn from his alleged solutions to pain and find peace God's way.

Fixing Our Thoughts on Jesus

Some of the best advice we will ever receive about changing our pattern of thinking is to fix our thoughts on Jesus rather than on our pain, anxiety, self-esteem, or needs: "Therefore, holy brothers, who share in the heavenly calling, fix your thoughts on Jesus, the apostle and high priest whom we confess" (Hebrews 3:1).

Many Christian psychologists agree that we need to focus our minds on our past before we can experience contentment in the future. The psychiatrist on "20/20" went so far as to say that we need to fix our thoughts on *past* lives to obtain healing! But God says to fix our thoughts on Jesus. *That one concept alone can transform our lives!*

When we finally understand what Jesus did for us on the cross, we can be freed from all emotional and mental bondage. When we meditate on His love for us, we are no longer in desperate need for the approval of others. When we fully appreciate His glory, we are not as easily impressed by the wealth and power of the rich and famous. When we have been washed clean of our sins and have bathed in His forgiveness, we are able to forgive those who have abused us. When we worship Jesus as our Lord, we long to please Him in every part of our being.

In the Bible, God frequently gives examples of the kind of relationship He desires with us: that of a father and a child, a husband and a wife, or a master and a servant. One rather plain illustration of absolute devotion many of us can identify with is the relationship between a kind man and his dog. Nothing delights a dog more than being in the presence of his master. He doesn't care what the master is doing, so long as he is by his side. The master can be sitting by the fire, reading the paper, or walking along a path. No matter what the situation, the dog simply keeps his eyes fixed on his master and is ready to obey his slightest gesture.

I have a dog like that. Hershey has been in our home for more than ten years. We got her as a puppy and she did all the naughty things puppies do—chewed the furniture, wetted the carpet, and so on.

I made the mistake of installing some lawn lights soon after she joined us. Hershey saw these new fixtures as delightful toys and proceeded to dismantle them. I was enraged and punished her severely (for which I repented afterwards). What's amazing to me is this: Though I am the one who disciplined her that time and many other times, she still loves me and obeys me, too.

Whenever I look over at Hershey lying on the floor of the family room, her tail begins to thump on the floor. When we get the leash to take her for a walk, her face literally breaks into a smile. She loves being with us.

She's getting old now and winters are hard on her. We dread the day when we will have to ask our vet to put her to sleep because even then she will be looking up at us with eyes full of love and unquestioning trust.

I know that this illustration hardly conveys the depth of love and total devotion we are to have for our Master, but it paints a picture we can understand. Moses said to "love the LORD your God with all your heart and with all your soul and with all your strength" (Deuteronomy 6:5).

Do we love Jesus like that? The more we love Jesus with simple yet total devotion, the more peace and joy we will experience—and the more His healing will flow through our entire being.

Filling Ourselves with the Word

One of the most significant ways we can fix our thoughts on Jesus—and transform our thinking—is to fill our hearts with the Word of God. Paul encourages us to do this when he says, "Let the word of Christ dwell in you richly" (Colossians 3:16).

If people insist on "therapy," I would suggest they undergo what I call "saturation therapy." We will discuss it in-depth in chapter ten. For now, it is enough to say that genuine and lasting healing of the wounded heart requires the continual and personal application of God's Word. Romans 12:2 tell us, "Do not conform any longer to the pattern of this world, but be transformed by the renewing of your mind. Then you will be able to test and approve what God's will is—his good, pleasing and perfect will." Renewing our minds is what saturation therapy is all about.

Practicing Right Thought Patterns

One of the most powerful Scripture passages that can help us change our thinking process so we can forget the pain of the past is Philippians chapter 4. In our next chapter, we will look at this passage more closely and consider it thought by thought, for it is one of the key Bible passages we must apply if we are to experience genuine healing of our wounded hearts.

❖ ❖ ❖

Dr. John Kryer sat in his office with his head bowed in prayer. He sighed deeply, dreading the encounter that was about to happen. As he sat at his desk, he reviewed in his mind what had happened just two weeks before. One evening, as he was about to spend a few quiet hours at home with his family, his doorbell had rung. When he opened the door, he was surprised to see Jackie Walker standing there awkwardly.

"Hi, Pastor John," she said. "Do you have a few minutes to talk with me?"

Though John was tired, he invited Jackie in. Jackie was one of the most active young adults in John's church. She taught a children's Sunday school class and could always be counted on when a tough or unpleasant job had to be done. She was a pleasant-looking girl, though a bit plain, and she seemed to have trouble relating to other young people her age. Jackie's parents, Brad and Anita, were members of the church.

"Mary," John called, "Jackie Walker is here."

Mary, John's wife, came into the hallway, drying her hands on a dish towel. "Hi, Jackie!" she said warmly as she gave the girl a hug. "What brings you out this time of night?"

Jackie looked flushed and nervous. She cleared her throat and said, "Oh, I just felt I needed to talk to you and Pastor John about something."

"Well, then, let's go into the living room," Mary said, leading the way.

When they were seated, Jackie cleared her throat again and said, "I don't know quite how to begin."

Mary leaned forward with a smile and said, "Just tell us what's on your heart, Jackie."

Jackie smiled weakly and then bit her lip. Tears formed in her eyes as she struggled with her emotions. Finally, she breathed deeply and said, "I've gotten involved with someone and I'm afraid you're going to make me give up my Sunday school class or maybe even leave the church. I wanted to be the one to tell you before you heard about it from someone else."

John nodded compassionately. "I'm glad you came, Jackie."

Mary tilted her head sympathetically and asked softly, "What exactly do you mean, 'involved with someone'?"

"Well, it just started out as a friendship, you know? We had some of the same classes and started doing some homework together at each other's houses. One thing led to another and we started feeling attracted to one another. Before we knew it, we started experimenting physically, and now . . . I just feel terrible about it!" Her voice broke as the tears came.

John and Mary waited patiently for Jackie to collect herself.

"You know how important my little class is to me. I just couldn't bear losing it!" She hid her face in her hands and began to sob.

Mary moved quickly to her side and put her arms around her, drawing Jackie's head to her shoulder. "There, there," she whispered softly, "the Lord can forgive and cleanse your heart, darling."

John nodded in agreement. "He can and He will if you're truly repentant, Jackie," he said softly.

Jackie looked up with relief and a slight smile forced its way through her tears. "Oh, I'm so glad you understand, Pastor John," she said. "I was so afraid you would take away my Sunday school class."

John looked at Jackie with concern and said, "You've always been one of our most faithful workers, Jackie. I've told your parents so many times how proud they can be of you. But I can't condone what you've done and overlook it as though it doesn't matter."

"You mean you *are* going to take the class away?"

"I didn't say that, Jackie. I need more information

before I can make a decision. Let me ask you: Have you broken off the relationship?"

Jackie looked down slowly and shook her head. "No. I need more time. I can't break it off just like that."

John sighed deeply and closed his eyes in prayer. Finally he looked at Jackie and said, "Surely you understand that I can't allow you to continue teaching the children when you are involved in a sexual relationship."

"But I *don't* understand," Jackie protested. "You make it sound so awful. It's not just a passing thing. We love each other. We're really committed!"

"But you aren't married, Jackie," Mary said firmly. "That's what makes it so wrong. Don't you realize that what you're doing is sinful?"

Jackie nodded. "I know. But we care for one another."

"I'm sure you do, Jackie," John said softly. "But that doesn't change what God has said. Marriage must come before sexual expression, if we want to please the Lord."

Mary reached over to Jackie and patted her hand. "Did you come here tonight because you want to make a clean start?"

Jackie's face grew hard and then she gave a slight giggle.

John and Mary looked at one another, uncertain of how to respond.

"Is something funny, Jackie?" John asked.

"Yeah, kind of," Jackie answered with a snicker.

"I fail to see the humor," John said as he sat back in his chair.

"You just don't understand, neither of you!" Jackie said, her eyes still twinkling with amusement. "The person I'm involved with isn't a boy." She paused, watching John and Mary as the truth hit them. "Her name is Susan."

John and Mary sat stunned. Then it began to make sense. John had seen Jackie with her girlfriend on several occasions. A couple of times, they had been holding hands, but John hadn't thought much about it. Now he leaned forward with concern in his voice. "Jackie, as awful as this sin is, God can still forgive you and cleanse your life. But you have to turn to Him with genuine repentance, and that means you can't continue in the relationship. It has to end immediately."

A look of rebellion swept across Jackie's face. "I thought you would say that! But I've learned that a person can't just break off a relationship overnight. It takes months, sometimes years. I just thought our church would be compassionate enough to understand and would work with me."

John nodded in agreement. "We will work with you, Jackie, if you seriously want to turn your life around. But while that's happening, I'm afraid you'll have to give up your Sunday school class."

"Why?" Jackie persisted. "Those little kids don't have to know about it. It hasn't affected my teaching up until now. How can I face the people in our church? How do I explain why you've taken my teaching job away? Think of what this will do to my folks!"

"I am thinking about it, Jackie, but *you* aren't. Don't you realize what sorrow this will cause your parents? You don't have to continue in this sin."

Jackie began weeping again. "I can't help myself!" she cried. "I love her!"

John waited for her sobs to quiet, and then asked, "Am I understanding you correctly, Jackie? Are you telling me that you won't break off this lesbian affair?"

"No! I won't! I *can't!*" she said hotly as she stood to her feet. "I can't believe I was so stupid as to come here and tell you! I thought you would be more understanding!" She walked to the door, then turned to face John. "You don't know what you're doing, Pastor. You're making a serious mistake!"

"No, Jackie, you're the one making the mistake," John replied sadly. "I'll be praying for you."

Jackie stormed out into the night, got into her car, and sped away.

A few days later, John received a phone call from Brad Walker, Jackie's father, who was one of the most faithful workers in the church.

"Pastor John?" he began hesitantly.

"Yes, Brad," John replied. "What can I do for you?" He thought he heard muffled sobs in the background.

"I understand Jackie came to see you the other night," Brad's voice cracked. "She said you were taking her off her teaching assignment."

"Yes, Brad," John said. "She did come and I told her we can't allow her to continue in willful sin and still teach the children. They look up to her, Brad. We expect all our teachers to be an example."

There was a long pause from the other end. Finally, Brad continued. "But John. It's Jackie–*our* daughter."

John took off his glasses and put them on the desk. "I know, Brad, and that makes it all the harder for me. But I simply have no choice in this matter. Would you and Anita be willing to come in and talk about it?"

There was another long silence. Finally, Brad replied, "I don't think so, John. Anita doesn't want to come. She knows your stand on psychological counseling, and her sister says that homosexuality is an issue that requires expert counsel. No offense, Pastor, but your training is only in the Bible. The counselor Anita has spoken with says Jackie's problem seems to be related to our relationship–Jackie's and mine, that is," Brad said wearily. "I guess I haven't been the best father in the world."

"Tell me, Brad, is there something that you have done to Jackie? Has there been any sexual relationship between you, or anything like that?"

"Oh, *no,* John! I'd *never* do anything like that! It's just that . . . I guess I wasn't there for Jackie emotionally at times." He paused for a moment to control his emotions. "To tell you the truth, John, I don't understand *what* I'm supposed to have done. I'm just getting the picture that somehow I'm to blame for what she's doing."

"Do you believe you are?"

"I don't know. I guess in some ways I can see it. I never have been very affectionate. I love my family, but I just don't know how to express it. You know what I mean?"

"Yes, Brad. I understand," John replied gently. "Tell Anita that we love you two and I'm disappointed that you're going elsewhere for counsel, but you certainly have that right. I'll be here to help in any way I can."

"Thanks, John," Brad said. "Please be praying for us."

"You know I will," John said, and then hung up the phone.

A few days later, John received another call–this time from the psychologist Brad and Anita were consulting.

"Hello, Dr. Kryer?" a pleasant voice with a bit of an accent came over the phone.

"Yes, this is John Kryer."

"John, this is Carlin Scheff. I'm the therapist working with the Walkers and their daughter Jackie."

"Yes, I heard that they were seeing a psychologist," John replied.

"That's right," Carlin said, "and they've told me how you feel about it. Really, John, I believe that we can help these people if we can put aside our differences and work as a team."

"I doubt that we could work together successfully, Mr. Scheff," John countered. "We approach things from two entirely different perspectives. You, the psychological, and I, the biblical."

"You don't even know me!" Carlin responded indignantly. "I am a *Christian* therapist! I have lectured at seminaries and churches all around the country!"

"I'm sure that's true," John said with a sigh.

"All I'm asking is that you allow me to accompany the Walkers as they come to your office. Perhaps we can work out a plan of action to help with Jackie's inner healing. And

John, I want you to know that I'm quite supportive of your role as pastor. I've told the Walkers that I respect your decision and that you are acting out of sincere conviction.

"The thing is this, John," Carlin continued, "I have had years of experience with homosexuality. That is my specialization. I have helped many, many suffering people come to grips with their sexuality. In fact, I was a practicing homosexual myself until just six years ago. But now I'm happily married and I'm helping others who are suffering from the same sin."

At least he calls it sin, John thought. "I'll be willing to meet with you and the Walkers, but I will insist on having one of our elders in the meeting," John said.

"And why is that?"

"Because I want to make sure that whatever is said is not misrepresented later. One of our elders is a friend of the Walkers, so I'm sure they won't object."

"If that's the way it has to be," Carlin said reluctantly.

The time for the meeting had come. John heard the main office door open, and voices echoed down the hallway as several people walked toward his office. John went out to meet them.

Brad and Anita Walker and their daughter Jackie were accompanied by a short, thin gentleman with a self-assured smile. He walked over to John, stuck out his hand, and said, "I'm Carlin Scheff. You must be John Kryer."

"Yes, I am. Welcome to our church, Mr. Scheff," John replied with a smile.

"Just call me Carlin, John! We're all friends here, aren't we?"

"I certainly hope so," John said and then turned to greet Brad, Anita, and Jackie. Brad looked downcast, and Anita looked tired and uptight. Jackie had a look about her that said, *You're gonna get it now, Buster!*

Soon, Richard Clayborn, the elder John had invited, arrived and joined the group.

"Let's all go into my office," John said. He led the way and set behind the desk. Five chairs were placed in a semi-circle facing the desk. When they were all seated, John said, "Let's pray."

A disapproving look flashed across Carlin's face, but he bowed his head with the others.

"O, dear Lord," John began, "you know what brings us together tonight. You know the heartache, confusion, and tension that the Walkers are experiencing, and I pray that You will guide all of us so we can help Jackie and Brad and Anita find a solution to the problems facing them. Give us wisdom as we determine to be obedient to You. I pray this in Jesus' powerful name. Amen."

Out of habit, John reached for his Bible and said, "I'd like for us to examine a few Scriptures tonight before we decide how to proceed. You see–"

"Excuse me, John," Carlin interrupted, but I don't think that's appropriate at this time. What we really need to discuss is how we can help Jackie deal with the emotional crisis she's facing right now."

"Well, I'm sorry you feel that it's inappropriate to open the Scriptures at a time like this, Carlin, but in my counseling office, that's how I begin," John replied.

"In due time! In due time, John!" Carlin protested, raising his hand like a policeman directing traffic. "Perhaps you've misunderstood the purpose of our visit."

"How so?"

"We're here to explain to you the dynamics of homosexuality. I mean no disrespect whatsoever, John, but this subject is out of your league. I'm a professional counselor. This is what I *do,* and I *know* how to help these dear people. Surely you can see the pain in Jackie's face. She is going through such confusion, such a series of conflicting emotions, desires, and beliefs. We have to help her, and frankly, kicking her out of her teaching responsibilities is going to be counter-productive."

The tension in the room began to rise noticeably. John looked Carlin full in the eyes as he opened the Bible. "Nonetheless, Carlin, I will begin by reading what the Lord has to say about sin, choices, and His power to help us overcome temptation," he said evenly.

"But you're acting like this issue is greater than any other sin!" Anita interjected angrily. "It's just like when I was a young girl in my church so many years ago. A friend of mine had done something wrong and the pastor made her stand in front of the entire church and confess her sin. She never went back there because of the humiliation and shame. I won't let that happen to Jackie!" She paused, shaking, then tears began to flow. She dabbed at her eyes with a tissue, then looked up at John. "I don't know why we have to treat this sin so differently from all other sins."

"I agree with you, Anita," John said. "But you don't seem to realize that *you* are asking me to treat it differently."

"You've missed the point entirely, John!" Carlin said. "We admit that a lesbian affair is sin. We aren't debating that. What we are saying is that the inner causes of homosexuality are rooted so deep that to merely quote some Bible verses is not going to help. We've got to help Jackie get in touch with herself, help her understand why she's drawn to another girl, and gradually wean her away from the relationship."

"What do you mean, 'gradually'?" John asked as he sat back in his chair.

"I mean that the healing process will take months, perhaps even a couple of years. You can't expect Jackie to abruptly pull away from this relationship without making the agony even greater. And don't you see that yanking Jackie out of her Sunday school class will only deepen her bitterness?"

"I'm sorry," John said, shaking his head gently. "I do not want to pull her out, but I have no other choice. If Jackie has decided to continue in this relationship, she will have to give up her class."

"Oh, *really*, John!" Carlin said in disgust. "This young child is suffering in the most pivotal crisis of her life, and you sit there unbending, without considering the impact on her tender psyche."

The elder, Richard Clayborn, cleared his voice and sat forward on his chair. "I have to say that I understand the pain the Walkers are feeling, but I also have told them that Pastor John really doesn't have a choice in this matter. We cannot allow overt sin to go unchallenged in our church."

Jackie began to cry, taking a cue from Carlin. "I'm only sixteen!" she wailed. "I'm just so confused, I don't know what to do."

John noticed, however, that no tears fell from her eyes this time.

Carlin leaned over toward Jackie and patted her shoulder. "There, there, it will be all right."

John pulled back up to his desk and spoke gently, "I'm sure you're upset, Jackie, but I would be doing you a great disservice to agree that you can't help yourself. God has told us that no temptation will *ever* come your way that He cannot give you the strength to overcome it. God will never leave you so helpless that–"

"That's enough!" Carlin said. "I must intervene!"

John turned, surprised at the interruption. Shaking his head in disbelief and annoyance, he said firmly, "I'm sorry, Carlin, but I will finish my statement."

"No, *I'm* sorry!" Carlin interjected again. "I simply must insist that this abuse stop right now!"

John tried to speak again, but each time, Carlin interrupted. "*I* am the professional counselor here. I cannot permit this!"

John sat back, stunned. In his entire ministry, he had

never witnessed such arrogant, unprofessional behavior. Here was a therapist who had asked permission to come to his office, and now had taken over as though he owned it. John looked at Brad and Anita, expecting them to speak up, but they sat silent, red with embarrassment. Richard Clayborn, the elder, was silent, too, not knowing what to say.

Had it not been for his love for the Walkers, John would have bodily ejected Carlin from the premises. His face became grim in an effort to restrain his anger. He sat back, trying to prevent an even more traumatic scene from developing.

Carlin felt he had finally gotten the situation under control. "Now," he said with a smile, "here's what we need to do: We must join forces–the church and my counseling office–in order to help this young girl. In time, I believe she will turn from lesbianism. Until, then, however, the church needs to support her, not condemn her."

"I have no intention of condemning her," John said, "but neither can I permit her to continue in a place of ministry while she is determined to go on with her sin. What Jackie must do is decide who will be the Lord of her life. The issues here are selfishness, rebellion, and the need for heart-felt repentance. Furthermore, I have no intention of allowing you to set the agenda in my counseling office."

"Stop!" Carlin said as he held up his hand.

"No, I won't stop," John said. "You have come here to my office and–"

"No! I won't allow this sort of discussion to further damage this girl!" Carlin shouted.

John stood to his feet. "I'm sorry, folks," he said sadly, looking at Brad and Jackie. "We aren't going to accomplish anything this way."

Carlin Scheff sat back in his chair and said, "I know this must be intimidating for you, John, but I couldn't allow you to move in the direction you were going."

Again John had an almost overwhelming urge to pick

Carlin up by his belt and carry him to his car, but he contained himself. He moved to the office door and opened it. The Walkers stood, trembling with embarrassment at the encounter, and they filed out into the hallway, followed by Richard Clayborn.

"I'm so sorry, Pastor," Brad said as he passed by. Anita and Jackie didn't say anything.

As Carlin Scheff walked by, he stopped and gazed into John's face. "I hope that eventually we can talk some more, John," he said condescendingly. "There's so much I can teach you."

John looked Carlin square in the eye and started to reply, then closed his mouth and walked back into his office. Carlin smiled slightly and walked out. John sat down at his desk and stared unseeing at his Bible. He shook his head in disbelief.

A few moments later Richard came back into John's office and sat down.

"Wow, John! That was the most bizarre thing I've ever seen!"

John shook his head, still frustrated. "I've never seen anything like it, Rich. That was the most unprofessional display of arrogance I have ever witnessed in my life. I mean—if I had invited myself to his office, even though I disagreed with him, I would at least have had the courtesy to allow him to finish his sentences. He acted like this was *his* office!"

There was a long pause, then John spoke again. "The tragedy is that he's got the Walkers convinced that Jackie's problem is in the deep recesses of her subconscious. If they could only understand the truth that each of us will stand before God in judgment for the choices we make in this life. Carlin Scheff is going to keep Jackie captive to her lust for two more years while he helps her 'work through' her grief. If only she would face the truth so she could learn to think the way God wants her to."

❖ ❖ ❖

Cliff sat back in his chair in absolute disbelief. He held a cordless phone to his ear. "You can't possibly mean that, Miriam!" he said. "How can you say that your father sexually abused you when you were a little child? Why haven't you ever told me about it before?"

"They told me you wouldn't believe me, Cliff. You refuse to believe that any of the abuse took place, but that doesn't change the facts," Miriam said bitterly. "I just thought you should know. It might help you to understand the grief I've been going through this past year."

Cliff shook his head in confusion. "Well, Miriam, I want to believe the truth, no matter where it leads. But this just seems so incredible! I've known your folks for years, and I just can't believe . . . I mean, I find it hard to accept that your dad could be capable of such a thing!"

"You haven't heard the half of it, Cliff!" Miriam said with conviction. "But I'm not sure you're ready."

"Ready for what?"

"Ready to hear how evil and twisted my childhood experience was. Cliff, it was so horrible that my mind blanked it out until just a few months ago. As innocent and sincere as my dad always seemed, we have found out that he was deeply involved in a satanic cult."

"Oh, come on, Miriam! You can't mean that!"

"I know...I know," Miriam said weakly, "it does seem so irrational. At first I found it impossible to accept, but now I have absolutely no doubt about it."

"How did you 'discover' this new information about your father?" Cliff asked cynically.

"Dr. Powell has helped me to recover memories that have been repressed deep in my subconscious. He has helped me to understand my dreams and flashbacks. At first, the images were blurry and clouded. But as time progressed, the memories became more vivid and certain."

"So the memories didn't surface spontaneously?"

"Well . . . no," Miriam admitted. "But that is how trauma and repressed memories work, Cliff. Try to understand for once, won't you?

"I *am* trying, Miriam! But I have a hard time believing in memories that have to be dredged up by a therapist. It would seem to me that–"

"I don't want to listen to your doubts, Cliff!" Miriam said firmly. "It has taken me long enough to sort these things out without your help, and I'm not going to let you mess with my mind now that things are starting to make sense."

"But, Miriam, all I'm asking you to do is to consider whether your memories are real or whether Dr. Powell created them in your mind."

"That's enough, Cliff! Even *now* you can't support me, can you?" Miriam spat out bitterly. "Do you and Dad have an agreement to continue the abuse forever? No way, Cliff! No way!" And she slammed the phone down on the receiver.

"Miriam? Miriam?" Cliff said with pain too deep to express. He hung up the phone and shook his head sadly as tears began to stream down his face.

8

Renewing
Your Mind

The apostle Paul knew about suffering. He listed for the Corinthian church some of the suffering he endured: he was imprisoned several times for the sake of the gospel; he was severely beaten; repeated attempts were made on his life; he received the maximum thirty-nine lashes on five different occasions; he was beaten with rods three times; he was stoned and left for dead; he was shipwrecked three times, once spending a night and a day floating in open waters; and he traveled nonstop to spread Christianity throughout the Roman empire. He wrote,

I have been constantly on the move. I have been in danger from rivers, in danger from bandits, in danger from my own countrymen, in danger from Gentiles; in danger in the city, in danger in the country, in danger at sea; and in danger from false brothers. I have labored and toiled and have often gone without sleep; I have known hunger and thirst and have often gone without food; I have been cold and naked. Besides everything else, I

face daily the pressure of my concern for all the
churches.   Who is weak, and I do not feel weak?
(2 Corinthians 11:26-29).

I point out Paul's suffering to remind us that he, too, was
the victim of abuse. He knew the humiliation of being
stripped publicly and brutally attacked. He was lied about,
misjudged, and betrayed. Still, with all of the wounds in his
past, he had the depth of character to write this:

> Rejoice in the Lord always. I will say it again:
> Rejoice! Let your gentleness be evident to all.
> The Lord is near. Do not be anxious about any-
> thing, but in everything, by prayer and petition,
> with thanksgiving, present your requests to God.
> And the peace of God, which transcends all
> understanding, will guard your hearts and your
> minds in Christ Jesus.
> Finally, brothers, whatever is true, whatever is
> noble, whatever is right, whatever is pure, what-
> ever is lovely, whatever is admirable–if anything
> is excellent or praiseworthy–think about such
> things. Whatever you have learned or received or
> heard from me, or seen in me–put it into practice.
> And the God of peace will be with you.
> I can do everything through him who gives
> me strength. . . . And my God will meet all your
> needs according to his glorious riches in Christ
> Jesus (Philippians 4:4-9,13,19).

Let's look at this powerful passage in detail and see how
it can apply to the healing we seek for our own sufferings.

Always Rejoicing

Paul writes, "Rejoice in the Lord always. I will say it
again: Rejoice!" Perhaps one of the most difficult habits for

a person to develop is rejoicing. Instead, we find it exceedingly easy to grumble and complain.

It is interesting that the word "grumble" appears only eight times in the NIV. "Complain" also shows up eight times. But "rejoice" is used over 120 times in the Bible. In Philippians 4:4, "rejoice" comes from the Greek word *chairō*. This word was often used as a greeting or farewell by the people of the first century. In the same way that we say, "Have a nice day," they would say, "Rejoice!" I like that! Wouldn't it be nice if we modern-day believers would frequently remind ourselves that we are to rejoice?

There are some people who are always complaining. They may not intend to drag others down, but they constantly remind us of the minor and inevitable irritations of human existence. Instead of noticing what is good around them, they become resentful over the good that *doesn't* happen to them. People like that cast a dark cloud over any gathering because of their negative spirit. Do you know people like that? Don't you just groan inwardly when you see them approaching?

On the other hand, there are wonderful people who bring sunshine into every room they enter. Their cheerful attitudes and laughter radiate throughout any group they happen upon, and folks look forward to their arrival. I know many people like that and I thank God for them. By their very presence they lighten the burdens that others carry. The Philippians seemed to have that effect on Paul. Even so, he reminded them, "Do *everything* without complaining or arguing" (Philippians 2:14, emphasis added).

Rejoicing is a habit we can develop by consciously making the effort to change the focus of our minds. Paul tells us how to do this.

Gentleness Versus Anger

Gentleness is a rare commodity in our day. Yet that should not be the case with Christians. Philippians 4:5

exhorts us, "Let your gentleness be evident to all. The Lord is near."

In the quest for healing of the soul, the believer needs to interact with other people in a spirit of gentleness. In contrast, some psychologists encourage people to express their hostility and vent their anger as a means of relieving their mental and emotional pressures.

I have received calls from around 'ne country from Christian men whose wives have been encouraged to defy their husband's leadership in the home. The women have been taught that their rage is justifiable and that their husbands are misogynists–that is, abusers of women–if they don't agree with the subjective feelings of their wives.

One heartbroken husband in Texas wrote me a sixty-nine-page handwritten letter explaining how his wife had been convinced by psychotherapy that she has multiple personalities and that her husband is her enemy. She has passed her anger on to the children, telling them they do not have to obey their father because he doesn't understand her pain. Far from receiving relief through venting her anger, she has become increasingly angry with the passage of time.

The truth is, the more we explode in anger, the angrier we become. God tells us, "Refrain from anger and turn from wrath; do not fret–it leads only to evil" (Psalm 37:8).

Some Christian counselors teach that it is all right to become angry so long as we get over it. The verse they quote in support of this view is Ephesians 4:26: "In your anger do not sin: Do not let the sun go down while you are still angry." Some people interpret that to mean that there are times when anger is appropriate–so long as we resolve the issue in a timely fashion.

It is true that in some cases, anger seems justified. Jesus was righteously angry at the money changers who were defiling the temple (Matthew 21:12, 13 and Mark 11:15-17). We are to hate evil (Psalm 97:10), and we can easily justify a person who uses force to protect the innocent and helpless. Yet, in all honesty, little of our anger falls into the category of righteous indignation. That's why James writes, "Man's anger does not bring about the righteous life that God desires" (James 1:20).

Remember the permission-to-be-angry passage in Ephesians 4? Many people conveniently overlook the next verse, which says, "Do not give the devil a foothold" (Ephesians 4:27). Anger is precisely that–a foothold for Satan. It gives him an entrance into our lives and he uses it to damage all who come within reach.

Anger is as natural to man as breathing. No one has to teach us the dark emotion; it erupts with the slightest provocation. It begins in our earliest days of infancy when we cry for a bottle and blanket. It continues into childhood as we shriek when our playmates refuse to give us their toys. And unless it is contained through firm parental correction, we continue to rage throughout life whenever we don't get what we want when we want it. That's usually what anger is all about–not getting what we want.

James 4 explains this problem: "What causes fights and quarrels among you? Don't they come from your desires that battle within you? You want something but don't get it. You kill and covet, but you cannot have what you want. You quarrel and fight" (James 4:1,2).

Anger is a habit and it is hard to break. It is fueled by our tempers, self-focus, weariness, human nature, and practice. Being around angry people tends to breed anger; that's why the Bible tells us not to make friends with someone who is easily angered (Proverbs 22:24).

Children who live in angry homes develop habits of anger. Anger can also frighten children away from home. Some Christian parents complain, "My kids never want to be at home!" Maybe there is too much anger and too little laughter in their homes.

Notice that right after Paul says, "Let your gentleness be

evident to all," he adds, "The Lord is near." What an inter-esting connection: "gentleness...the Lord is near." Some people say that this is a reminder that the Lord's return is close at hand and we need to behave ourselves because judgment is just around the corner.

That's possible, but I tend to think Paul is telling us that the Lord is close beside us at all times and that sinful anger grieves His heart. Have you noticed how much easier it is to control your anger when you are in the presence of someone from outside of your family? It might be a neigh-bor, an employer, or an important dignitary. We are able to control our expressions of rage when outsiders are observ-ing us. That's the point Paul is making: Jesus is *always* with us, observing our outrage and fits of temper. The next time your temper rises, think of Jesus standing in the room with you. He *is* in the room, watching you.

The obvious contrast to our anger is gentleness. Some confuse gentleness with weakness, but in reality, gentleness has great power. Proverbs tells us, "Through patience a ruler can be persuaded, and a gentle tongue can break a bone" (Proverbs 25:15). And it is a wise person who learns this profound truth: "A gentle answer turns away wrath, but a harsh word stirs up anger" (Proverbs 15:1).

Do you want to find genuine healing for the wounds of your soul? Then begin to cultivate the habit of gentleness. You will find that life is easier and happier when you extend a gentle hand even to those who have hurt you. Does that sound foolish to you? Then listen to what Jesus says: "Take my yoke upon you and learn from me, for I am gentle and humble in heart, and you will find rest for your souls" (Matthew 11:29). What a blessed promise!

A Prescription for Anxiety

In our stress-ridden society, Paul's next words are likely to get a few smiles: "Do not be anxious about anything"

(Philippians 4:6). We may think to ourselves, *but Paul, you have no idea what it's like to live in this day and age!*

It's amazing what people become anxious about today. For example, we once had a couple scheduled to perform a concert at our church. As we discussed their housing arrangements, we understood that they were going to stay with relatives and they thought we were going to reserve a motel room for them. On Saturday evening when the couple arrived, there were no rooms available anywhere in town because of a major conference in our area. So my wife hurried to prepare our guest room.

When she explained the situation to the couple, the husband seemed agreeable and took it in stride. But the wife became indignant that she would have to stay in our home instead of a motel. She went to the guest room, shut the door, and stayed there.

In the middle of the night, we heard a knock at our bedroom door. The embarrassed husband told us that his wife was having a panic attack and would need medical attention. Somehow she made it through the night, but the next morning, the woman's anxiety returned and she began to hyperventilate, feeling her throat become constricted. Fortunately we had a respiratory therapist in the congregation who provided an inhaler, and the singer was able to perform. Later on she apologized, saying that nothing like that had ever taken place before.

What had really happened? The night before, as I sat talking with her husband, he told me that his wife's problem was selfishness. She was, quite simply, angry that she didn't get her way. Consequently she had worked herself into an anxiety attack.

While that may have been worry to the extreme, all of us experience anxiety from time to time. Some people suffer from severe anxiety and find it hard to leave the house or to go into an unfamiliar setting. Other people, due to the pain of genuine abuse, become anxious when certain sounds, tastes, smells, or other sensations cause them to remember unpleasant memories. For those who have never found healing and lasting peace in Jesus, the wounds of the past may surface without warning to cause suffering all over again.

What do people worry about? *Everything.* Finances, house repairs, aging, our children, crime, weight gain, hair loss, next week's party, a deadline for an assignment, marriage, divorce, being hurt again, failure, being laughed at–the list can go on forever.

Paul writes a prescription for anxiety in Philippians 4:6: "Do not be anxious about anything, but in everything, by prayer and petition, with thanksgiving, present your requests to God." His answer for worry is prayer, urgent supplication, and a spirit of gratitude.

Prayer is the preventative to worry. It is talking to God from the heart. It is telling Him our needs, our desires, our fears, and our pain. It is unloading on the Lord and letting Him bear our burdens.

Sometimes, however, we are already in a fix and we come to God with *petitions*–that is, intense heartfelt prayer–begging the Lord to act in our behalf. Isn't it wonderful that He doesn't scold us? Instead, He invites us to present our urgent requests to Him.

Paul then goes on to tell us one of the most important elements of anxiety-healing prayer: thanksgiving. Thanksgiving is like a spiritual antibiotic; it kills the infection of worry. Why? Because gratitude reminds us that God has answered prayer in the past and has provided for us again and again.

Paul writes that we are always to be "giving thanks to God the Father for everything, in the name of our Lord Jesus Christ" (Ephesians 5:20). Again he uses that pesky word: *everything.* How can God expect us to thank Him for disasters, pain, suffering, and sorrow? How can we be grateful for the unfairness of life, the cruelty of other people, and the horrifying circumstances over which we have no control?

Only by faith. Faith that God is greater than even our

pain. Faith that He will indeed work "for the good of those who love him, who have been called according to his purpose" (Romans 8:28) even when it seems impossible. Though it appears so unreasonable, Paul insists that we "give thanks in all circumstances, for this is God's will for you in Christ Jesus" (1 Thessalonians 5:18).

Thanksgiving is ultimately a statement of faith. It is tangible evidence that we believe in the goodness of God regardless of the circumstances of life. That's why we are urged to "give thanks to the LORD, for he is good; his love endures forever" (1 Chronicles 16:34). God is *good.* He doesn't want your suffering to be meaningless; He will reward the faith of the person who says, "though he slay me, yet will I hope in him" (Job 13:15).

What can you thank the Lord for right now? Your health? Or perhaps a child who has been a source of joy for years? A car that works? Get a sheet of paper and start writing a list of things to thank God for. Do it right now. Put this heading on it: Things I Thank God For.

Look around you. Here are some suggestions: the miracle of vision, good friends, family members, running water, the refrigerator, hands that work, feet, indoor plumbing, birds, trees, sunshine, snow, rain, a hot shower, good roads, a job, the ability to read, songs, a child's laughter, mountain streams, love, a roof over your head. . . .

Thank God out loud! Tell others how good He is. David learned the joy of thanking God in the presence of others. He wrote, "I will give you thanks in the great assembly; among throngs of people I will praise you" (Psalm 35:18).

Church is a wonderful place to thank the Lord. Sometimes in our services, we take time to express thanks for specific ways that God has blessed us. As we stand in prayer, one person will say, "I thank You, Lord, for loving me just the way I am." Another person will speak out, "I praise You, Lord, for the health You have blessed me with." Still another will say, "Thank You, Lord, for my new job!"

Gratitude is a healing medicine. It is almost impossible to overflow with thanksgiving and to remain wounded at the same time. Make thanksgiving a habit by practicing it constantly.

The Promise of Peace

One of the deepest needs of the wounded heart is peace. Note in our passage from Philippians how Paul connects peace with a spirit of thanksgiving. He writes, "With thanksgiving, present your requests to God. And the peace of God, which transcends all understanding, will guard your hearts and your minds in Christ Jesus" (Philippians 4:6,7). Meditate for a moment on this Biblical principle: *Peace is a by-product of grateful faith.* Perhaps you are saying, "That doesn't make sense!" Precisely. God's peace doesn't make logical sense to the finite human intellect. His peace goes far beyond our understanding. While the world says that the only way a person can experience healing of the heart is to "work through" his past and to "embrace his pain," the Bible says that peace comes from prayer and thanksgiving.

Some time back, a song titled, "Don't Worry, Be Happy" became very popular. It was a cheerful song and its message was a definite improvement over the mournful lyrics so prevalent in contemporary music. Theologically, however, it was a bit shallow, not unlike some of the praise choruses that are sung in our churches.

It is not shallow, however, when God says, "Don't worry, be thankful," because the focus of our gratitude is God Himself and the result is peace. Moreover, the peace of God does not merely give us a sense of well-being. According to Paul, God's peace has the power to literally "guard your hearts and your minds in Christ Jesus" (Philippians 4:7).

His peace guards the heart, our emotional center, from the discouragements and fears that inevitably strike when we are faced with the uncertainties of life. And it is significant that part of this peace comes from sheer obedience–that is, righteousness: simply doing what God says to do. Paul affirmed that truth when he said we are to protect our heart with the "breastplate of righteousness" (Ephesians 6:14).

The point is this: We will never experience peace of heart when we are disobeying the Lord. Husbands, we will never have peace when we are harsh and unloving toward our wives. Wives, you will never experience peace when you are in rebellion toward your husbands. And *please* don't get angry with me for saying that. *I* didn't think of those principles; they come from Scripture (Ephesians 5:22-33; Colossians 3:18, 19; 1 Peter 3:1-7).

When we refuse to submit to the biblically ordained authority of civil governments, our employers, our husbands, our parents, our church leaders, and other similar authorities, we rob ourselves of peace, because ultimately, we are rebelling against God.

Remember too that the peace of God will guard our minds. There is a mental and intellectual serenity that comes when we know we are right with God. There is a sense of assurance we can have when we know *Whom* we have believed and we have experienced the peace only He can give.

A New Way of Thinking

Maintaining one's peace of heart and mind is the theme of Philippians 4:8,9. Here we find a list of qualities that are best exemplified in Christ in much the same way that the fruit of the Spirit in Galatians 5:22-23 are best seen in the Lord Jesus. The best way to understand and imitate these qualities, then, is to do as the writer of Hebrews suggested: "Let us fix our eyes on Jesus" (Hebrews 12:2).

Isn't focusing on Jesus a better solution to our pain than gazing inward at our psychic wounds and hoping to gain a flash of insight that will lead to temporary healing? God says, "Turn to me and be saved, all you ends of the earth; for I am God, and there is no other" (Isaiah 45:22). The Hebrew word translated "turn" can also mean "look" and is rendered that way in the King James Version. We are to continually look to God, to the Lord Jesus, and to the Holy Spirit rather than our woundedness.

If Jesus is the perfect standard of mental, emotional, and spiritual health that we believe Him to be, then we will want to study His character so we can become like Him. Paul says, "Your attitude should be the same as that of Christ Jesus" (Philippians 2:5).

Let's look, then, at Philippians 4:8,9:

> Finally, brothers, whatever is true, whatever is noble, whatever is right, whatever is pure, whatever is lovely, whatever is admirable–if anything is excellent or praiseworthy–think about such things. Whatever you have learned or received or heard from me, or seen in me–put it into practice. And the God of peace will be with you.

Whatever Is True

Renewing our minds begins by thinking upon whatever is true. If we want to experience genuine healing, we must willingly face the truth. Ultimately, it will do no good to blame others for our own sinfulness. If we want the cancer of sin removed, we must acknowledge its presence and come to the only source of forgiveness. Look at that verse in Isaiah again: "Turn to me and be saved, all you ends of the earth; for I am God, and there is no other" (Isaiah 45:22). There is no other source of healing from the wounds of sin.

A godly woman once told my wife that her husband was one of the most considerate and Christlike men she had ever known. Over time, however, she allowed unbiblical counsel to convince her that he was a harsh and domineering man. I knew her husband before and after her therapy and I could tell that he had not changed at all. Rather, she had come to believe a lie.

The lie was that if he didn't agree with her subjective feelings and tag along as she followed her heart, then he was guilty of mental cruelty and no longer deserved her submission. She focused on the lie until it became reality to her. Eventually she separated from her husband, who to this day loves her and prays for her return.

I often wanted to ask this woman, "What are you *thinking?* How can you justify breaking up your family and victimizing your children for the sake of a lie? Why won't you remember the *truth* about your husband?"

What *is* true about the person who wounded you? The truth is that individual is a sinner just like you and I. From the human point of view, he is probably not *all* bad. He may have some positive qualities that you and other people appreciate. He may have wept genuine tears of remorse for what he did. Still, God says he is responsible for his thoughts and actions.

To a greater or lesser degree, the person who wounded you chose to follow a sinful path that damaged his life and the lives of those around him. Who knows what painful experiences led to the destructive decisions he made, the sinful choices he followed, and the abusive things he did to others? He, too, may have been a victim of abuse by his parents, who were in turn victimized by their parents, and so on through countless generations of the past. Or, he may have just chosen to be evil.

Still, the truth is, it doesn't matter whether he was the last link in a long chain of abuse or the first in his line to hurt another person. He is still responsible before God for the choices he made.

And so is the next link in the chain. If the victim blames the abuser for every sinful choice she has made since the trauma took place, she is not thinking true thoughts.

May I suggest an activity that will help you think the truth about the person who hurt you? Take a sheet of paper and write at the top, "The Truth about _____." Then draw a vertical line down the middle and divide the sheet in half. Label the left side "Good Things about _____." Label the right side "Bad Things about _____."

Before you begin writing your lists, you'll want to pause for a moment to pray. Say something like this to God: "Father, help me to see _____ the way you see him. Help me to be truthful. Amen." Now begin, and take your time. Be totally honest as you try to see this person the way God sees him.

When you are done, get another sheet of paper and title it, "The Truth about Myself." Be honest and write down the words, choices, attitudes, and actions that may have contributed in any way to the suffering you have experienced. Do *not* take on guilt that does not belong to you, but be as truthful as possible and acknowledge your faults where appropriate. Ask the Holy Spirit to help you be fully honest with yourself. Perhaps you will need a trusted friend–someone who knows the Word of God–to help you evaluate whether you bear any responsibility. The key is to see the truth.

I can hear professional therapists objecting vehemently to this suggestion: "How can you revictimize a person already suffering from undeserved abuse by suggesting that she holds any responsibility for what happened to her?"

On the contrary, I do not want a victim to accept responsibility for what she did not choose. But a key part of the healing process is thinking truthfully about ourselves as well as other people. Paul wrote to the Romans: "Do not think of yourself more highly than you ought, but rather think of yourself with sober judgment, in accordance with the measure of faith God has given you" (Romans 12:3).

Think on what is *true*.

Whatever Is Noble

Paul continues the prescription: We are to think upon "whatever is noble." The word translated "noble" in Philippians 4:8 is the Greek word *semnos*, which means "venerable" or "honorable." Honor is a concept almost foreign to the modern mind, but it has a key role in retraining our minds to think the way God wants us to. We are to give honor to whom honor is due. Paul writes, "Give everyone what you owe him: If you owe taxes, pay taxes; if revenue, then revenue; if respect, then respect; if honor, then honor" (Romans 13:7).

God demands that we respect the humanity of every human being, since people are made in the moral image of God (Genesis 1:26,27). According to Genesis 9:6, we are to honor and value human life: "Whoever sheds the blood of man, by man shall his blood be shed; for in the image of God has God made man." Contrary to modern humanistic thought, capital punishment is a statement supporting the sanctity of life rather than devaluing it.

The honor spoken of in Philippians 4 goes beyond mere acknowledgment that a person's life is intrinsically valuable. Honor has to do with our attitudes toward others. It means that we esteem them highly. In our day of *self*-esteem, the concept of honoring others is alien, but that is what God tells us to do if we want to experience genuine peace in our own hearts.

Honor is the opposite of contempt, disdain, or scorn. Implied in the command to think upon what is honorable is the fact that some things are *not* honorable–that is, they are contemptible. Some things are simply unworthy of our attention, and when we concetrate on them, they can cause much damage.

Undeserved criticism is like that. If we ignore such criticism as contemptible verbal refuse, then we remain free of its power and pain. On the other hand, if we dwell on undeserved criticism, it can destroy our joy, peace, relationships with other people, and our walk with God and replace those qualities with anger, hurt, depression, and spiritual defeat. Undeserved criticism is a lie; it is dishonorable.

One woman I knew became angry with her husband and began describing him as a misogynist (someone who hates women), an unfair controller, and a man who did not deserve her respect. The problem with her accusations, however, was that they were untrue. The teenage children wrote letters to the court and to church authorities and said that they had lived with both parents and that their father had always been kind and loving in the home. I myself had seen him cleaning the house and doing the laundry. I have met few husbands who were as tender and thoughtful as he. All I would ask of his wife is to think honestly–and honorably–about her husband.

If we look hard enough, we can find contemptible things in *anyone's* life–things that irritate, repulse, and disgust. Yet at the same time, if we look truthfully, we can find honorable qualities in their lives as well.

My mother used to get aggravated with my dad's snoring because it kept her awake. Then he had a heart attack. After that, she told me, the sound of his snoring brought peace to her heart. The snoring assured her that he was alive and well, and that, in turn, enabled her to fall fast asleep. There was so much that was honorable about my dad and mom loved him so much that his snoring simply didn't bother her anymore. She concentrated on the blessings instead of the irritations.

Thinking honorably is a key part of retraining our thinking process. Paul reminds us, "Be devoted to one another in brotherly love. Honor one another above yourselves" (Romans 12:10). How can we apply this biblical concept to the heart of one who has been abused and deeply wounded? Giving honor where honor is due can help us to see a hurtful person more realistically and can help us to forgive him or her.

Whatever Is Right

Paul continues with God's program of mind renewal when he tells us to focus on "whatever is right." The Greek word for "right" is *dikaios*, which means "that which is correct or just." Sometimes we use the word *fair* to communicate the same idea. Paul is telling us to view people and circumstances with fairness. The problem is that our hearts and minds are so twisted by sin and selfishness that our perceptions are distorted. The only way to correct our spiri-tual vision is through the lens of God's Word.

As I stated earlier, I am not denying that abuse runs rampant in our sin-twisted world. Millions of people suffer the pain and sorrow of verbal, physical, and sexual abuse perpetrated by relatives, neighbors, trusted friends, and others. I do not want to minimize the trauma that abuse inflicts upon its victims. It is that very concern that causes me to encourage genuine victims not to allow well-meaning therapists to make them return to their pain under psychotherapeutic theories that enslave rather than liberate. It just isn't right.

Nor is it right to accuse innocent people of having abused their children, spouses, counselees, parishioners, or students when they have not done so. It isn't fair to accuse someone when there is no possible way he or she can disprove the accusation. Unless there is incontrovertible evidence to support an accusation of abuse, we must assume innocence. That is a principle of civil law, and it is also scriptural:

> One witness is not enough to convict a man accused of any crime or offense he may have committed. A matter must be established by the testimony of two or three witnesses.
>
> If a malicious witness takes the stand to accuse a man of a crime, the two men involved in the dispute must stand in the presence of the LORD before the priests and the judges who are

in office at the time. The judges must make a thorough investigation, and if the witness proves to be a liar, giving false testimony against his brother, then do to him as he intended to do to his brother. You must purge the evil from among you (Deuteronomy 19:15-30).

We should not accuse someone of a horrible crime on the basis of hazy "memories" that have returned only with the help of therapy or books or articles about satanic ritual abuse or repressed memories.

The problem of accusing someone of abuse is complicated by the fact that we humans are absolutely incapable of seeing into another person's heart or mind. "Who among men knows the thoughts of a man except the man's spirit within him?" (1 Corinthians 2:11). This truth contradicts the claims of psychologists who think they can delve into the compartments of the mind and discern between fragments of personalities and demons.

One pastor who is convinced that psychological techniques are necessary to deal with multiple personality disorder and demonization wrote about satanic cults and their ability to establish mind control: "This programming involves an organizational system . . . for the alter personalities involving internal mental imagery, which is driven by demons, who provide the power." Now look carefully at what he says next: "Undoing it requires an understanding of the mental processes involved, the imagery or blueprint used, and the spiritual dynamics."[142] The understanding he speaks of must depend on psychological findings, for he writes, "Christians . . . too often have been unaware of the psychological issues. There are encouraging signs that an increasing number of people are beginning to see that 'deliverance' alone does not cure the psychological component, including the MPD."[143]

God's Word and the power of the Holy Spirit are not

enough? We need the insights of psychology? No, we need the humility to admit that we *don't* understand anyone else's heart.

A human counselor can only go on the basis of what a counselee reveals or on any actual evidence that is presented. A wise biblical counselor will reserve judgment until he has heard both sides of an issue (Proverbs 18:13,17). He will also wait until he has thoroughly investigated the accusations. Read what Deuteronomy says about this:

> If a man or woman living among you in one of the towns the LORD gives you is found doing evil in the eyes of the LORD your God in violation of his covenant, and contrary to my command has worshiped other gods, bowing down to them or to the sun or the moon or the stars of the sky, and this has been brought to your attention, then you must investigate it thoroughly. If it is true and it has been proved that this detestable thing has been done in Israel, take the man or woman who has done this evil deed to your city gate and stone that person to death. On the testimony of two or three witnesses a man shall be put to death, but no one shall be put to death on the testimony of only one witness. The hands of the witnesses must be the first in putting him to death, and then the hands of all the people. You must purge the evil from among you (Deuteronomy 17:2-7).

Investigations are to be thorough and accurate before a judgment is made.

Whatever Is Pure

Paul continues his description of inner renewal when he says that we are to think upon "whatever is pure." The

victims of genuine sexual abuse or incompetent psychotherapy are often subject to vivid mental images of perverted sexual acts. Whether these images reflect memories of
actual events; or they are the result of exposure to pornographic literature, movies, and television; or they were
spawned by misguided therapy, the cure is the same: to fill
the mind with pure thoughts instead of perverted ones.

Paul encourages us to "purify ourselves from everything
that contaminates body and spirit, perfecting holiness out of
reverence for God" (2 Corinthians 7:1). That is why we must
be careful about what we read or view. I'm not referring only
to what is traditionally thought of as pornographic; we must
not allow *any* perverted ideas to fill our minds–whether they
come from television, books that focus on satanic ritual
abuse, or discussions with counselors.

A woman called me and asked if I thought it was proper
for her husband, a psychotherapist, to counsel alone with
women about their sexual fantasies. She asked, "Don't you
think it is dangerous for a man to counsel women day after
day and talk about their sexual problems?"

"Of course it's dangerous," I replied. "No man should be
counseling a woman by himself, especially if the issue is
of a sexual nature. We don't allow our counselors to meet
with members of the opposite sex without their mates being
present."

She went on to tell me that her husband was working
with a woman he has diagnosed as having MPD. During
the counselee's "child" stage she asked the therapist to mas-
sage her back, which he did, though his wife warned him
about the danger. The MPD "child" also asked the therapist
to take her to the park, which he has done, and she writes
him letters signed "your little girls" and "your true love."

The wife went to their pastor, who confronted the therapist about the danger of what he was doing. Since that meeting, the therapist has refused to even speak to the pastor. I
warned the wife that she needed to confront her husband

immediately because he is headed for moral failure. I encouraged her to ask her pastor to begin some sort of church discipline. I shared with her the warnings in Gala-tians 6:1-3 and 1 Corinthians 10:11, 12 about how easy it is to fall into temptation.

A few minutes after she hung up, her pastor called me to talk about the issue for a while. He agreed that the problem was serious. Yet when I asked if his church was in the habit of exercising discipline, he said, "No, but maybe this situation will bring us to that point."

Isn't it incredible that a Christian therapist could be so foolish? Though his wife objected to his behavior, his pastor confronted him, and he has since been fired from the counseling clinic for insubordination, he persists in his sinful slide toward disaster.

God wants us to "become blameless and pure, children of God without fault in a crooked and depraved generation, in which you shine like stars in the universe" (Philippians 2:15). In contrast, psychological experts tell us that Christians are no different from any other group of people and that we have no special resources to keep us from being polluted by evil. "We assume that because we are now possessed by the Holy Spirit somehow this magically protects us from psychological or emotional problems. In fact, however, this is no more the case than that being a Christian protects us from getting mumps or measles."[144]

No longer believing that the Word of God is sufficient to meet the needs of our self-centered and abusive age, Christians have accepted polluted philosophical systems which corrupt our thinking. Paul warns that "to those who are corrupted and do not believe, nothing is pure. In fact, both their minds and consciences are corrupted" (Titus 1:15). Perhaps that is why some Christian psychologists have come to believe that nearly everyone is either an abuser or a victim of sexual abuse. Everything is interpreted through a perverted sexual matrix.

We are told to focus on whatever is pure. Personal purification is perhaps one of the most troubling problems facing a victim of sexual abuse: "*How* can I become clean? What do I have to do? What kind of therapy is required? How many years will it take? What will it cost? How much pain must I endure? How can the integration of multiple personalities be achieved and will such unity produce the sense of purity desired?"

A common view is that a person must spend years in therapy to achieve integration of his or her fractured soul. "A study . . . found MPDs had been in treatment an average of almost seven years before the correct diagnosis was made."[145] The biblical view, however, is that God is still able to change lives today just as He has done throughout the centuries for millions of believers in Jesus Christ–through His Word and the power of the Holy Spirit.

"Oh, you simple fool!" some people may respond. "Do you really believe that problems this deep can be solved merely by reading the Bible?"

That's not what I said. I have never taught that the healing of the soul takes place just by *reading* the Bible. Remember what James says: "Do not merely listen to the word, and so deceive yourselves. Do what it says" (James 1:22).

How can people deceive themselves by listening to the Word of God? By mistakenly thinking that there is some spiritual merit in the mere act of reading the words. Yet it is not the *reading* that pleases the Lord, but the *doing*. It is submission and obedience to His Word that transforms and heals the wounded heart.

Peter says it this way: "Now that you have purified yourselves by obeying the truth so that you have sincere love for your brothers, love one another deeply, from the heart" (1 Peter 1:22). Do you see the sequence? First we must obey God's Word, and then the emotional healing will come. Submitting ourselves to His truth enables us to genuinely love others–even those who have hurt us.

Only when we saturate our minds with the principles, precepts, attitudes, and insights of God's truth can we achieve the wholeness we so desperately seek. That is why I contend that *only* God can heal your wounded heart.

Whatever Is Lovely

Paul tells us that we are to focus our minds on "whatever is lovely." The Greek word translated "lovely" in Philippians 4:8 is *prosphilēs,* which is found only in this verse. It comes from the preposition *pros,* which means "from the side of, at, or toward" and the word *phileō,* which means "to love." If we are going to change our way of thinking, we must focus on that which comes from the side of love or has love as its goal.

This is where self-examination comes into play: "Am I doing this out of love for others or out of love for myself? Is my motivation Christlike love or personal pride?" As long as we demand our own way, we will never experience the peace and inner wholeness we long for.

Worldly therapy teaches that the wounded person must assert herself and take care of her own wants and needs. One woman I know was even taught that disobeying the Word and following her own heart was an act of love that would help her learn how to love her husband better. In reality, such disobedience is rebellion, and her actions produced sorrow for her entire family.

It is not lovely to fix your mind on the abuses of the past. Reliving the sordid details of what may or may not have happened years ago does not produce healing, as psychologists claim. Instead, it produces bitterness, accusations, broken relationships, separations, and divorce. It divides churches, families, and friends. It weakens a person's faith in God and His Word. The cure—as irrational as it may seem—is to think on what is lovely.

Whatever Is Admirable

The divine prescription for healing continues with thinking about "whatever is admirable." The English word *admire* comes from the Latin word *admirari*, which means "to wonder at." It means "to regard with pleasure, wonder, and approval; to have a high opinion of; esteem or respect."[146] Now it seems as if Paul has finally gone too far. How can God expect an abuse victim to extend approval to an abusive past or regard it with pleasure?

He *doesn't* expect us to do that. God never asks His children to lie or pretend. It is not past abuse He wants us to focus on, but rather, whatever is admirable right now. The common mistake in current therapy is to force the mind of the victim to return to the pain and wounds of long ago.

A therapist may tell a woman that Christ did not heal her wounds, and she is in denial if she insists that He did. He may also tell her that she must turn away from family and friends who doubt her reclaimed memories and disagree with her new focus on survival. As a result, contempt develops for anyone who dares to question the accuracy of her memories or their interpretation and the therapist becomes the primary authority in the confused counselee's life.

The summer 1994 issue of *Leadership Journal* featured a heartbreaking true story called "Recovered Nightmare," which detailed the damage that was done when a psychotherapist convinced a woman that her uncle had sexually molested her when she was a child.[147] Her pastor was sympathetic and supportive, yet cautious because her accusations would affect two families in the church.

The pastor referred the woman (Jennifer) to a Christian psychologist in the church—a counselor whose instincts he trusted. Still, he wanted to be certain that the accusations were true before he confronted the uncle, an officer in the church. "Are you absolutely sure Brian was the one who abused you?" he asked earnestly. His question was rebuffed by her angry retort, "Pastor Kirk, you know nothing about sexual abuse. You have no business questioning me."

Eventually, the psychologist accused the pastor of becoming the "main obstacle to Jennifer's healing" since his "apparent skepticism about her abuse" was "revictimizing her." Other people in the church wondered if the pastor was trying to protect an influential member and began to doubt their pastor's integrity.

The pastor's "fault" was that he wanted to be absolutely certain before joining in the accusations. He was trying to follow a basic principle of moral, religious, and civil law: to seek the *truth.* He knew from the Scriptures that no one is to be condemned without witnesses (Deuteronomy 19:15), and no exception is made for sexual abuse.

The pastor's stand was courageous and admirable, yet the psychologist said to him, "You're hiding and using Scripture as an excuse."

Shortly thereafter, Jennifer left the church, saying that "it was undermining her healing and that she couldn't stomach listening to someone preach whom she didn't respect." *That's* what the real problem was: lack of respect. Neither Jennifer nor her psychologist respected the opinions and judgment of others. Jennifer's father soon became a target of their criticism as well. No one was admirable or worthy of respect unless they agreed with Jennifer and her therapists.

This sort of contempt for family members and church officials is fostered by a twisted philosophy that makes truth a secondary issue. In this view, there is a difference between what is "true" and what is "real." Truth is defined as "narrative truth"–true to the person reporting it, "but that 'truth' is not necessarily historically accurate" or real.[148] What a tragic confusion! Truth is no longer based on fact, but can now be defined by fantasy–so long as the person telling the story believes it.

But real truth is *essential* to the healing process. In medicine, a doctor may believe the medicine he is administering is safe, but if it is a deadly poison, his patient will suffer and perhaps even die—because the doctor did not know the truth. In legal, moral, and ethical matters, truth is just as vital. That's why God commanded His people to go to great lengths to find the truth: "These are the things you are to do: Speak the truth to each other, and render true and sound judgment in your courts" (Zechariah 8:16).

It is not admirable to believe a lie or to act on misinformation. It is not right to accuse an innocent person of having abused someone years ago on the basis of an uncertain memory. As psychologist Dr. Dan Allender admits, "the truth of a recovered memory is impossible to determine. . . . Memory is not a videotape or photograph of past events. It's a deeply biased interpretation of events. Too many studies show that false memories can be easily created."[149] How true! And yet in his book *The Wounded Heart*, Dr. Allender insists that a person must return to the past to be healed. "The process of entering the past will disrupt life. . . . Marriages will need to be reshaped. . . . The fabric of life will need to be unraveled piece by piece as the Master reweaves the cloth to His design."[150]

On the one hand, the author seems to repudiate the "underlying assumption for many therapists [that] the memories of sexual abuse must be reclaimed in order for the person to be healed."[151] On the other hand, he writes in *The Wounded Heart*, "the unclaimed pain of the past presses for resolution."[152]

Marriages and family relationships have been severely damaged as a result of therapies such as the "wounded heart" philosophy. There are several reasons: 1) the viewing of nearly every woman as a victim who cannot find wholeness and healing without psychotherapy; 2) the removal of any and all responsibility from the victim regardless of age or ability to cry out (in contradiction of Deuteronomy 22:23-27); 3) the stereotyping of churches and pastors as naive, "Biblio-addicted," into denial, and given to simplistic counseling; 4) the lack of biblical support for the counseling theory; 5) the distortion of the biblical doctrines of love and forgiveness; 6) the unbiblical concept of confrontation, which borders on seeking vengeance; 7) the acceptance of unsupported memories as evidence of abuse.[153]

I do not believe that Christian psychologists intend to accuse and damage innocent people. But that is what is happening all across the country. And since innocent people are defending themselves vigorously, the courts are beginning to question the validity of recovered memories, making it all the more difficult for *actual* abuse victims to successfully prosecute their abusers.

Punishing the innocent and excusing the guilty is not admirable; it is *abominable*. Helping victims of actual abuse or therapeutic confusion to refocus their hearts and minds on the purity of the Lord Jesus *is* admirable. Helping them to put their past behind them through Christlike forgiveness is admirable. Helping them to grow into Christian maturity is admirable. But to perpetuate their victimhood, even with the noblest of motives, is a tragedy.

A Word of Encouragement

We *can* learn to refocus our attention on whatever is excellent and praiseworthy. Otherwise the command in Philippians 4 is meaningless. We *can* choose what we are going to meditate upon–pain or joy; beauty or ugliness; truth or lies; purity or perversion; that which is noble or that which is contemptible; righteousness or evil. Paul urges us to learn how to think biblically by "put[ting] it into practice" (Philippians 4:9). The result is the presence of God Himself in the life of the person who obeys His prescription. "The God of peace will be with you" (Philippians 4:9).

May I urge you to memorize this scripture passage? If you review it daily and make it a part of your inner renewal, you will find it a powerful resource for permanent restoration of joy.

Finally, brothers, whatever is true, whatever is noble, whatever is right, whatever is pure, whatever is lovely, whatever is admirable–if anything is excellent or praiseworthy–think about such things. Whatever you have learned or received or heard from me, or seen in me–put it into practice. And the God of peace will be with you (Philippians 4:8,9).

The phone rang in Cliff's bedroom as he lay in bed reading the Bible. It was late at night and the children had been in bed for hours, but Cliff couldn't sleep. He put down the Bible and picked up the phone.

"Hello? Well, hi, Dad!" he said. "It's good to hear from you. Is everything okay?"

On the other end of the line, his father-in-law's voice was shaking with emotion. "Cliff, Miriam flew in to visit with us today. Her mother and I had been looking forward to seeing her, especially since she had told us about the problems you two have been having."

"Uh-huh," Cliff replied emptily.

"But Cliff, nothing could have prepared us for what she told us."

Cliff's heart sank. He knew how twisted Miriam's thinking had become. "Just what *did* she tell you, Dad?"

"She didn't come alone, Cliff. She came with another woman she described as a member of her 'family of choice.' When they sat down we tried to make conversation, but the tension was so thick you could almost taste it."

"What happened?"

"Cliff, I have to tell you something first," Miriam's father said. "For a while, her mother and I believed the things she was saying about you–that you had become harsh and unloving. But now I want to ask your forgiveness. We know we were wrong."

"I understand, Dad. Things have become so strange since she entered therapy that I almost believed her accusations myself."

"Well, the long and the short of it is that Miriam accused me of having molested her when she was a little girl. Can you believe it? I never–and I mean *never*–did *anything* to my little girls except love and protect them. Cliff, you've known me for years. Do you believe I could have done such a thing and not have been aware of it?"

"No, Dad," Cliff replied earnestly, "I don't believe it for even a second."

"What am I going to do, Cliff? She said that unless I confess that I raped her, she will never speak to me again. She also hinted that she might file charges against me! Cliff, how do I prove I *didn't* do something over thirty years ago?"

"How does *anyone* prove he didn't do something?" Cliff replied. "That's what is so crazy about this business of recovered memories. A therapist can invent any story, no matter how bizarre, and people will believe it. It doesn't seem to matter if there is absolutely no evidence to back up the account. All that matters is the narrative of the victim."

"But what can I do?" Cliff's father-in-law asked.

"I'm not sure, Dad, but I would get the rest of the family together as soon as possible and explain the situation. Ask everyone to pray that the Lord would break through the wall of lies that Satan has built around Miriam. If we are all united in prayer, in our attitudes toward Miriam, and in our determination to stand by the truth, I still believe Miriam can be restored. I am more and more convinced that this is a deep spiritual battle that can be won only with spiritual weapons."

"I think you're right, Cliff," Miriam's father said. "I think you're right."

❖ ❖ ❖

The next day, Miriam flew back to Denver with her friend and called Cliff. "Well, you may have heard already, but I finally confronted my father about the sexual abuse," she said in dead tones.

"Yes, Miriam, he called me. And I have to tell you that you are wrong. He never molested you, and I believe that deep in your heart you know that."

"How can you say that, Cliff?" Miriam responded angrily. "You weren't there. You didn't endure the torture–the ritual cutting with a knife on my chest and back. You weren't there when he burned me with incense while others in his coven took turns assaulting me."

"Oh, Miriam! Think clearly for a moment! If those things really happened, don't you think your chest and back would be scarred? But they aren't, Miriam. You know it and I know it. There is no way he could have abused you that way without leaving some kind of evidence. How does your therapist explain that?"

Miriam was silent for a few seconds. "I don't know how he did it, Cliff, but somehow he found a way to torture me without leaving the scars. Satanic cults have ways of controlling minds and memories and they are experts at covering up their trail. When they sacrifice babies, the authorities almost never find the body, do they? No! And do you know why? Because they are experts at covering up their evil deeds."

"No, Miriam! Not even satanic cults are able to cut and torture people without leaving scars. You have been convinced by the false teaching that things happened to you that you don't remember. Don't you see, Miriam? You've been deceived by a destructive fabrication of imcompetant therapy. Honey, I beg you, come home and let's work on this together!"

There was silence again at the other end of the line. Then she said, "I wish I could, Cliff, but I know that if I don't resolve this now, the abuse will start up all over again.

I can't allow you to do it to me again. Never again!" Then she hung up.

In her bedroom, Miriam sat on the edge of her bed in a daze. Her eyes were hollow and her hair was disheveled. She looked years older than her age and she had lost some weight.

"Oh, Cliff," she moaned, "if only you could see the truth!" But at that moment a thought flashed through her mind: "No, Miriam! It's time for *you* to see the truth!"

The word "truth" kept ringing through her mind. *Truth! I must find the truth!*

For the first time in months, Miriam looked around her room to find her Bible, but it was nowhere to be seen. Finally she spotted it on the floor, almost hidden under the bed. Slowly she picked it up and held it with trembling hands. *Where do I begin?* she thought.

She turned to the concordance in the back of her Bible and began looking for the word *truth.* Then, verse by verse, she began tracing the word through the Scriptures.

As she read, she became aware of a battle within. She wanted to believe what Cliff had said about her father, yet she couldn't bear the thought of disappointing her new family of choice. Her greatest fear, however, was that she might disappoint Dr. Powell, whom she had come to respect and admire for his wisdom and compassion. And to stop therapy now would mean turning away from her inner child and her alter personalities. *It would be like I was betraying them,* she thought.

Her eyes went out of focus for a moment and she shook her head, trying to clear her mind. *Whatever is true, Miriam! Think on these things!* And then other thoughts flooded her mind. *No, Miriam! Don't let Cliff fool you again! We know your dad abused you! Don't turn away from us, Miriam! We need you!*

A new wave of depression swept over Miriam with a power and darkness deeper than she had ever known. In agony she cried out, "Oh, God! Oh, God, where are you? Please help me! Oh, God, please help me!" She fell to her knees beside the bed, weeping in sorrow and confusion. She felt as though she could hardly breathe, and she struggled to draw air into her lungs through her constricted throat.

For a long time Miriam couldn't say anything. She groaned with misery too deep to express in words. Eventually the darkness began to lift and she was able to pray out loud. "Oh, God!" she said again and again. "Please show me what is true and what is not. If I'm wrong, I want to know it and confess it. I want to be with my family again. I want to be with Cliff and the children!"

A new surge of grief hit her and she began crying and moaning with sobs as her body jerked convulsively. The voices in her mind screamed at her. *You traitor! You fool! We are your truth! Listen to your heart and know what is true!*

Miriam looked at her Bible again. Though it was hard to focus her eyes because they were filled with tears, she pulled the Bible toward her and opened it to Philippians 4. Then she began to read out loud. "Whatever is true. . . ." She paused and closed her eyes as she repeated: "Whatever is true."

Suddenly her eyes opened wide. It was as though God had just cleared the fog from her mind. She stood to her feet in amazement and said, "None of it was true! *None* of it!"

She began to laugh and cry at the same time. Her emotions alternated between elation at the knowledge that her father was innocent and deep anger at Dr. Powell and others who had convinced her of a lie. Then a surge of guilt swept over her as she realized that she had chosen to walk a path that had led her away from her relationship with Christ.

"Oh, Jesus," she cried, "please forgive me! I've been such a fool! How could I have betrayed You and doubted Your Word? How could I have accused my own father?" Again, she broke into sobs of grief and bitterness.

Miriam had never known such despair–not even when she had first been convinced that her father had abused her.

Now that she knew the truth, her heart ached with shame and she wanted to die. The voices in her mind seemed to say, *Yes, Miriam! It's time to die! Your father will never forgive you. And what will your children think when you tell them it was all a big mistake? Think about what you've done to Cliff! And what about all the people at church who believed you? They would all be better off if you weren't here anymore.*

Miriam nodded in agreement and whispered, "I know. I know." She looked at the bathroom door and thought about the antidepressants in the medicine cabinet. It would be so easy and everyone's suffering would be over.

She slowly rose to her feet and shuffled with great effort into the bathroom. She opened the medicine cabinet and reached for the prescription bottle.

In an exhausted daze, she swallowed the pills one or two at a time until they were gone. As her eyes went slowly out of focus, she slumped to the floor and muttered with slurred speech, "Please forgive me, Jesus. Please . . . please . . . forgive . . ."

9

Changing
Your Attitudes

Wrong attitudes can literally kill a person. The way we think can produce success or failure, happiness or misery, health or disease. You've no doubt heard someone say, "He's going to worry himself to death!" It can actually happen.

According to some reports, about 2,000 American teenagers commit suicide each year. And it is estimated that for every suicide, there are up to 350 failed attempts. That means there may be as many as 700,000 teenage suicide attempts each year. Why are these young people so anxious to end their lives? Because of confusion, bitterness, and a sense of hopelessness. Their thinking and attitudes are wrong.

Columnist Joseph Perkins wrote, "If young Americans feel empty, it is because their hearts and minds have not been properly filled with values that can sustain them during those dark nights of the soul that everyone faces at some point along life's highway."[154]

He continues:

Past generations of Americans had a support system they could rely on during the turbulent times of adolescence and young adulthood. They could turn to their parents or their churches or their schools for guidance when confronting the vexing questions of life.

Nowadays, young Americans are pretty much left to themselves to figure out their place in the world. And with no core values to inform their life decisions, they bend toward self-destructive behavior, prurient sex, substance abuse, criminality, violence, suicide.[155]

If a preacher were to say that, people would call him harsh, legalistic, and unloving. But this is a secular columnist who had the common sense and courage to say what needed to be said.

Young people are not the only ones who struggle with wrong attitudes. Adults also suffer the debilitating effects of wrong thinking and sinful attitudes. In a column about social problems, Dr. Peter H. Gott said:

Regardless of the object of the fear, people with social phobias experience incapacitating anxiety, which leads not only to extreme discomfort but also to an obsession to avoid the situation. Thus, the phobia interferes with social activities, interpersonal relations and occupational responsibilities. Such people are especially apprehensive when dealing with authority figures (such as teachers or supervisors) or members of the opposite sex. Because of excruciating self-consciousness, phobiacs become progressively inwardly focused and concerned with negative self-evaluation. This leads to a vicious cycle of avoidance, insecurity and defeat. The disorder is also marked by loneliness, alcoholism (and tranquilizer abuse), depression and suicide.[156]

Notice Dr. Gott's observation that these people are suffering from "excruciating self-consciousness" and that they are "progressively inwardly focused."

Focusing on God

In pointed contrast, the Bible tells us to "fix [our] thoughts on Jesus, the apostle and high priest whom we confess" (Hebrews 3:1), and again, to "fix our eyes on Jesus, the author and perfecter of our faith" (Hebrews 12:2). Do you see the difference? Instead of focusing on ourselves, we are to fix our thoughts and eyes on Jesus, because when we do, our outlook on life changes for the better.

The Danger of Worry

Wrong focus leads to wrong attitudes, which in turn produce needless worries. And ultimately, worry is doubting the character and power of God to do what is best for us. That is why Jesus emphatically warned us against worry:

> Therefore I tell you, do not worry about your life, what you will eat or drink; or about your body, what you will wear. Is not life more important than food, and the body more important than clothes? Look at the birds of the air; they do not sow or reap or store away in barns, and yet your heavenly Father feeds them. Are you not much more valuable than they? Who of you by worrying can add a single hour to his life?
>
> And do you about clothes? See how the lilies of the field grow. They do not labor or spin. Yet I tell you that not even Solomon in all his splendor was dressed like one of these. If that is how

God clothes the grass of the field, which is here today and tomorrow is thrown into the fire, will he not much more clothe you, O you of little faith? So do not worry, saying, 'What shall we eat?' or 'What shall we drink?' or 'What shall we wear?' For the pagans run after all these things, and your heavenly Father knows that you need them. But seek first his kingdom and his righteousness, and all these things will be given to you as well. Therefore do not worry about tomorrow, for tomorrow will worry about itself. Each day has enough trouble of its own (Matthew 6:25-34).

Read the passage carefully and you will see that Jesus' emphasis is upon the faithfulness and compassion of God our Father and that we need to focus our minds and energies upon serving Him. To do so requires a radical change in attitude because we are usually focused upon ourselves and our own interests. The irony is that the more we seek to please ourselves, the less pleased we are, because self-focus promotes worry and bad attitudes.

Suffering and anxiety have a way of affecting every area of our existence–spiritual, mental, physical, and social. David wrote, "My life is consumed by anguish and my years by groaning; my strength fails because of my affliction, and my bones grow weak" (Psalm 31:10). Yet, David found a solution for his anguish: "On my bed I remember you; I think of you through the watches of the night" (Psalm 63:6). Are you having trouble sleeping? Learn to meditate on the goodness of God, and you will find that peace will return in proportion to the time you spend with Him.

The Benefit of Trusting God

Recently, during one of our family Bible studies, we talked about God's consistent kindness to us over the years.

Both Marlowe and I were blessed to be born into families who truly believed in Jesus Christ as Savior. Both of our fathers also served as pastors of Bible-believing churches. In addition, we have been blessed with good health, joyful children, material goods adequate to meet our needs, and a Christ-honoring church.

Don't think, however, that our families have never experienced trials or suffering. Marlowe's parents served as missionaries in Africa before her father's health broke and they had to return to America. After that her father pastored small churches in New England while both parents supported themselves through hard physical labor.

My parents went through many heartbreaking episodes during their thirty years of ministry in various churches, which ended with Dad's heart attack and cancers. Yet, through it all, God showed Himself to be their Strength and Provider, and they are now home with Him in heaven.

Our parents experienced profound depressions, intense physical need, and times of nearly unbearable confusion. Yet they found relief and healing through the power of Jesus Christ as they meditated upon His Word and committed themselves to lovingly obeying Him.

Marlowe's mother, Mom Donner, experienced deep sorrow in her childhood when her mother died. During her teenage years, her stepmother treated her with cold cruelty. Many people would say she must be in great need of therapy to deal with an abusive past. Unwilling to accept worldly labels or to give in to self-pity, however, Mom Donner has shown consistent cheer and courage throughout her life, and she is an inspiration to our family and to everyone she meets.

I'll forever cherish a video that I taped several years ago, in which Mom Donner was in a hurricane in Cape Cod. The wind was roaring overhead as it pounded New England furiously. All around us in the surrounding forest, trees were cracking and poppin gas limbs broke off and flew throught the air. We all huddled inside Mom and Dad Donner's bungalow—all except Mom. She was out walking around in the driveway that circles the house, thoroughly enjoying the awesome majesty of the moment!

Marlowe and I have experienced times of deep sorrow and loss. We have watched loved ones suffer and die. We cared for my aging mother after Dad graduated to heaven and we shared her sorrow and loneliness until she rejoined him.

We have been lied about, betrayed by coworkers, accused of wrongdoing, and threatened by some people who claim to be followers of Christ. Yet we have found deep and abiding comfort every time we have gone to the Word of God and applied it to our aching hearts.

As we look back, our brief moments of suffering fade in comparison to the many joyous times we've experienced. Ours is a home filled with laughter and peace. And that is because of the Lord Jesus and His powerful Word!

No matter what psychological experts say, we *are* able to change our attitudes by focusing our hearts, minds, and wills on the Lord Jesus and His Word. Do you remember what we learned in Philippians 4? Did you memorize verse 8? If not, I encourage you to do so. It will become a tremendous resource for your soul as you restructure your attitudes.

Expressing Gratitude

Another powerful tool God has given us to help change our attitudes is the discipline of giving thanks. Just as with forgiveness, gratitude begins with obedience rather than our feelings.

Paul writes, "Give thanks in all circumstances, for this is God's will for you in Christ Jesus" (1 Thessalonians 5:18). Notice he doesn't say, "As soon as you *feel* thankful, give thanks to God." And how often should we express gratitude? In Ephesians 5:20 Paul says, "*Always* giving thanks to God the Father for *everything*, in the name of our Lord Jesus

Christ" (emphasis added). Paul amplifies this concept when he writes, "Whatever you do, whether in word or deed, do it all in the name of the Lord Jesus, giving thanks to God the Father through him" (Colossians 3:17).

Paul then links thankfulness to the problem of anxiety in Philippians 4:6: "Do not be anxious about anything, but in everything, by prayer and petition, with thanksgiving, present your requests to God."

I call this healing process "willful gratitude." It is the choice to be thankful for everything. The moment we begin to praise the Lord and thank Him for His blessings, we begin feeling better. The feelings don't have to be there first; they are the *result* of obedient, willful gratitude to God.

Are you grateful to the Lord for all that He has done in your life? Then follow David's example when he says, "Praise the LORD, O my soul, and forget not all his benefits" (Psalm 103:2). We ought to thank Him for loving sinners like us and for providing a way to eternal life. We ought to praise Him for all that He has placed in our hands, whether it be a little or a lot. He owes us nothing; we owe Him everything. As David said, "From birth I have relied on you; you brought me forth from my mother's womb. I will ever praise you" (Psalm 71:6).

Refreshment for the Soul

Learning to praise the Lord with genuine gratitude is a healing and refreshing exercise for our soul. It will lighten our burden. In spite of failing health, unfair attacks by others, or deep disappointment, we can say with David, "I will always have hope; I will praise you more and more" (Psalm 71:14).

The more we understand about our God, His love, His unending mercies and grace, and His power to save and deliver, the more we will experience peace and joy. Peace and joy–those are the elements that produce the true happiness that every person so desperately seeks.

A heart full of peace and joy is difficult to conceal, according to Proverbs 15:13: "A happy heart makes the face cheerful, but heartache crushes the spirit."

Perhaps you are saying, "I *have* a deep heartache and my spirit *is* crushed." But you don't have to stay that way! God has provided a medicine that heals the wounded heart. Read the following passage and rejoice in the healing God offers:

> Praise the LORD, O my soul; all my inmost being, praise his holy name. Praise the LORD, O my soul, and forget not all his benefits–who forgives all your sins and heals all your diseases, who redeems your life from the pit and crowns you with love and compassion, who satisfies your desires with good things so that your youth is renewed like the eagle's (Psalm 103:1-5).

A person who allows himself to be labeled a victim all his life will live in a state of mental and spiritual oppression, and the inevitable result is misery. "All the days of the oppressed are wretched, but the cheerful heart has a continual feast" (Proverbs 15:15).

The Good News

How can a wounded heart experience genuine joy? By believing and receiving good news from God. "A cheerful look brings joy to the heart, and good news gives health to the bones" (Proverbs 15:30). Good news–that's what the gospel is! It's the best news anyone has ever heard–that God has provided a way of salvation to all who will believe in His Son.

It is tragic for Christians to believe that the world offers a better solution than the one God has given to deal with inner pain. It is the gospel of Christ that liberates and heals. "How beautiful on the mountains are the feet of those who bring good news, who proclaim peace, who bring good tidings, who proclaim salvation, who say to Zion, 'Your God reigns!'" (Isaiah 52:7).

This is the reason Jesus came to earth: to deal with our deepest needs. Isaiah predicted it when he wrote, "The Spirit of the Sovereign LORD is on me, because the LORD has anointed me to preach good news to the poor. He has sent me to bind up the brokenhearted, to proclaim freedom for the captives and release from darkness for the prisoners" (Isaiah 61:1).

The fulfillment of that prophecy was revealed when Jesus read that same passage and then explained, "Today this scripture is fulfilled in your hearing" (Luke 4:21). His ministry was to bring God's good news, which produces healing.

Why It Doesn't Always "Work"

Why doesn't every believer enjoy the peace and joy promised by God? That's essentially what T.R. asked me one day on our radio broadcast, *Return to the Word*. "I'm an agnostic," he said in a gentle and sincere manner, "but I have a relative in Texas who has been a good Christian for most of his life. I have a lot of respect for Christians who really walk the walk, and he has. How do you explain the fact that he has suddenly become so depressed that my sister had to put him in a retirement home?"

I asked T.R. for more information about his relative: how long he had been depressed, if there were any biological symptoms, and if there had been a full medical examination to eliminate the possibility that he had an organic disorder. When T.R. told me that the depression had come on virtually overnight, I told him that the relative needed to have another medical evaluation, since a sudden depression often indicates a physiological problem.

"If all organic possibilities have been eliminated," I continued, "it may be that your relative has a faulty understanding of God's love, forgiveness, and power. Perhaps he has done something wrong that he believes has come between himself and God. He needs to learn the good news of God's forgiveness and cleansing when we confess our sins to Him." I shared with T.R. the glorious truth of 1 John 1:9, and he arranged to call me later at my office when I was off the air.

Again, why doesn't every believer enjoy the peace and joy promised by God? Because many believers have failed to study and meditate on His Word. They have not grasped the truths of God's grace and forgiveness. Others have simply chosen to disobey the biblical truths they already understand, and they live in a spiritual twilight zone caught between guilt and the healing God offers.

As someone has well said, "Many Christians have just enough faith to make them miserable." They can't enjoy the world and its sin because they know the truth of the gospel, but they also can't enjoy their walk with God because they still cling to the world. James says that such a person is "a double-minded man, unstable in all he does" (James 1:8).

People like this are spiritually stunted. To them, Paul writes, "Brothers, stop thinking like children. In regard to evil be infants, but in your thinking be adults" (1 Corinthians 14:20).

Cultivating Thankfulness

A Willingness to Obey

The first step to cultivating thankfulness is to make a conscious choice to express this attitude. To give thanks is to obey the revealed will of our Father. We are expressly commanded to "give thanks in all circumstances, for this is God's will for you in Christ Jesus" (1 Thessalonians 5:18).

It's no use for us to tell God, "I can't do it" when He tells us we can.

A woman who had decided to divorce her husband told a counselor, "I just can't love my husband any more!" Her counselor replied, "You can't or you *won't?*" The woman thought for a moment and then replied, "I guess you're right. I won't!"

Whether or not we give thanks isn't a matter of our *inability* to obey, but our *willingness.* David recognized the connection between our willingness to obey and the joy God offers when he wrote, "Restore to me the joy of your salvation and grant me a willing spirit, to sustain me" (Psalm 51:12).

We must first be willing to obey God's command to be thankful at all times.

Making a Praise List

A second step in developing willful gratitude is to consciously list and declare the blessings God has given us. One way to do this is to tell other people the specific things He has done for us. David knew the importance of praising God enthusiastically before others. He said, "I will give you thanks in the great assembly; among throngs of people I will praise you" (Psalm 35:18).

Telling other people about God's goodness helps to make our thankfulness more tangible. It puts us on record that God has been kind to us. Verbal testimony has a healing effect on the teller and the listeners, so praise God out loud to others and praise Him often. As Proverbs 11:25 tells us, "He who refreshes others will himself be refreshed."

A grateful spirit will change our attitude, our personality, and our countenance. I have noticed within myself a flow of new energy and peace when I have consciously praised and thanked the Lord. And I have experienced the feeling of being drained and exhausted when I have given in to an attitude of complaining.

Looking to the Past and Future

A third principle for developing a willful gratitude is to praise God for the past and trust Him for the future. Solomon understood this truth when he reminded the Israelites of God's continual blessings in the past. "Praise be to the LORD, who has given rest to his people Israel just as he promised. Not one word has failed of all the good promises he gave through his servant Moses" (1 Kings 8:56).

One of the few areas of the past we *are* commanded to review is that which God has done. Peter writes, "Dear friends, this is now my second letter to you. I have written both of them as reminders to stimulate you to wholesome thinking" (2 Peter 3:1). That is a perfect definition of willful gratitude—"wholesome thinking."

Practicing Praise

A fourth step in the process of changing our attitudes is to give thanks continually. Make a practice of giving thanks so that it becomes a habit. Paul wrote, "Whatever you have learned or received or heard from me, or seen in me—put it into practice. And the God of peace will be with you" (Philippians 4:9).

A Solution That Works

When you find yourself becoming depressed again and again, remember that the source of your joy is the Lord. David had to remind himself of that truth from time to time. He said, "Why are you downcast, O my soul? Why so disturbed within me? Put your hope in God, for I will yet praise him, my Savior and my God" (Psalm 42:11).

After I preached on this subject one Sunday, a lady stopped to speak with me on her way out of the worship center. "I was severely depressed and under psychiatric care for a couple of years," she said, "and nothing seemed to help. But then I got better. When my psychiatrist asked what had happened to me, I told him, 'I just began praising the Lord and thanking Him for all He has done.' He was amazed and said to me, 'Nobody comes out of such a serious depression like that.'"

But *she* did. And so can you–by exercising willful gratitude.

❖ ❖ ❖

Cliff heard the siren of an ambulance in the distance as it sped through the streets blocks away. He sat in the family room, Bible in hand, praying that the Lord would do something to bring healing to his marriage.

Becky and Eric were asleep in bed. Earlier, Becky had been crying. She asked Cliff, "Dad, why did Mom leave us? Doesn't she love us anymore?"

"She still loves you, sweetheart," Cliff said sadly. "Don't ever think she doesn't. She's just terribly confused right now and we have to pray that the Lord will help bring her back to us."

"I don't understand, Dad," Becky sobbed. "She didn't come to my school concert!"

"I know, dear," Cliff said as he comforted her. "Let's pray for her right now." Cliff then looked up and motioned to Eric to come join them. Eric scampered over and jumped into his father's lap.

Becky dried her cheek with her sleeve and began praying. "Dear Jesus, please be with Mom tonight and help her to come back home. We miss her so much!"

Tears welled up in Cliff's eyes. He wiped them away so the children wouldn't see.

"And Lord," Becky continued, "please help Daddy. Thank you that he stayed with us. Help him to be happy again someday. Amen."

Cliff swallowed hard and turned to Eric. "Do you want to pray, son?"

"Okay, Daddy." He bowed his head and clasped his hands. "Dear Jesus, please help Mama come home so our house can be happy again. Thank you, Jesus. Amen."

Cliff tucked the children into bed and returned to the family room and sat down, exhausted. He was working hard at three part-time jobs in an effort to make enough money to pay the bills. His heart ached when he thought about happier times–when the family was united and he and Miriam served the Lord together at their church. He felt useless now, and it seemed that every dream he had ever had was destroyed. At times he wondered where God was in all of this.

Suddenly the phone rang. Cliff jumped involuntarily, then took a deep breath and picked up the receiver. "Hello?"

"Is this Clifford Chase?" an authoritative voice said.

"Yes."

"This is Dr. Orvin at St. Joseph's hospital. I'm afraid I have some bad news for you."

Cliff's heart dropped and he swallowed with a dry mouth. "What...what is it?"

"An ambulance just brought your wife into emergency. It seems as though she has swallowed some pills. It doesn't look good for her. If I were you, I'd get here immediately."

Cliff stood to his feet, shaking. "Of course," he said. "I'll be there as soon as I can get someone to watch the children."

"I'd hurry, Mr. Chase. I really would."

Cliff hung up the phone, shook his head, and tried to catch his breath. For a moment, he couldn't think who to call. Then he thought of Wallace Kramer, one of the elders at the church. He quickly dialed the number. "Wallace? This is Cliff. Listen, I just got a call from St. Joseph's. Miriam took some pills and is in emergency. I've got to get there right away. Can Marge watch the kids for me?"

"Of course, Cliff," Wallace said. "We'll both be right over. I'm going to drive you, okay?"

"Thanks, Wallace," Cliff said. "That would help a lot."

Wallace and Marge Kramer arrived within twenty minutes. As soon as Marge went into the house, Cliff ran to the car and jumped in. Wallace sped through the deserted streets and pulled up to the emergency entrance of St. Joseph's to let Cliff out.

"I'll park the car and be right in," he said as Cliff jumped out and ran inside.

Cliff hurried to the admission counter and spoke rapidly to the nurse, saying, "I'm Clifford Chase. I was told that my wife Miriam Chase was brought in a short time ago."

"Yes, she was." The nurse looked at him and handed him the form she was working on. "Here's her paperwork, Mr. Chase. I'll need some signatures."

"Is she . . . is she . . . going to make it?" Cliff asked as he signed the forms.

"It's too early to tell," the nurse replied. "It doesn't look good."

"Can I see her?"

"In a few minutes, perhaps. I'll let the doctor know that you're here."

Wallace hurried in, looked around the room, spotted Cliff, and joined him at the counter. "Have you heard anything yet?"

"No," Cliff replied. "The nurse is checking with the doctor right now." He and Wallace sat down and waited.

It seemed like a long time had gone by before the nurse returned. When she did, Cliff and Wallace stood and walked to meet her.

"Can I see her now?" Cliff asked.

"Yes," the nurse answered. "She isn't conscious, but the doctor said you can come back with me." She noticed Wallace and said, "No one else can come. Sorry."

Wallace squeezed Cliff's arm and said, "I'll be out here praying for you and Miriam."

"I know you will. Thanks, Wallace, for being such a good friend."

Cliff hurried to catch up with the nurse, who was already walking down the hallway. She led him through several doors and past a series of curtains until they came to a cubicle where a doctor and three nurses were working on Miriam.

A heart monitor beeped and measured Miriam's pulse and blood pressure. Intravenous fluid dripped into her arm. A nurse lifted Miriam's eyelids to view her eyes. "Dilated," she said as she wrote on a chart.

"She's having trouble breathing, doctor," another nurse said. Miriam's skin was pale and clammy and her lips and fingernails were turning blue. A nurse covered her with a blanket. Suddenly, Miriam went into convulsions and began sweating profusely.

Cliff closed his eyes and began to pray silently.

Foam drooled out of Miriam's mouth, and for a moment she stopped breathing altogether. Just as the doctor prepared to do CPR, Miriam took a deep breath.

"Did anyone bring the prescription bottle?" the doctor asked loudly.

"Yes, doctor," a nurse replied. "We have it right here."

The doctor took the vial and squinted to read the label. "It figures!" he said. "Perphenazine and amitriptyline."

"What's that?" Cliff asked a nurse close to him.

"It's a combination drug–an antipsychotic and an antidepressant. It's usually reserved for people with a severe, agitated depression or profound anxiety. It can be deadly in quantity. Do you have any idea why she would overdose?"

He shook his head. "I don't know for sure. She left home nearly two years ago and I knew she had been depressed, but I never thought she'd do anything like this."

Cliff sat in a chair in the corner and began praying again. After more than an hour, Miriam's condition improved marginally. The nurses continued to monitor her vital signs as the doctor walked over to Cliff. "I think she's going to make it, Mr. Chase," he said with a weary smile, "but we're going to have to keep a close watch on her for a couple of days."

Cliff nodded. "Thank you, doctor," he said. "I'm grateful for all you've done."

Miriam was moved to a private room in the hospital and Cliff went back out to report to Wallace. "She's doing better, but I think I should stay with her for a while. Do you think Marge could stay with the kids a little longer?"

"Of course. Take as long as you want. Give us a call at your house when you're done and I'll come back and pick you up."

"Thanks, Wallace. I appreciate you so much!" Cliff said with tears in his eyes as he shook Wallace's hand gratefully.

Cliff hurried to Miriam's room. Monitors, fluid bottles, and an oxygen mask were hooked up to her pale, thin body and made her look even more fragile. There was a beeping sound from one of the monitors.

Cliff pulled a chair close to Miriam's bed and sat down. He took the hand that was not attached to a machine and stroked it gently. "Oh, Miriam," he whispered. "I love you so much. Please get well."

He bowed his head in prayer. "O Lord," he said, "please restore Miriam to full health. Please bring her back to our home. The children need her." He choked with emotion and couldn't speak for a few moments. Finally he was able to continue. "And I need her, too."

Miriam's hand was cold and seemed lifeless. Her breathing was shallow and rapid. Every few minutes, a nurse came in to check on her condition.

After about an hour, Cliff began to get sleepy. When the nurse came in, she said with a concerned smile, "Don't you think it's about time you got some rest, Mr. Chase? We'll call you if there's a major change in her status."

"I suppose you're right," Cliff said reluctantly. "But please call me right away if . . . if she gets worse."

"I will. But I think she's past the crisis for the time being. Go on home and get some rest."

Cliff called Wallace, who came and drove Cliff back to his house.

"Thanks, Marge," Cliff said as Wallace's wife met them at the front door.

"The kids are still asleep." Marge said. "They didn't even know you were gone."

"Call us as soon as you hear anything," Wallace said.

"I will, Wallace. Thanks again."

"Oh, I almost forgot," Marge said, turning back to Cliff. "I called the prayer chain at our church and at Faith Evangelical. People are praying, Cliff."

"I know, Marge. Thanks!"

Cliff slumped down in his recliner in the family room, too tired to go upstairs to bed. He began praying again, but soon, in spite of himself, he fell asleep.

❖ ❖ ❖

Miriam regained consciousness the next morning and had a terrible headache. She was confused by her new surroundings. She looked around the room and tried to move, but the cords and tubes pulled at her arm with a sharp pain.

"Ouch!" she said. The pain seemed to clear her mind. "Where am I?" She saw the call button attached to her bedrail and pressed it.

Soon a nurse walked into the room. She looked at Miriam with a smile and said, "So! You finally decided to wake up, did you?"

"Where am I?" Miriam asked.

"You're at St. Joseph's hospital. You overdosed on your medicine. Do you remember?"

Miriam wrinkled her brow, trying to recall the events of

the night before. Slowly, it began to come back to her. And with the memory came sorrow and guilt. She began to cry.

"There, there," the nurse said kindly. "There's no need to cry. You're going to be fine."

Miriam tried to control her tears, but found that she couldn't and turned her face away. "Please," she said, "just let me rest."

"All right, but I'm just down the hallway. Push the button if you need me."

"I will," Miriam said, still facing the wall.

When the nurse was gone, Miriam began to think to herself, *I can't even kill myself right!* She began crying again. *Oh, Cliff! I need you! Why aren't you here? Oh God, please, please help Cliff to be able to love me again. Help him to be able to forgive me.*

Exhaustion overcame her and she fell back asleep for the rest of the day.

That evening, Cliff drove to the hospital with Becky and Eric. "Do you think Mom will want to see us?" Becky asked.

"I'm sure she'll be glad to see all of us," Cliff said, but deep inside, he wasn't so sure.

Eric carried a bouquet of flowers and Becky had a box with a new bathrobe and slippers. They made their way to the elevator and rode it to the fifth floor. Then they turned left, walked into the circular ward, and went to Miriam's room. The children knocked softly as Cliff stood out of view.

"Come in," Miriam said weakly.

The children pushed the door open and looked in. Miriam looked toward the door and could only make out their silhouettes in the doorway.

"Who is it?" she said, still confused.

"It's us, Mommy!" Eric said cheerfully as he walked in holding the flowers.

"Oh, Eric!" Miriam said. "Come here! I'm so glad to see you!"

Eric hurried to her side. "See what I brought you?"

Miriam took the flowers from Eric. "Oh, Eric! They're beautiful! Where did you get them?"

"From Dad!" Eric said proudly. "And look what Becky has for you!"

"Here, Mom," Becky said awkwardly as she handed Miriam the box. "I hope you'll like it."

"What is it, darling?" Miriam said.

"It's a new bathrobe with a matching pair of slippers. Shall I open it for you?"

"Yes, dear, please."

Becky opened the box and held up the robe. "See? It's your favorite color!"

"Oh, Becky! It's beautiful! Where did you get it?"

"From Dad, of course," Becky answered.

Miriam looked to see if Cliff was with the children. "Is your father here with you?"

"Why, Mom?" Becky asked. "Do you want to see him?"

Miriam nodded sadly. "More than anything."

"Then why don't you ask him to come in?" Eric said with simple innocence.

Miriam looked up in surprise. "Is he really here?"

Both Becky and Eric nodded with big smiles on their faces.

"Cliff!" Miriam called. "Cliff! Please come in!"

Cliff appeared in the doorway and hesitated. "Are you sure?"

Miriam held out her free hand and whispered, "Oh, yes!"

Cliff hurried to her side and took her hand. "Oh, Miriam," he said as tears filled his eyes, "I was so worried about you!"

Miriam began to cry. Eric and Becky looked at each other, wondering what to do. Cliff gently wiped Miriam's tears away while his own fell onto her bed.

Miriam looked up through her tears and whispered, "Can you ever forgive me?"

Cliff's eyes opened wide with surprise. "Why . . . of course . . . I forgive you! Will you forgive me, too?"

"If there is anything to forgive, Cliff, I *do*, with all my heart! I am so sorry I put you and the kids through all this suffering! I'm so ashamed!" And she began to cry again.

"Don't cry, Mommy," Eric said as he hurried to her side. "Just come back home with us! Will you?"

Miriam smiled through her tears. "If your father will let me, I'll come right home as soon as they release me from here!"

Eric looked up at Cliff. "Will you, Daddy? Can Mommy come home?"

Cliff smiled as wide as his mouth could spread, looked into Miriam's eyes, and said, "Your Mom will always be welcome in our house!" He squeezed Miriam's hand and she squeezed his in return.

Becky ran to the bedside and lay her head on Miriam's shoulder. "It's what I've prayed for! It's exactly what I've prayed for!"

"Thank You, Jesus!" Cliff said out loud. "Thank you for bringing us back together. Please heal our marriage and our home. Help us to forgive one another and to regain our love for each other once again."

"Yes, Jesus," Miriam whispered in agreement.

Just then a nurse entered the room. "I'm afraid it's time for Mrs. Chase to get some more rest. You can come back tomorrow."

"Do they have to go so soon?" Miriam protested.

"Yes, but they can visit you again tomorrow."

The children started walking toward the door, but Cliff stayed by the bed as Miriam clung to his hand with a strong grip.

"I'll see you in the morning, darling," he said tenderly. "Is there anything I can bring?"

"Just yourself," Miriam replied, "and a Bible. Please bring that."

"I will," Cliff promised. He walked to the door and took the children's hands. They waved good-bye to Miriam, and as they walked down the hallway, they laughed with the greatest joy they had known since Miriam had left home.

10

The Healing Effect of Serving Others

The happiest people I have known are those who have willingly committed themselves to serving others. Though their lives are often full of pain and suffering, they have found great joy in serving those around them. Indeed, serving others is a necessary part of God's healing the wounded heart.

There is a woman in our church who has suffered intense physical agony for years. Her medical prescriptions have added to her suffering; they cause her to experience excruciating pain at even the slightest touch. Yet I have watched her minister faithfully to other people year after year; cooking meals, leading our food and clothing ministry, and giving unselfishly of her time, energies, and finances. She has been an inspiration to our entire congregation.

I smile when I think of my father- and mother-in-law, who in their eighties still visit "the old folks" at nursing homes. They simply refuse to sit back and wait for death; instead, they are determined to use their days to help people. They are happiest when they are serving others.

We have a group of older people in our church who continually reach out with love and kindness to others who are lonely. Recently, our oldest member, Marion, turned 93, and these caring folks went to Marion's nursing home with a birthday cake and had an impromptu birthday party. By ministering to Marion, they lifted their own spirits as well.

The Value of Service

Nehemiah understood the value of serving the Lord. Many Christians have heard the amazing story of how he worked tirelessly to rebuild the city walls of Jerusalem. After the wall was completed, he prayed, "Remember me for this, O my God, and do not blot out what I have so faithfully done for the house of my God and its services" (Nehemiah 13:14).

Our service for the Lord does not have to be as dramatic or historic as was Nehemiah's. There are many seemingly ordinary yet important ways to serve God. Jesus reminds us that He values the "little" deeds of mercy: "I was hungry and you gave me something to eat, I was thirsty and you gave me something to drink, I was a stranger and you invited me in, I needed clothes and you clothed me, I was sick and you looked after me, I was in prison and you came to visit me" (Matthew 25:35,36).

No Ministry Is Insignificant

There are times our labor for the Lord seems so insignificant. After all, what eternal value can there be in mending clothes, cooking meals, teaching children's Sunday school, or cleaning the church? Yet one woman was memorialized in the book of Acts for her humble deeds of service.

In Joppa there was a disciple named Tabitha (which, when translated, is Dorcas), who was always doing good and helping the poor. About that time she became sick and died, and her body was washed and placed in an upstairs room. Lydda was near Joppa; so when the disciples heard that Peter was in Lydda, they sent two men to him and urged him, "Please come at once!"

Peter went with them, and when he arrived he was taken upstairs to the room. All the widows stood around him, crying and showing him the robes and other clothing that Dorcas had made while she was still with them.

Peter sent them all out of the room; then he got down on his knees and prayed. Turning toward the dead woman, he said, "Tabitha, get up." She opened her eyes, and seeing Peter she sat up. He took her by the hand and helped her to her feet. Then he called the believers and the widows and presented her to them alive. This became known all over Joppa, and many people believed in the Lord (Acts 9:36-42).

Tabitha's ministry of service was so important and the church longed so much for her that the Lord raised her from the dead as a testimony to the entire city of Joppa.

We do not know much more about Tabitha, but I believe that she was a woman who knew the joy of serving others. I also wouldn't be surprised to discover in heaven that she had suffered a great deal of pain during her lifetime. It seems that the people who have gifts of service are often those who have suffered deeply. Instead of dwelling on their own pain, however, they have learned that there is healing and happiness in ministering to others.

Service as a Source of Healing

I have yet to see anyone truly healed by "working through the past," or by "embracing one's own pain." I have not met anyone who has recovered from a traumatic childhood by looking inward or by recovering memories or by catering to an inner child. Nor have I found anyone who has discovered God or true happiness by sharing his intimate failures with a support group.

Worldly therapy says that we must take care of ourselves before we can help others. In contrast, Jesus says, "whoever wants to become great among you must be your servant" (Mark 10:43). Such service is not to be done resentfully or legalistically, but out of love. Paul tell us, "You, my brothers, were called to be free. But do not use your freedom to indulge the sinful nature; rather, serve one another in love" (Galatians 5:13).

We are commanded to take every opportunity to minister to others: "As we have opportunity, let us do good to all people, especially to those who belong to the family of believers" (Galatians 6:10). The ideal woman described in Proverbs "opens her arms to the poor and extends her hands to the needy" (Proverbs 31:20). Service that comes joyfully, voluntarily, and enthusiastically is the kind that heals.

The Call to Service

Two Samaritan Stories

In the book of Luke, Jesus told a poignant story about a man who had learned the secret of serving unselfishly:

> Jesus said: "A man was going down from Jerusalem to Jericho, when he fell into the hands of robbers. They stripped him of his clothes, beat him and went away, leaving him half dead. A priest happened to be going down the same road, and when he saw the man, he passed by on the other side. So too, a Levite, when he came to the place and saw him, passed by on the other

side. But a Samaritan, as he traveled, came where the man was; and when he saw him, he took pity on him. He went to him and bandaged his wounds, pouring on oil and wine. Then he put the man on his own donkey, took him to an inn and took care of him. The next day he took out two silver coins and gave them to the innkeeper. 'Look after him,' he said, 'and when I return, I will reimburse you for any extra expense you may have.'

Which of these three do you think was a neighbor to the man who fell into the hands of robbers?"

The expert in the law replied, "The one who had mercy on him."

Jesus told him, "Go and do likewise" (Luke 10:30-37).

There is another interesting but less-known story about Samaritans and it also involved an unusual kindness. It's found in 2 Chronicles. There we read that Israel, with its capital now in Samaria, had conquered Judah and planned to turn their relatives into slaves. But a prophet warned the Samaritan Israelites that God's judgment would fall on them if they did so, and they repented and showed kindness instead.

The soldiers gave up the prisoners and plunder in the presence of the officials and all the assembly. The men designated by name took the prisoners, and from the plunder they clothed all who were naked. They provided them with clothes and sandals, food and drink, and healing balm. All those who were weak they put on donkeys. So they took them back to their fellow countrymen at Jericho, the City of Palms, and returned to Samaria (2 Chronicles 28:14,15).

Notice that the Samaritan Israelites not only let their prisoners go free, but they also returned their possessions, clothed those who were naked, gave them food and medicine, and even provided transportation back to Judah. I wonder if the Samaritan in the book of Luke had ever heard this account about his ancestors. In both stories, God used the despised and rejected half-breed Samaritans as an example of unselfish service that brings the blessing of God.

True Religion

Christians sometimes have the mistaken idea that the Lord is more interested in formal religion than caring for other people. Look at what God tells us in the Old Testament:

> Is not this the kind of fasting I have chosen: to loose the chains of injustice and untie the cords of the yoke, to set the oppressed free and break every yoke? Is it not to share your food with the hungry and to provide the poor wanderer with shelter–when you see the naked, to clothe him, and not to turn away from your own flesh and blood? Then your light will break forth like the dawn, and your healing will quickly appear; then your righteousness will go before you (Isaiah 58:6-8).

Notice that the Lord connects *our* healing with the serving of *others*. Paul picks up the same theme when he writes, "In everything I did, I showed you that by this kind of hard work we must help the weak, remembering the words the Lord Jesus himself said: 'It is more blessed to give than to receive'" (Acts 20:35).

The world tells us that we must take care of ourselves and indulge our own desires, but the Bible says, "We who are strong ought to bear with the failings of the weak and not to please ourselves" (Romans 15:1). Some people might respond, "But that command is for the *strong*, and I am a weak victim of abuse. I need someone to carry *my* burden." But Paul quickly reminds us, "Carry each other's burdens, and in this way you will fulfill the law of Christ" (Galatians 6:2). *Everyone* is called to help others, no matter how wounded we think we are.

We may be deeply religious and read the Bible faithfully. We might even memorize extensive passages and pray diligently. But God is not impressed unless we are actively ministering to others as well. James says, "Religion that God our Father accepts as pure and faultless is this: to look after orphans and widows in their distress and to keep oneself from being polluted by the world" (James 1:27).

The Motive for Service

Our motivation for this kind of service should not be obedience alone, though that is an honorable motive. God also wants our service to come from the heart. "We continually remember before our God and Father your work produced by faith, *your labor prompted by love*, and your endurance inspired by hope in our Lord Jesus Christ" (1 Thessalonians 1:3, emphasis added).

We may never get the recognition we deserve. Our unselfish gifts of time and energy might never be announced at an awards banquet or mentioned on the evening news broadcast. Yet it is important that we serve enthusiastically, knowing that ultimately, we are doing it because we love the Lord. Even when it seems as though no one appreciates our work, we can have full confidence that the Lord is keeping an accurate account. Paul says, "My dear brothers, stand firm. Let nothing move you. Always give yourselves fully to the work of the Lord, because you know that your labor in the Lord is not in vain" (1 Corinthians 15:58).

Perhaps you are asking, "But how does this relate to the healing of *my* wounded heart?" We find a clue in the miraculous story of God's deliverance of Israel from the Egyptians: "If you listen carefully to the voice of the LORD your God and do what is right in his eyes, if you pay attention to his commands and keep all his decrees, I will not bring on you any of the diseases I brought on the Egyptians, for I am the LORD who heals you" (Exodus 15:26). Do you see the pattern? Listening, obedience, and blessing. It's that same spiritual principle we looked at in James 1:22-25, where we are told to live as hearers *and* doers of the Word.

The principle is the same today. If we pay attention to God's instructions and lovingly do what He says, we also will experience blessing and healing from His hand.

God's Paradoxical Ways

We may find at times that God's healing does not happen exactly the way we expected. God sometimes works in ways that surprise us. He says, "'My thoughts are not your thoughts, neither are your ways my ways,' declares the LORD. 'As the heavens are higher than the earth, so are my ways higher than your ways and my thoughts than your thoughts'" (Isaiah 55:8,9).

God's ways may seem paradoxical to us. The Bible says, "Give to the poor, and you will have treasure" (Matthew 19:21); "everyone who has left houses or brothers or sisters or father or mother or children or fields for my sake will receive a hundred times as much and will inherit eternal life" (Matthew 19:29); "whoever wants to save his life will lose it, but whoever loses his life for me and for the gospel will save it" (Mark 8:35); "if anyone wants to be first, he must be the very last, and the servant of all" (Mark 9:35); "I consider everything a loss . . . that I may gain Christ" (Philippians 3:8). Though these statements are paradoxical, they are true and worthy of our trust. And though it may be hard to believe that healing can come through serving others, we can trust God to do exactly as He promises.

True Inner Healing

The world promises cures that it cannot deliver. In contrast, Paul tells us that the gospel is not just "wise and persuasive words," but it is proven true "with a demonstration of the Spirit's power" (1 Corinthians 2:4). God promises healing that changes our very character so that we become more like His own Son. This is a result only God can produce, because dealing with our inner being is beyond human therapy.

The healing of our wounded hearts is not a matter of gazing within, focusing on the pains and sorrows of our past, or recalling our sinful failures for other people to analyze. Permanent healing comes from enthusiastically living life God's way by joyfully following the principles He has revealed in His Word, and allowing the Holy Spirit to produce His fruit in us so that we become more like Christ.

No other therapy will produce lasting results so rapidly as learning to love other people as Christ loves us. It is truly the miracle cure for our wounded hearts.

Miriam was released from the hospital once her vital signs returned to a normal level and the doctor was satisfied that the crisis was over. Cliff and the children hurried to the hospital to take her home.

Cliff stopped at the nurses' station and told the children to wait nearby. "I'll be just a moment," he said. "I need to talk to the nurse."

Cliff then walked to the counter and asked the nurse, "Is there anything I should know about her medication?"

"Well, the doctor said that someone should monitor her drug intake at all times," she said. "If Miriam goes off the anxiety drug instantly she could have psychotic reactions, so we have written a regimen for you to gradually wean her off the drug. She's going to have to be watched by a doctor regularly during this time," the nurse said as she handed Cliff the written instructions and a vial of medicine.

Cliff nodded and stuffed the paper and vial in his pocket, then beckoned to the children that he was ready to go to Miriam's room.

The children ran ahead to the room and shoved the door open. Miriam was sitting on the bed, dressed and ready to go. She smiled weakly and with obvious anxiety on her face. The children ran to her and threw their arms around her.

She buried her face in Becky's hair and held her close while Eric squeezed her so tightly that she could hardly breathe.

Just then, Cliff appeared in the doorway. He stood back, almost shyly, with his head tilted to one side, a little smile turning up the corners of his mouth. Miriam looked at him with tears in her eyes, uncertain that Cliff would really want her to return. Without words, her face said to him, "I'm so sorry. Can you *really* forgive me?"

Tears flooded Cliff's eyes and streamed down his face as he saw the pain and sorrow that flowed from Miriam's heart. He walked forward and joined the cluster and squeezed them all together with his strong arms.

"We're together again, Daddy, just like we prayed!" Eric said happily.

"Yes, little buddy," Cliff said with deep emotion, "we're together again!"

"Well, let's go home, then!" Becky said. "I can't wait until we're all together in our house again!" She looked at her mother and said, "Oh, Mom, we've missed you so much!"

"And I've missed you, too, darling!" Miriam replied. "Let's go home!"

They signed the release papers at the office downstairs and went out to the car. Miriam sat on the far side of the front seat. She longed to be closer to Cliff, but wondered if he would want her to be that close so soon.

As they headed toward the freeway, Cliff wondered if Miriam was keeping her distance because she was still confused and angry. They tried to talk, but it was difficult to make conversation when relations had been strained for so long. There was much to say, yet neither parent wanted the children to hear anything that might hurt and confuse them. The children couldn't help but notice, and the mood grew more somber as they drove toward home. During the last few blocks of the drive, the car was entirely silent.

They pulled into the driveway and got out of the car. Miriam was exhausted and her face was drawn, with dark circles under her eyes. Cliff couldn't help but notice how much older she looked. Nothing spontaneous or joyful remained of her former personality.

As the children ran into the house, Miriam struggled to stand to her feet. Cliff helped her without a word. His heart ached, sensing that even now, they were still worlds apart.

Miriam walked into the house and looked around, confused, finding it difficult to orient herself. Finally she looked at Cliff and said, "I'm so tired. I think I'd better lie down." Her eyes began to lose their focus and Cliff quickly steadied her.

"May I carry you upstairs?" he asked stiffly.

"Please," Miriam replied with a wan smile. She put her arm around his neck as he bent over and picked her up. He felt her bones through her flesh and could tell that she had lost a great deal of weight.

He carried her up the stairs and gently set her down on the bed. "Is there anything I can get you?" he asked.

"No, thank you," Miriam replied. "I just need to rest."

"I understand. I'll be downstairs. Just call if you need anything."

"I will."

Cliff turned to walk out of the room, his heart a mixture of heaviness and hope.

"Cliff?" Miriam said softly.

Cliff turned. "Yes?"

"Thank you for letting me come back home." She bit her lower lip to keep from crying, but tears still managed to escape. "I'll understand if you don't want me to stay too long. . . ."

Cliff wanted to run to her side, take her in his arms, and give her a long, passionate kiss. But something kept him standing by the door, looking down at the carpet. He finally looked up and said, "I don't know what to say, Miriam. I'm so confused right now, I don't know how I feel about anything."

"I understand," she said, turning her face toward the wall.

Cliff went out and closed the door. He leaned against the wall and sighed deeply with great weariness of soul.

Becky peeked out from her room and saw Cliff standing alone, looking blankly at the floor. "Daddy?" she said quietly.

Cliff looked up, surprised. He thought Becky was down in the playroom. "Yes, honey? What do you want?"

"Daddy, is Mom going to stay with us or will she go away again?"

"I don't know, dear. I really don't know."

The phone rang at John Kryer's house late that night. "Hello?" John said sleepily.

"I'm sorry I'm calling so late, John, but I need your advice."

"That's okay, Cliff," John said. "What's up?"

"I brought Miriam home from the hospital this afternoon."

"Oh, Cliff! That's wonderful!"

"Well, I'm not sure how wonderful it is. At least not yet."

"Do you mean she still believes in her multiple personalities?"

"I don't know, John. We haven't really talked yet. She

was just too exhausted when we got home. She's been sleeping ever since. But that's not the problem right now. The problem I want to talk to you about is my own attitude."

"What do you mean?" John asked.

"Well, I've been praying for two years now that Miriam would come back home, and now that she's here, I don't know how I feel about it. It's almost like my own emotions have shut down. I don't feel especially angry with her, but I don't feel particularly excited, either. I guess I don't feel much of anything. Do you understand what I'm saying?"

"Yes, I think I do, Cliff. It's not at all unusual for a person's emotions to be confused after the sort of thing you and Miriam have gone through. Fortunately, the Lord doesn't tell us to follow our feelings. He commands us to obey His Word."

"Would you be willing to counsel us if Miriam agrees to come?" Cliff asked.

"Of course, Cliff! I'm praying that she will want to get together. I love her just like I love you and I want to see your marriage healed. Just think how the Lord could use the two of you once your relationship is restored!"

"What do you mean, John?"

"Well, think about it. You two have gone through the valley of the shadow of death, literally! Your home was virtually destroyed by Christian psychology. Think of how you could be used by the Lord to alert pastors and lay people all across the city about the danger of following the counsel of man rather than the Word of God."

"Do you think that's possible, John?"

"Of course I do! I've been praying for that very miracle ever since Miriam got taken in by this deception."

"I can't think of anything I'd rather do," Cliff said firmly. "If our story can spare even one other couple, it will be worth it all. But first, I've got to get my own heart right again, and it isn't, John—it isn't at all."

"Then I want you to go to Ephesians 4 and read the

entire chapter and meditate deeply on it. You have to master the resentment and anger that Satan is trying to build in your heart. Will you promise to do what I've asked?"

"Yes, I will, John," Cliff agreed. "I'll talk with Miriam in the morning and see if we can set a time to meet with you. Thanks again for being such a friend."

❖ ❖ ❖

Cliff didn't want to disturb Miriam, so he slept in the guest room. The next morning, he knocked on the bedroom door. "Miriam?" he said softly. "Are you awake?"

"Hhmm?" Miriam stirred in her bed.

"Can I come in?" Cliff asked.

Miriam blinked, her eyes still heavy with exhaustion. "Sure, Cliff," she said in a foggy voice, "come on in."

"Are you decent?" Cliff said as he peeked in. He felt awkward, almost as though they had never been married.

"Yes," Miriam answered nervously with a little smile as she pulled the sheets up to her chin.

Cliff came in and pulled a chair up beside the bed. He noticed that Miriam's hair was thinner and had lost its beautiful dark sheen.

"Did you sleep well last night?"

"Fairly well," Miriam said. "but my leg muscles seem to be cramping and twitching."

"Has that happened before?" Cliff asked.

"Yes. Mostly since I started taking the medicine Dr. McCall prescribed."

"Is that the medicine you took the other night?"

Miriam looked down quickly and nodded. She finally looked up at Cliff and said, "I'm so sorry, Cliff. I'm so ashamed that I've put you and the kids through all of this. How could I have been so deceived? How could my faith have become so weak that I would actually try to take my own life?" She began to cry and turned her face away.

Cliff's heart began to melt with compassion. He reached out and took Miriam's hand. "It's okay, Miriam. You're home with us now. That's all that matters for the moment." He reached for a box of tissues and pulled a few out for Miriam. "Here, honey," he said as he handed them to her.

Miriam took the tissues and dried her eyes. "Thank you," she said through her tears.

Cliff patted her hand and sat back. "Would you like to pray together?"

Miriam hesitated for a moment, then nodded and said, "I'd like that, Cliff."

They reached for one another's hands and bowed their heads. "Oh Lord Jesus," Cliff said with a deep sigh, "we are back together now in our own home for the first time in more than two years. Our hearts are still very confused and sad. Please help us to be able to forgive each other and learn how to rebuild our marriage. We need You so much right now. Please help us to try to understand each other and to guard our hearts against the anger that will surely rise up in our hearts again. I thank You, Jesus, that we are at least talking to each other. Oh, help us to regain the love we once had for each other. I pray this in Your holy name. Amen."

"Amen," Miriam whispered.

There was a knock at the door just then. Becky stuck her head in and said, "Can we come in?"

"Sure, honey," Miriam said.

Becky and Eric ran in and jumped on the bed and gave Miriam a series of hugs. "We're so glad to have you home, Mom," Becky said. "Are you going to stay with us from now on?"

Miriam looked at Cliff, whose gaze dropped to the floor. "I . . . I . . . hope so," she said uncertainly. "I want to."

Cliff looked over at Becky and Eric and nodded. "She's going to stay with us from now on." He looked back and gave Miriam a tight-lipped smile. "Now, we'd better get out so your mom can get dressed. Come on," he said as he picked up one child with each arm. "You come on down when you're ready. I'll make some breakfast."

After the others left, Miriam got up and went into the bathroom. She looked at herself in the mirror and was again astonished to see how old she looked. Her weight loss, combined with the effects of the drugs and worry, had produced a drawn and weary look. Her skin–which had always been so soft and young-looking–was wrinkled and dry. Dark loose line pouches sagged under her eyes and her nose was red from crying. "Oh, I'm so ugly!" she said, agitated at her appearance.

She got into the shower and washed her hair, wanting to look the best she could when she went downstairs. After drying off, she opened the medicine cabinet and, to her surprise, her make-up was still in place–as though she had never left.

As she covered the dark circles and wrinkles, she began to feel more at ease. She dried her hair and combed and arranged it carefully in the style Cliff liked so much. She dabbed his favorite perfume on her neck and went to the closet.

Everything was just as she had left it. Her shoes, dresses, skirts, and blouses were still organized by color and style. Her heart warmed as she realized that Cliff had loved her all along. "Oh, Cliff," she said softly as she began to dress.

Her clothing hung loosely on her, but the outfit she chose helped to hide her thinness. She stood in front of a full-length mirror and bit her lip nervously. She took a deep breath, opened the door, and went downstairs.

Cliff and the kids were in the family room, wrestling and playing. When Miriam came into the room, they stopped and looked up.

"Mom!" Becky said, "you look beautiful!" She ran to Miriam and threw her arms around her.

Cliff stood up and nodded with a smile. "She's right, you know," he said softly. "You *are* beautiful!"

Miriam sighed with relief. "I'm so glad you still think so," she said as she walked toward him.

Cliff's heart jumped with joy and desire as she put her arms around his neck. He pulled her close and hugged her tightly as the children watched with big eyes. Neither Cliff nor Miriam spoke for a long moment as they embraced.

"Come on, Dad," Eric said, "give her a big one!"

Cliff laughed as he looked down at his son. "All right," he said. "I will!" And he kissed Miriam tenderly, then firmly, then passionately. "Oh . . . you smell good," he whispered in her ear.

"Okay! That's enough!" Eric said as he wormed his way between them. "I'm hungry. Let's eat!"

Cliff and Miriam laughed and they all walked into the kitchen. Cliff had prepared the ingredients for scrambled eggs and invited Miriam to sit down with the kids while he began to cook.

"I didn't realize you knew how to cook, Cliff," Miriam teased.

He looked at her with raised eyebrows and said, "I've had to learn a lot of things."

Miriam felt a stab of pain in her heart, but said nothing. Cliff immediately wished he had chosen his words more carefully.

"What I meant–"

Miriam smiled tightly and shook her head. "It doesn't matter. I had it coming."

The easy teasing and banter that they had always enjoyed was dangerous now, they both realized. They would have to guard themselves and choose their words with caution until trust was rebuilt.

After breakfast, when the kids had gone out to play, Cliff and Miriam sat at the table together.

"We need to talk," Cliff said.

"I know."

"I'm sorry I took that swipe at you. I didn't mean it the way it sounded."

"That's okay," Miriam said without smiling. "We've

been through a lot and it's going to take time to turn things around."

"That's what I wanted to talk about with you. I called John Kryer last night."

Miriam tightened noticeably at the mention of John's name.

"What did you talk about?" Miriam asked, already knowing.

"About us. About the fact that we are going to need some help to rebuild our marriage. I trust him, Miriam, and you can, too. He told me that he cares about you just as much as he does about me. Would you be willing for us to meet with him?"

Miriam looked down at her plate and sighed. "I suppose so, Cliff, if you think it's necessary." She paused, then said, "I wish there were someone else."

"Why?"

"Well, Cliff, he knows all about our problems and already has his mind made up that I'm totally at fault. You know how he hates psychology."

Cliff didn't say anything for a long moment, shook his head slowly, then said, "Don't you?"

"What?"

"Don't you hate psychology, too? Look what it has done to us! Look what it did to you! Our marriage has been destroyed, I lost my career, our savings are gone, our reputation as Christian leaders is destroyed! You almost killed yourself! Aren't you ready to come back to the Lord to find the solutions for our problems? Do you still believe psychology has the answers for us?" Cliff stood, feeling bitterness and anger rising within his heart. "What is it going to take, Miriam? I ask you, what is it going to take?"

Miriam began weeping and held her head as it pounded with pain. "I know," she said, "I know." She lowered her head and began to cry. There was a long, awkward pause. Then, gaining control of her emotions, she dried her tears and looked at her husband, her eyes strangely different. "You're right, Cliff. Our marriage has been destroyed. I can see that now. I was a fool to think that we could work it out. You haven't changed one bit! You still have to have it your way." She stood to her feet. "I'll get my things and be out of here today."

Cliff stood with his mouth open in total shock. "No, Miriam!" was all he could say.

Miriam walked shakily to their bedroom. Her strength was gone and she began to sweat heavily. She felt hot and her mouth was dry. She entered the bedroom, closed the door, fell onto the bed, and nodded off to sleep.

Downstairs, Cliff sat down at the table, first sad, then angry. "I can't believe that woman!" he said to himself. "What's it going to take to open her eyes?"

He reached for the phone and dialed John Kryer. "John, I just talked with Miriam, and she wants to leave again. I don't know what to do!"

"I'm so sorry, Cliff," John said with deep compassion. "Let's fast and pray for her. I'll ask some of our folks to join us. Like I said before, Cliff, this is a spiritual battle. The enemy isn't going to give up easily."

Cliff rubbed the back of his neck. "I don't know, John. I'm not sure I feel like trying anymore."

"Forget your feelings, Cliff! Of course you don't feel like continuing the battle. The question is, what would the Lord have you to do? What does His Word say? Remember the principle? Feelings follow actions."

Cliff nodded. "You're right, John. Thanks. I'll let you know if there's any change."

"And Cliff?" John said.

"Yes?"

"Her healing doesn't depend on whether she gets with me or any other human counselor. What she needs is the truth of God's Word. Don't insist that she come to me. Help her to get back into the Scriptures. Do you understand what I'm saying?"

"Yes, John, I do. That helps. She may not want to open up to you right now, but I think I can get her to start reading the Bible again."

"Well that's what she needs most. She needs to read it and then obey it. That the only way she's going to know true healing," John said. "We'll be praying."

11

A Therapy
That Works

The Christian life is actually quite simple. God has not given us a complex system of steps to follow in our search for inner healing. Jesus was once asked to condense the laws of God into a small, understandable package, and this is what He said:

> "Love the Lord your God with all your heart and with all your soul and with all your strength and with all your mind"; and, "Love your neighbor as yourself" (Luke 10:27).

I believe Jesus was teaching the same principle in Matthew when He told us how to treat others: "In everything, do to others what you would have them do to you, for this sums up the Law and the Prophets" (Matthew 7:12). Such an attitude is possible only when we first love the Lord with all our being.

While Jesus' summary of true religious experience is simple, it is also deeply profound. As we consider biblical counsel, let us never mistake simplicity for shallowness. By the same token, when we examine psychological counsel, we should never confuse complexity with depth.

The Complexity of Psychology

When I began investigating the validity of "Christian psychology" I came across a book written by a well-known author who is respected as an orthodox evangelical with a genuine commitment to the Scriptures. I cannot deny his sincerity, but I question his understanding of biblical interpretation and theology.

In his book, he explained how we can be changed from the inside out. I had heard from other people that his book was spiritually deep and intellectually challenging. But as I read it I found myself asking, "What is the author trying to say?" Eventually I realized the book was not deep; it was confusing.

That experience reminds me of speakers who delight in using lofty language to impress audiences with their intellectual powers. People are seldom moved toward a closer walk with God by such speakers, but they are certainly impressed by what they heard. In response, many will whisper with awe, "He is so *deep!*"

Much of psychology is like that. It complicates life with its endless theories of behavior and therapies, which try to uncover and explain the subconscious motivations of our soul. And psychology says it so *impressively* and with such *authority.* Psychological experts tell us that special training and knowledge are required to unravel our twisted psyches and to bring healing to our wounded inner selves.

Thanks to psychology, we no longer have to deal with just one depraved soul per individual. Now the counselor must ferret out dozens of alter personalities, become acquainted and build a trusting relationship with each one of them, and deal with each individual trauma of the various alters in order to help integrate the several into the one host personality. Failing to do that, the therapist must lead each remaining alter to a personal commitment to Christ.

That should make us wonder how God decides whether a person goes to heaven. If only some of the alters become saved, will only part of the soul be redeemed?

In psychotheology, a person can no longer come to Christ in simple childlike faith, be born again, and experience transformation by the power of the Holy Spirit. Instead, wounded people are told that they must submit to therapy so they can work through the pain of their past and eventually learn to cope with their confusion and suffering. Though unbiblical psychotherapies may produce a weak and temporary relief, they will never produce genuine healing for the wounded heart.

Paul addresses the issue of worldly complexity and biblical simplicity when he says that he preaches the gospel "not with words of human wisdom, lest the cross of Christ be emptied of its power" (1 Corinthians 1:17). He readily admits that "the message of the cross is foolishness to those who are perishing." But he adds without hesitation that "to us who are being saved it is the power of God" (1 Corinthians 1:18).

Paul was not intimidated by the intellectual powers of the educated elite. He writes, "Where is the wise man? Where is the scholar? Where is the philosopher of this age? Has not God made foolish the wisdom of the world?" (1 Corinthians 1:20). Worldly intellect is simply inadequate to deal with spiritual problems. That's why Paul says, "Since in the wisdom of God the world through its wisdom did not know him, God was pleased through the foolishness of what was preached to save those who believe" (1 Corinthians 1:21).

God offers true healing through the Scriptures and the working of the Holy Spirit as we submit to His authority in our lives. Jesus told us that only the truth can set us free (John 8:32). And furthermore, He defined that truth: "I am the way and the truth and the life. No one comes to the Father except through me" (John 14:6).

The Walk of Faith

If you have read this far, you obviously are interested in genuine healing from God. We can receive this healing through what I call "saturation therapy." I use that term only to contrast it with the ineffectual therapies that are marketed to an unwary public as miracle cures. "Saturation therapy" simply means to fill our heart and soul with the truths of Scripture. Its purpose is to prepare and produce in us a daily walk with the Lord Jesus Christ.

Note what these Scriptures say about our walk with the Lord:

> We are buried with him by baptism into death: that like as Christ was raised up from the dead by the glory of the Father, even so we also should walk in newness of life (Romans 6:4 NASB).

> There is therefore now no condemnation to them which are in Christ Jesus, who walk not after the flesh, but after the Spirit (Romans 8:1 NASB).

> We walk by faith, not by sight (2 Corinthians 5:7 NASB).

> Walk by the Spirit, and you will not carry out the desire of the flesh (Galatians 5:16 NASB).

> I, therefore, the prisoner of the Lord, entreat you to walk in a manner worthy of the calling with which you have been called (Ephesians 4:1 NASB).

> Walk in love, just as Christ also loved you, and gave Himself up for us, an offering and a

sacrifice to God as a fragrant aroma (Ephesians 5:2 NASB).

Be careful how you walk, not as unwise men, but as wise (Ephesians 5:15 NASB).

As you therefore have received Christ Jesus the Lord, so walk in Him (Colossians 2:6 NASB).

If we walk in the light as He Himself is in the light, we have fellowship with one another, and the blood of Jesus His Son cleanses us from all sin (1 John 1:7 NASB).

The one who says he abides in Him ought himself to walk in the same manner as He walked (1 John 2:6 NASB).

Saturating Ourselves with God's Word

God wants our hearts to be filled with His truth. David recognized this when he wrote, "Surely you desire truth in the inner parts; you teach me wisdom in the inmost place" (Psalm 51:6).

The English word *saturate* comes from the Latin word *saturare,* which means "to fill" and "to soak or load to capacity."[157] And the question we need to ask ourselves is this: "Am I filled to capacity with the Word of God?"

There is no shortcut to this sort of saturation. As we're about to see, it happens by believing, reading, meditating, and memorizing God's Word.

Believing the Word

The first step to saturating ourselves with the healing truths of God's Word is to *believe* it. When we believe, we accept something as true or real. Thus, a person who believes God expects that what He says will actually happen. This person has full confidence in the character and power of the Lord to do what He promises. To believe God is to have a bold faith in His sovereignty and the absolute dependability of His written Word.

Paul had that sort of faith. He publicly declared, "I believe everything that agrees with the Law and that is written in the Prophets" (Acts 24:14). I wish more Christians today would believe as Paul did.

When writing to the church at Thessalonica, Paul said, "We also thank God continually because, when you received the word of God, which you heard from us, you accepted it not as the word of men, but as it actually is, the word of God, which is at work in you who believe" (1 Thessalonians 2:13). That's the issue: Either the Bible is truly the Word of God or it isn't. Those who accept the Scriptures as true but say they are insufficient to deal with our inner pain are taking a weak and foolish stand.

God has always placed a special value upon belief. He asked Moses, "How long will these people treat me with contempt? How long will they refuse to believe in me, in spite of all the miraculous signs I have performed among them?" (Numbers 14:11). Think about it: Is God asking that about you or me? In spite of all that He has done for us, do we still refuse to believe Him?

The problem with Israel was that "they did not believe in God or trust in his deliverance" (Psalm 78:22). That proved disastrous for the entire nation. We see the same problem happening today; the reason so many Christians are suffering in slavery to sin is they do not believe in God, and they are trusting others to deliver them.

Two suffering men approached Jesus one day and asked for healing. They cried out,

> "Have mercy on us, Son of David!"
> When he had gone indoors, the blind men

came to him, and he asked them, "Do you believe that I am able to do this?"

"Yes, Lord," they replied.

Then he touched their eyes and said, "According to your faith will it be done to you"; and their sight was restored (Matthew 9:27-30).

In the same way, Jesus asks us at this very moment, "Do you believe I am able to do this?" Some people will reply, "Yes, Lord, I *do* believe!" and will receive healing for their wounded hearts. Other people will hesitantly reply, "Well, Lord, I'm not sure. I've been told that my illness will require expert psychotherapy." And Jesus will sadly walk away to heal those who do believe.

He says to us, "How foolish you are, and how slow of heart to believe all that the prophets have spoken!" (Luke 24:25). Are we really Christians? Then "the work of God is this: to believe in the one he has sent" (John 6:29).

We must believe God's Word even though it is politically correct to dismiss it as simplistic and naive. If we have to add to His Word or improve upon it with our studies, findings, and innovative therapies, we are repeating the mistake of the Galatians. Paul asked them, "Does God give you his Spirit and work miracles among you because you observe the law, or because you believe what you heard?" (Galatians 3:5). Today he would ask us, "Does God heal your wounded hearts because you participate in therapy or because you believe what you heard?"

The world just doesn't have a clue when it comes to dealing with the issues of the soul. How can prisoners free other prisoners? That is what the Bible declares mankind to be: "The Scripture declares that the whole world is a prisoner of sin, so that what was promised, being given through faith in Jesus Christ, might be given to those who believe" (Galatians 3:22).

We have been blinded by the sophisticated but empty

promises of psychotheology. Paul might well say to us today, "I pray also that the eyes of your heart may be enlightened in order that you may know the hope to which he has called you, the riches of his glorious inheritance in the saints, and his incomparably great power for us who believe. That power is like the working of his mighty strength" (Ephesians 1:18,19).

Read that passage again! God wants to open our spiritual eyes to see three life-changing truths: real hope, our rich inheritance, and God's incomparable power to make it so. Where will this hope come from? Belief in God through the Lord Jesus! "Through him you believe in God, who raised him from the dead and glorified him, and so your faith and hope are in God" (1 Peter 1:21).

Such belief in the power of God through Christ comes only through the Scriptures as the Holy Spirit applies them to us. Peter writes, "Though you have not seen him, you love him; and even though you do not see him now, you believe in him and are filled with an inexpressible and glorious joy" (1 Peter 1:8). Does that describe your emotional condition right now? It can! And you don't have to wait for your next appointment with your therapist; it can happen right now.

Do you know why so many Christians doubt the love and power of God? Because they have been taught that they should never have to suffer. But Paul reminds us, "It has been granted to you on behalf of Christ not only to believe on him, but also to suffer for him" (Philippians 1:29).

True healing faith is the kind of faith that believes in the goodness and power of God—even in the deepest times of suffering.

Reading the Word

The more people I counsel and talk to on the radio, the more I realize that many Christians simply aren't reading the Bible as a regular part of their daily walk with the Lord.

In Deuteronomy, God gave these explicit instructions for the king of His people:

> When he takes the throne of his kingdom, he is to write for himself on a scroll a copy of this law, taken from that of the priests, who are Levites. It is to be with him, and he is to read it all the days of his life so that he may learn to revere the Lord his God and follow carefully all the words of this law and these decrees (Deuteronomy 17:18,19).

Note the particulars: 1) the king was to personally copy the Scriptures by hand; 2) he was to keep a copy with him; 3) he was to read it daily; 4) so that he would properly honor the Lord; and 5) obey God in every matter.

As believers, we belong to an even more exclusive class than kings. We are called "a chosen people, a royal priesthood, a holy nation, a people belonging to God" (1 Peter 2:9). How much more, then, should we do what God commanded His kings to do?

The first requirement was to personally study the Word. The king was not to hire a scribe to do the study for him, and neither should we. Too many Christians rely upon books other than the Bible for their spiritual food. Yet only the Bible can give us our daily bread. Never substitute *a* book for *the* Book!

The second requirement was to keep a copy close at hand at all times. Do you have a Bible where you can get to it right now? You never know when you're going to need it.

The third command for the king was to read the Word daily. That's what the Bereans did in Acts 17:11; they "examined the Scriptures every day." Like the Bereans, we too must eagerly open the Bible to check out the teachings we are receiving.

Fourth, the king was to revere the Lord. As we learned earlier, James tells us this kind of reverence is possible only when we are doers of the Word and not hearers only (James 1:22). There is no way we can honor God if we don't do what He says.

That leads us to the last of God's commands: The king was to obey Him in every matter. That command applies to us as well. We can't pick and choose what we will obey and what we won't, what we will believe and what we won't. It's a package deal—all or nothing. Otherwise, there is simply no healing from the Lord.

Are you reading the Word the way you should? I often ask that question of people who come to me with wounded hearts.

"Oh, yes, I'm in the Word daily, but I'm still suffering from depression and panic attacks," they might say.

"I see. And are you attending a Bible-believing church?"

"Yes. I go nearly every week."

"Uh-huh. And are you involved in a close relationship with other believers who can pray for you and disciple you in your walk with the Lord?"

"Well . . . uh . . . not exactly. I'm a bit too shy to get close to people like that."

"But that is what the Lord requires of us if we are going to grow," I gently remind them. "It isn't enough just to read the Word; we have to do what it says."

Meditating on the Word

When Joshua was about to assume leadership of Israel, God told him, "Do not let this Book of the Law depart from your mouth; meditate on it day and night, so that you may be careful to do everything written in it. Then you will be prosperous and successful" (Joshua 1:8).

I believe the same principle and promise applies to us today. God wants us to take the time to carefully consider what He has written so that we can wisely apply His guidelines to our daily lives. When we do so, we will be "prosperous and successful." The goal of biblical counseling, therefore, should not be to keep a believer in ongoing therapy, but to equip him to study and meditate on the Word so that he can apply God's solutions to his problems.

To meditate means to ponder or to think deeply about something. The word *meditate* comes from the Latin root *med,* from which we derive the word *medicine. Med* means "to take appropriate measures." To meditate, therefore, means to think deeply about a given subject so that appropriate measures can be taken.

Biblical meditation does not bear the slightest resemblance to New Age or Eastern mysticism. It is not mindlessly chanting a mantra. Rather, it is thoughtfully and intelligently considering the meaning, implications, and applications of each passage in God's Word.

Psalm 119 is a powerful resource for the child of God. It teaches us a great deal about the discipline of meditation. The psalmist writes that he was committed to meditating on God's precepts and considering His ways (Psalm 119:15). Even if others thought it was foolish, he was determined to follow through: "Though princes sit together and slander me, your servant will meditate on your decrees" (Psalm 119:23).

Meditating, by the way, is not a tedious task for a person who loves the Lord. It is a delight. "I reach out my hands for your commandments, which I love, and I meditate on your decrees" (Psalm 119:48). Later on, the psalmist writes, "Oh, how I love your law! I meditate on it all day long" (Psalm 119:97).

Do you love the Scriptures? Do you delight in finding new truths to guide you in your walk with the Lord? May I ask you to do something right now? Please open your Bible to Psalm 119 and take the time to read it slowly and thoughtfully. Meditate on it. Take your time; I'll wait for you.

When I was preparing for college, I took a speed-reading

course. By the time I was done, I was supposed to be able to read an entire John Steinbeck novel in about eight minutes, and I passed the test. I still am able to read light material very quickly with a fair measure of comprehension. All through college and seminary, I was able to speed through my reading assignments in minutes instead of hours. But I found that speed-reading was about as satisfying as speed-eating.

Gulping down giant bites of steak without taking time to enjoy the texture and flavor is tasteless—and dangerous. Hurrying through the Bible is like that. If you read so fast that you don't understand what the prophet or writer meant, you can choke on a serious misunderstanding. And unfortunately, the spiritual Heimlich maneuver that forces us to cough up a chunk of false doctrine is as painful as the physical technique: "No discipline seems pleasant at the time, but painful. Later on, however, it produces a harvest of righteousness and peace for those who have been trained by it" (Hebrews 12:11).

Meditating on the Word of God is how we avoid the sins that destroy our lives. The author of Psalm 119 says, "How can a young man keep his way pure? By living according to your word" (Psalm 119:9). Preventive measures are always wiser than restorative action. Think of how many sorrows we all could have avoided if we had only paid closer attention to God's Word. The psalmist writes, "I have hidden your word in my heart that I might not sin against you" (Psalm 119:11).

Memorizing the Word

One of the most effective ways to meditate on Scripture is to memorize it. You never know when you're going to need the right verse to deal with a spiritual emergency. Memorizing Scripture is especially valuable when you don't have the Bible right at hand.

Imagine that you are a soldier under fire who finds that

his rifle is full of dirt. You have to quickly dismantle the rifle, clean it out, and reassemble it while bullets and rockets zip overhead. Fortunately you have been trained to take apart your weapon and put it back together again in a matter of seconds. But this skill came only with memorization: You had to memorize the sequence of this procedure by practicing, practicing, practicing. After all, when you're lying in the mud in the jungle and dodging enemy fire, you don't have time to take out the manual and read the instructions. You need to *know* what to do immediately. That's what memorization of our spiritual weaponry is all about.

Perhaps you are thinking to yourself, "I can't memorize verses. I'm too old," or "I have a disability," or "I've never been able to memorize things."

Let me suggest to you a simple method of memorization that has worked since the Scriptures were first penned: 1) Find a verse that is especially meaningful to you at this time. 2) Get a pad of paper and write the verse along with its reference. Take care to be accurate. 3) Write the verse out in longhand again and again until you can reproduce it without mistake. 4) Have a friend check your memory. Recite the verse out loud again and again until it flows from your mouth at conversational speed. Like the psalmist says, "With my lips I recount all the laws that come from your mouth" (Psalm 119:13). 5) Write the verse on a small business-size card and keep it with you to review each day. 6) Review all your verses at least once a week and restudy those that have become hazy in your memory. 7) Set a goal of memorizing at least one verse per week.

Now, one verse a week may not seem like much of a challenge, but if you begin this week, you will have fifty-two new verses in your heart by this time next year!

We have a Bible read-through program at our church which was started by one of our laymen who has a great love for God's Word. He challenges other people in the church to read through the entire Bible chronologically in just fifteen weeks! The participants come together each week and discuss what God has shown them in their reading. Such a project requires about two hours of reading each day.

I will admit that when I first heard about this program, I was skeptical. I thought that people would be reading only to get through the passages quickly. But I have seen more spiritual growth and maturing through this program than in any other single Bible-reading ministry I have ever been blessed to observe.[158] (If you are interested in obtaining the *Bible Read-Through Handbook*, see endnote 158.)

We Don't Have to Wait Another Moment!

Saturation therapy can begin right now. You don't have to wait until you can afford psychotherapy. You don't have to put it off until an appointment opens up at the church counseling office. Healing for your wounded heart is *already* under way if you have committed yourself to returning to the Word of God for the solutions to your problems.

A Summary of Genuine Healing

Let's briefly review what we have discovered in our time together. Here are the guidelines for experiencing genuine healing for our wounded hearts:

1. We must reject everything that is false.
2. We must overcome the poison of bitterness.
3. We must courageously face the absolute truth.
4. We must accept full responsibility for our lives and accept God's powerful remedy for our own sin.
5. We must forgive those who have wronged us.
6. We must refocus our minds on Christ and others.
7. We must develop a biblical mindset.
8. We must change our attitudes by learning willful gratitude.

9. We must actively serve others.

10. We must saturate our inner being with the Word of God.

Is it still too complicated? Then let's look at how Jesus summarizes all of this: "'Love the Lord your God with all your heart and with all your soul and with all your mind.' This is the first and greatest commandment. And the second is like it: 'Love your neighbor as yourself.' All the Law and the Prophets hang on these two commandments" (Matthew 22:37-40).

It all comes down to this: Who is controlling you? Are you controlled by your own fleshly desires? Are you controlled by the imaginations of a therapist who doesn't understand or believe the Scriptures or the power of God (Matthew 22:29)? Are you controlled by fear and rebellion, which Satan inspires? Or are you controlled by the gentle Spirit of God? Remember, "The mind of sinful man is death, but the mind controlled by the Spirit is life and peace" (Romans 8:6).

No one else can do for you what God can do. No theory of man or any psychological therapy can produce the genuine inner peace for which you so desperately long. Truly, my friend, *only* God can heal your wounded heart.

Cliff heard Miriam stirring upstairs in the bedroom, and he went up to talk with her. He knocked on the door, but there was no answer.

"Miriam?" he said softly. He tried to turn the doorknob, but it was locked. Still, there was no answer. "Honey, I know you're awake. Can I come in?"

Miriam came to the door, opened it, and turned away. It was clear that she had been crying again. "What do you want?" she said wearily. She was packing a suitcase.

"I want to ask your forgiveness. I know I was too harsh

downstairs and I'm truly sorry."

Miriam didn't say anything and kept packing.

"What's going on, Miriam?" Cliff asked, suddenly aware of what she was doing.

"What does it look like? I'm packing. I'm not going to burden you any further, Cliff."

Cliff walked over to Miriam and gently took her hand. Miriam didn't fight it, but she didn't look at Cliff, either.

"Please, Miriam!" Cliff said with deep emotion. "*Please* don't. I'm asking you with everything in my heart: Please don't leave us again. We need you. The kids do," he said as his voice cracked. "And *I* need you desperately." He took her by both shoulders and turned her to face him head-on. Gently he nudged her face up with his finger until she looked him in the eyes. "I love you, Miriam. Don't you understand that? I love you more than I can possibly say!"

Miriam didn't reply and her hands hung limply at her side. Her eyes looked dry and lifeless.

Cliff began to weep, and then prayed out loud. "Oh Lord God, I pray right now that You will intervene. Help Miriam to know what You want her to do. Help her to realize how much we love her and that this is where she belongs. O Father, please . . . *please.*"

Miriam shivered involuntarily and shook her head. Tears welled up in her eyes. She saw the genuine love in Cliff's eyes and her mind suddenly began to clear again. She blinked as the tears blurred her vision and then she threw her arms around Cliff's neck. "Oh, Cliff, I'm so sorry. I'm still so confused and I keep letting my bitterness take over. I do love you and I want to be here with you and the kids. Please hold me close!" Her body trembled with fear and a glimmer of hope. "I won't leave you. Not ever again!"

Cliff hugged Miriam tightly, then kissed her again and again. "Do you promise? Please *promise* me you won't ever leave us again!"

"Oh, I do, Cliff! I *do* promise! I want us to love each

other like we used to. I want to laugh and play and run together in the mountains. I want to hold hands with you and feel you next to me when I'm asleep. I want to pray with you again and serve the Lord together!"

Cliff and Miriam stood for a long time in each other's arms, unaware that two children were peeking around the doorway and smiling from ear to ear.

One year later, Miriam stood as the women's director at Trinity Presbyterian Church introduced her. "Miriam Chase is the wife of a pastor, the mother of two children, and–as you can see–has a third on the way. She is a speaker and the author of a soon-to-be-released book about her own story of false memories and multiple personalities. God is using her message to alert women to a major deception that is destroying marriages and even entire families. Please welcome our guest speaker, Miriam Chase."

Miriam walked to the podium as the women applauded. She placed her notes on the stand, took a deep breath, and began to speak.

"I'm going to tell you my personal story," she said softly. "It's a story of good intentions, devastating family interference, false doctrines, incompetent therapy, and the near-destruction of my marriage. It all began about four years ago."

Miriam related the tragic history of her false memories and the therapy that caused her to leave her family and accuse her own father of satanic ritual and sexual abuse. She told them of the confusion and bitterness that had taken hold of her heart and what psychoactive drugs had done to her mind. She told of the near-hypnotic control Dr. Powell had achieved over her and how she had been desperately afraid to disappoint him. She described the ways her support group had fostered in her mind beliefs in events that had never happened.

"I actually believed the images that came into my mind under the counseling of a Christian psychologist and the peer pressure of my support group. I have no doubt to this day that the therapist–a kind and compassionate man–still believes that I was sexually abused and that my father was involved in a satanic cult that sacrificed babies and tortured me. But I can tell you for a fact: *None* of it *ever* happened. I *know* that today.

"I want to warn you of what can happen to ordinary, intelligent, sincere Christian women who begin to believe in psychotherapy and read books that teach doctrines that are clearly unbiblical."

Miriam continued with her personal story and then opened the Bible and shared how the Lord had begun to heal her heart through prayer, fellowship with other believers, and Scripture reading and memorization. She shared how her relationships with her husband, children, and parents were being restored.

"I am still embarrassed about what I did to my family," she said. "I still find it hard not to feel condemned and ashamed. I find it hard not to take any suggestion or criticism personally. Other retractors have told me they experience the same inner battle. So please understand if we sometimes seem standoffish and aloof. We find it difficult to trust people. But as I continue to walk with the Lord, it is becoming easier.

"Nothing else cleared my mind like the Word of God. Nothing else has ever duplicated the deep and abiding sense of peace and well-being that I've received from the Scriptures. I plead with you–if you are going through a period of depression, anxiety, panic attacks, or general discontent–don't turn to the counseling theories that are based on psychology. Instead, I encourage you, as one who has been through it, to return to the Word of God. You will find more help there than in all the therapy you can afford!"

Several women nodded and said, "Amen!" but others looked troubled and angry.

"I am blessed beyond what I deserve," she continued. "My father and mother have forgiven me and our relationship is being healed. My husband, Cliff, prayed for me and loved me the whole time I was gone from our family. He never gave up. He watched over our children and kept himself pure for me. Though from time to time we still struggle with confusion, we are truly happier now than we have ever been!"

Miriam paused for a moment, her eyes becoming moist. She swallowed hard and continued. "Today, Cliff and I are serving the Lord together again. God has opened a job at another church near our home, and we are ministering to other people whose lives have been damaged by sin."

Tears filled her eyes as she saw the pain on the faces of several women in the audience. "It doesn't usually work out this way, I know. Not everyone has a husband like I have, and some men won't put up with being abandoned. Whatever you do, don't make the mistakes I did.

"Keep this in mind. If you have *actual* memories of abuse, they won't have to be dredged up or manufactured by a therapist. And even if the memories *are* real, the Lord Jesus can heal your wounded heart! I'm living proof."

Notes

Returning to the Past

1. John Kryer and Cliff Chase were two of the main characters in *Why Christians Can't Trust Psychology*, by Dr. Ed Bulkley (Eugene, OR: Harvest House Publishers, 1993).

Chapter One–Adult Victims of Chilhood Abuse

2. Glenna Whitley, "The Seduction of Gloria Grady,*" D Magazine*, October 1991, p. 46.
3. Jim Grady, *A Brother's Reflections on a Sister Lost to False, Repressed Memories*, a self-published monograph, p. 2.
4. Ibid.
5. "The Orphanage," *Newsweek*, December 12, 1994, p. 31.

Chapter Two–False Memories

6. MPD has been relabeled by the American Psychiatric Association as DID, or Dissociative Identity Disorder, number 300.14 of the DSM-IV (*Diagnostic and Statistical Manual of Mental Disorders*), American Psychiatric Association, Washington, D.C., 1994, p. 484.
7. Ibid.
8. Ibid.
9. Glenna Whitley, "The Seduction of Gloria Grady," *D Magazine*, October 1991, p. 46.
10. Ibid., p. 47.
11. Jim Grady, *A Brother's Reflections*, p. 5.
12. Glenna Whitley, "The Seduction of Gloria Grady," p. 46.
13. Jim Grady, *A Brother's Reflections*, p. 6.
14. Glenna Whitley, "The Seduction of Gloria Grady," p. 48.
15. Ibid.
16. Ibid.
17. Ibid., p. 49.
18. Jim Grady, *A Brother's Reflections*, p. 10.
19. Ibid.
20. Ibid.
21. Ibid., pp. 10, 11.
22. From *The Biblical Counselor*, published by the National Association of Nouthetie Counselors, Lafayette, Indiana, September 1994.
23. Personal letter on file.
24. Ibid.
25. Letter on file.
26. James G. Friesen, *Uncovering the Mystery of MPD*, (San Bernardine, CA: Here's Life Publishers, 1991).
27. Bill Scanlon, "Therapists Under Fire,*" Rocky Mountain News*, March 10, 1994, p. 1D.
28. The False Memory Syndrome Foundation can be reached at 1-800-568-8882.
29. Bill Scanlon, "Therapists Under Fire," p. 7D.
30. Ibid.
31. Ibid.
32. Ibid.
33. *Rocky Mountain News*, December 13, 1994, p. 19A.

34. *Rocky Mountain News,* December 4, 1994, p. 12A.
35. Ibid., p. 14A.
36. Ibid, p. 12A.
37. Ibid.
38. Ibid., p. 14A.
39. Ibid.
40. Bill Scanlon, "Therapists Under Fire," p. 9D.
41. Ibid.
42. Jonathan Bor, "'False memory' victims gather to recount ordeals," *The Baltimore Sun,* December 11, 1994, p. 1C.
43. Ibid.
44. Leon Jaroff, "Lies of the Mind," *Time,* November 29, 1993.
45. Ibid.
46. Ibid.
47. Ibid.
48. Dan Allender, *The Wounded Heart* (Colorado Springs: Nav Press, 1991), p. 25.
49. Charles Krauthammer, "If everyone's a victim, no one can be held to blame," *Rocky Mountain News,* February 7, 1994, p. 31A.
50. Ibid.
51. Ibid.
52. Karen S. Peterson, "Some therapists have too much faith in memory," *USA Today,* October 8, 1993.
53. Ibid.
54. Gayle Hanson, "Total recall versus tricks of the mind," *Insight,* May 24, 1993, p. 6.
55. Anne Rochell, "'Recovered' memories sever a family relationship," *The Atlanta Journal and Constitution,* December 11, 1994, p. G1.
56. Ibid.
57. Ibid.
58. Ibid.
59. Ibid.
60. Pat Shellenberger, *Misty Memory* (The Grand Rapids Press, December 4, 1994, down loaded from Internet).
61. Joseph P. Kahn, "Trial by memory; Stung by daughters' claims of abuse," *The Boston Globe,* December 14, 1994, p. 80.
62. Jonathan Bor, "False memory victims," p. 1C.
63. Hanson, "Total recall," p. 6.
64. Ibid.
65. An audiocassette of Johanne Wayne's story is available from "Return to the Word," Dr. Ed Bulkley's radio broadcast, at 1-800-458-6577.
66. Mark Pendergrast, *Victims of Memory, Incest Accusations and Shattered Lives* (Hinesburg, VT: Upper Access Books, 1995), p477.
67. Hanson, "Total recall," p. 6.
68. Downloaded from America Online.
69. Ibid.
70. Ibid.
71. Ibid.
72. Dr. Kevin Leman and Randy Carlson, *Unlocking the Secrets of Your Childhood Memories Workbook* (Nashville, TN: Thomas Nelson Publishers, 1994), p.5.
73. Ibid.
74. Frank Minirth, *The Power of Memories* (Nashville, TN: Thomas Nelson Publishers, 1995), p. 55.
75. *Time,* November 29, 1993.

76. Hanson, "Total recall," p. 6.
77. Ibid.
78. Eric L. Nelson and Paul Simpson, "First Glimpse: An Initial Examination of Subjects Who Have Rejected Their Recovered Visualizations as False Memories," *Issues in Child Abuse Accusations* (Institute for Psychological Therapies, 1994), pp. 123-33.
79. Ibid., p. 125.
80. Ibid.
81. Ibid, p. 126.
82. Ibid.
83. Ibid., pp. 126-27.
84. For information, contact Dr. Paul W. Simpson, Ed.D., 5240-D. Knight Dr., #120, Tucson, AZ 85712, (602) 751-0101 or Eric Nelson, M.A., P.O. Box 15700, San Diego, CA 92175, (619) 230-9170.
85. Eric L. Nelson and Paul Simpson, "False Memories in the Church," unpublished article, 1994, p. 2.
86. Ibid., pp. 2-3.
87. Ibid., p. 3.
88. Frank Minirth, *The Power of Memories,* cover.
89. Ibid., p. 15.
90. Ibid., p. 22.
91. Ibid., p. 70.
92. Ibid., p. 75
93. Ibid.
94. Ibid., pp. 37, 43.
95. Ibid.

Chapter Three–The Tragedy of Bitterness

96. *American Heritage English Dictionary,* version 1.1 (Boston, MA: Houghton Mifflin Co., 1987).
97. Robert H. Schuller, *Self-Esteem, the New Reformation* (Waco, TX: Word Books, 1982), p.34.
98. Dan Allender, *The Wounded Heart* (Colorado Springs: Nav Press, 1991), p. 26.
99. Ibid., p. 41.
100. Ibid., p. 78.
101. Ibid., p. 87.
102. Ibid., p. 98.
103. Ibid., p. 100.
104. Ibid., p. 101.
105. Ibid., p. 101.
106. Ibid., p. 105.
107. Ibid., pp. 108-09.
108. Ibid., p. 26.
109. Ibid.
110. Ibid.

Chapter Four–Where Healing Begins

111. Jim Grady, *A Brother's Reflections on a Sister Lost to False, Repressed Memories,* a self-published monograph, p. 11.
112. Ibid.
113. Ibid.

114. If you would like to hear Lee and Jean Grady's story in their own voices, you can order "How False Memories are Destroying Christian Families," a five-part audiocassette series available from our national radio ministry, "Return to the Word," 1-800-468-6577.

115. Joseph P. Armao and Leslie U. Cornfeld, "How to Police the Police," *Newsweek*, December 19, 1994, p. 34.

116. William J. Bennett, *The Book of Virtues* (New York: Simon & Schuster, 1993), p. 599.

117. Josh McDowell & Bob Hostetler, *Right from Wrong* (Dallas, TX: Word Books, 1994), p. 21.

118. "20/20," March 12, 1994.

Chapter Five–From Victim to Victor

119. Margaret Carlson, "And Now Obesity Rights," *Time,* December 6, 1993.

120. Ibid.

121. Kristin Leutwyler, "Sick, Sick, Sick, Neurotic? Probably, Says DSM-IV, " *Scientific American,* September 1994, p. 17.

122. Claudia Wallis, "Life in Overdrive," *Time,* July 18, 1994.

123. Ibid.

124. Ibid.

125. Ibid.

126. Ibid.

127. Ibid.

128. Ibid.

129. Henry Brandt, *Breaking Free from the Bondage of Sin* (Eugene, OR: Harvest House Publishers, 1994), p. 20.

130. Ibid, p.69.

131. Ibid., pp.85-86.

132. *American Heritage Electronic Dictionary,* version 1.1 (Boston, MA: Houghton Mifflin Co., 1987).

Chapter Six–The Power of Forgiveness

133. Eleanor Goldstein and Kevin Farmer, *True Stories of False Memories,* (Boca Raton, FL: SIRS Books, 1993), p. 45.

134. Gary R. Collins, *Can You Trust Psychology?* (Downers Grove, IL: InterVarsity Press, 1988), p. 45.

135. *American Heritage Electronic Dictionary,* version 1.1 (Boston, MA: Houghton Mifflin Co., 1987).

Chapter Seven–The Gift of Forgetting

136. Louis and Kay Moore, "Recovery Comes to the Church," *Moody*, September 1994, p. 20.

137. Ibid., p. 23.

138. William L. Playfair, M.D., *The Useful Lie,* (Wheaton, IL: Crossway Books, 1991), p. 86.

139. Ibid., p. 87.

140. Louis and Kay Moore, "Recovery Comes to the Church," p. 21.

141. "20/20," September 2, 1994.

Chapter Eight–Renewing Your Mind

142. Tom R. Hawkins, "A Pastoral Approach to MPD and Demonization," a paper presented at Dallas Theological Seminary, June 2, 1992, p. 3.
143. Ibid., p. 7.
144. O. Quentin Hyder, *The Christian's Handbook of Psychiatry* (Old Tappan, NJ: Fleming H. Revell Company, 1976), p. 49.
145. James G. Friesen, *Uncovering the Mystery of MPD* (San Bernardino, CA: Here's Life Publishers, 1991), p. 42.
146. *American Heritage Electronic Dictionary*, version 1.1 (Boston, MA: Houghton Mifflin Co., 1987).
147. "Recovered Nightmare", *Leadership Journal,* Summer 1994,
148. "Questions Pastors Ask (About Abuse),"*Leadership Journal,* Summer 1994.
149. Ibid.
150. Dan Allender, *The Wounded Heart* (Colorado Springs: Nav Press, 1991), p. 26.
151. "Questions Pastors Ask," *Leadership Journal,* Summer 1994.
152. Allender, *The Wounded Heart,* p. 15.
153. From a personal critique of Dan Allender's I.B.C. seminar on sexual abuse in Birmingham, Alabama, March 12-14, 1992.

Chapter Nine–Changing Your Attitudes

154. Joseph Perkins, "Kids Too Often Play the Victim," *San Diego Union Tribune,* transmitted to America Online, April 28, 1994.
155. Ibid.
156. Peter H. Gott, M.D., "How to Conquer Common Social Phobia," transmitted to America Online, November 1, 1993.

Chapter Eleven–A Therapy That Works

157. *American Heritage Electronic Dictionary,* version 1.1 (Boston, MA: Houghton Mifflin Co., 1987).
158. If you are interested in ordering the *Bible Read-Through Handbook,* write to LIFE Fellowship Ministries, 11500 Sheridan Blvd., Westmister, CO 80020, or call at 1-800-468-6577.

Other Good
Harvest House Reading

WHY CHRISTIANS CAN'T TRUST PSYCHOLOGY
by *Ed Bulkley*

Today's search for inner fulfillment has exploded into what is now called the Recovery movement, complete with twelve-step seminars, counseling programs, and self-help books. Thousands of people are looking to Christian psychology to help them attain victory over modern dysfunctions. Some say we need the Bible plus psychology. Others say the Bible alone is sufficient. With deep insight and candor, pastoral counselor Ed Bulkley presents the opposing sides of this issue—and offers trustworthy, biblical answers for those who long to break away from pain and guilt and know true freedom.

THE FACTS ON SELF-ESTEEM, PSYCHOLOGY
AND THE RECOVERY MOVEMENT
by *John Ankerberg & John Weldon*

Do twelve-step programs, self-help books, and inner-healing therapy have any place in a Christian's life? Tens of thousands of Christians today are seeking relief from stress, emotional pain, and destructive habits—making this booklet a highly relevant resource for our day.

LOVING GOD WITH ALL YOUR MIND
by *Elizabeth George*

In a fresh, friendly manner, Elizabeth George explores what it means to think biblically. "Biblical thinking," she writes, "gives women freedom from the draining emotions of fear, worry, depression, and bitterness." Liz will help you develop a scriptural and healthy view of God, the past, the future, problems, other people, and yourself, based on six truths backed by God's promises and power.

THERE'S HOPE FOR THE HURTING
by *Richard Lee*

In a world where broken promises are the rule, there is One whose Word is unfailing. Using many illustrations from everyday life as well as examples from the lives of Bible personalities, Lee reminds readers that God will restore and redeem those who cry to Him "out of the depths." Where is God when we need Him most? He is right in the middle of our problems—so close that we sometimes do not see Him at work.